From the drawing by Cecelia Beaux

Arthur Twining Hadley

ARTHUR TWINING HADLEY

BY

MORRIS HADLEY

LUX ET VERITAS

NEW HAVEN

YALE UNIVERSITY PRESS

LONDON · GEOFFREY CUMBERLEGE · OXFORD UNIVERSITY PRESS

1948

B
H1312

TO

H. H. M. H.

CONTENTS

ILLUSTRATIONS

ARTHUR TWINING HADLEY

CHAPTER I

CHILDHOOD AND FAMILY
1856–1868

ARTHUR TWINING HADLEY was born on April 23, 1856, at New Haven, Connecticut, in a house facing the Yale campus. On this campus his life was to center, first as student, then as teacher, lastly as president. During the twenty-two years of his presidency, from 1899 to 1921, he was to be the leader in the growth of Yale, both on its campus and in its influence throughout the nation.

His father and grandfather were teachers. Before them the Hadleys, since the early days of New England, had been farmers. They had come from England to Ipswich, Massachusetts, in 1637. In the next century they had moved to New Hampshire. Their farming was interrupted at times by Indian fighting, especially for the fifth of the line in this country, George Hadley. George was a captain of the Northern Rangers, and deplored the fighting in the Revolution as hopelessly unexciting when compared with fighting Indians. There is even a family tradition (unsupported by any known facts) that this George Hadley was the model from whom James Fenimore Cooper drew Leatherstocking.

George Hadley's son James, the grandfather of Arthur Hadley, was a graduate of Dartmouth in the class of 1809. Soon after graduation he moved to Herkimer County, in the Mohawk Valley, in upper New York. There he became professor of chemistry and materia medica in Fairfield Medical School. Arthur Hadley in 1904 wrote a brief biographical memoir of his own father for the National Academy of Sciences, containing some account of his grandfather as well, from which much of the following description is directly taken.

The little town of Fairfield, on the edge of the Adirondack forests, was in those days an intellectual center. The academy there was one of the best in New York State, and the medical school at this period was enjoying a brief but rather brilliant prosperity. A "Circular and Catalogue" for 1828 of this "College of Physicians and Surgeons of the Western District of the State of New-York" shows a three-year medical course, in which James Hadley gave the lectures on chemistry and on materia medica, besides being the Register of the college.

The formidable title of the medical school was balanced by the simplicity of the life. The circular states that "board without lodging can be obtained at $1 25 per week; with lodging, rooms, fire-wood, $2, or $2 25 per week." The circular further states: "N.B. A summer course on Chemistry will be delivered by Dr. Hadley, to commence on the first Monday in June next, and to continue six weeks. Ticket fee, $6. Lectures or instructions on Botany will also be given at the same time. Ticket fee, $4." Among the students in 1828 appears the name of Asa Gray. He had originally planned to study medicine, but was turned by Hadley's influence to the pursuit of botany in which he was to become famous. By the testimony of Gray and others, Hadley had a genuine enthusiasm for scientific study at a time when such study was rarer and less appreciated than it now is.

James Hadley in 1812 married Maria Hamilton, the daughter of a doctor, Hosea Hamilton. Her family had come from Scotland to Connecticut in 1647. All the sons of James and Maria who lived to maturity achieved a more than ordinary degree of success in study and teaching. The eldest, George, was for a long time professor of chemistry in Buffalo Medical College. The youngest, Henry Hamilton Hadley, became professor of Hebrew in Union Theological Seminary. James Hadley, son of James and father of Arthur, was professor of Greek in Yale College.

This younger James Hadley was born in Fairfield, March 30, 1821, and grew up there. When only seven he was crippled for life by an injury to his knee in play, and ever after had to use a crutch in getting about. Even before his accident he had shown a natural aptitude for learning. Now, deprived of the chance of joining in the sports of his fellows, he turned still more eagerly to his studies. At seven he was reading Latin, at ten Greek, at fifteen Hebrew, and by eighteen he had added German, Spanish, and Italian. After finishing the regular course at Fairfield Academy he became an instructor there at the age of sixteen, and taught for three years, before entering Yale at nineteen as a junior in the class of 1842. He graduated with this class two years later, having won the highest honors. After postgraduate work in mathematics at Yale, and a year of teaching at Middlebury College, he was appointed a tutor at Yale in 1845. In 1848 he was made assistant professor of the Greek language and literature, and became a full professor in 1851.

There is a memorandum written by James Hadley at nineteen covering what he had studied since the age of seven. When checked against the famous list of Macaulay's classical reading at school and at the university, it appears that James Hadley had read as much before leaving Fairfield. During the early period of his education he had shown no marked predilection for any one group of studies. He had a universal interest in books and a singularly catholic power of appreciating and handling every form of literature or science. His mathematical work both before and after graduation attracted attention, and Professor Benjamin Peirce of Harvard remarked that he could not forgive Yale College for making professor of Greek the man who should have been the foremost mathematician of the country.

Having decided on philology as his field, James Hadley entered into it heart and soul and took his full share in contributing to the etymological and phonetic discoveries of the period. Had he lived abroad, or had America then been what it is today, his papers would have found larger audiences than could be furnished by the Classical and Philological Club of New Haven, and perhaps more distinctively suitable ones than those of the American Oriental Society. By force of circumstances his particular field of creative activity was in the classroom rather than in research. His *Introduction to Roman Law,* published after his death, had been given in lecture form at Yale and at Harvard. His *Greek Grammar* was used by generations of students at Yale and elsewhere. This *Grammar* continued in use, in revised form, for half a century after his death. His "Brief History of the English language," first published in 1864, has been reprinted, with necessary revision, in edition after edition of *Webster's Dictionary*.

Even though James Hadley devoted his life to the study of language, and was President of the American Oriental Society and Vice-President of the American Philological Association, it would give a misleading picture to present him simply as a philologist. Least of all would it explain his many-sided influence upon his son Arthur. James Hadley combined with his love of language an equal love of literature. This is shown in his translations, which, in addition to the grammatical accuracy to be expected of a philologist, have real charm and preserve to an unusual degree the rhetorical spirit of the original. Not only was he familiar with such languages as Sanskrit and Gothic but his knowledge extended through Welsh and Gaelic down to the more usual modern languages, not omitting by any means the current literature of his own.

In 1851 James Hadley married Anne Loring Twining, the daughter of Stephen Twining and Almira Catlin. Stephen Twining was a New Haven lawyer, a graduate of Yale College in the class of 1795, and at the time of his death in 1832 was serving as the assistant treasurer of Yale. Anne was the youngest of six children, two boys and four girls. Her oldest brother, Alexander Catlin Twining, was a mathematician whose interests covered a wide range. He was professor of mathematics and astronomy in Middlebury College for nine years, but also lectured at the Yale Law School on constitutional problems. He was, as well, a civil engineer, and in the early days of railroad location was in charge of the work not only on the roads running out of New Haven but on the old Lake Shore line and as far west as the Rock Island. The next brother, William, was a Congregational minister. Anne herself had a brilliant and exceptional mind.

The Twinings and Catlins, like the Hadleys and Hamiltons, had been in this country since the first half of the seventeenth

century. In the names of Arthur Hadley's other great-grandparents we find the same New England flavor: Wells, Hubbard, Doane, Goodman. These ancestors, and their ancestors in turn, seem from the available records to have been reliable citizens but not, for the most part, distinguished ones.

Five years after the marriage of James Hadley and Anne Twining their first and only child was born, on April 23, 1856. He was named Arthur, apparently through a process of elimination, to judge by a letter of his uncle, Henry Hamilton Hadley, written on May 6, 1856, when quite another name was still under discussion:

He is a remarkable child. Here there is no room for question. The doctor says so. Everybody says so. His equal has never been seen. Yet what this phenomenon, this wonderful baby, is to be called remains unsettled. The subject of deliberation. *James* is out of the question. Every other name already in the family is equally interdicted. The Professor it seems has in this matter put down his foot. He does not believe in an oligarchy of names. Conservative man that he is, he is nominally a Radical. Praenomens as well as Post Masters must have rotation in office. To hand down Tom, Dick and Harry in a family from generation to generation is a relic of hereditary exclusiveness not to be tolerated in these democratic times. But the negative is much more easily reached than the positive, it is easier to say what shall not be than what shall be. I have proposed Hezekiah. 1st because it is scriptural and 2nd on account of the agreeable homophony—Hezekiah Hadley—isn't it beautiful? But this is outvoted. And what do you think is the probable designation of our young Hadley, a scion of the Hadleys, a prosaic and sober minded family? What, but a name which has the odor of romance, which belongs to the heroes of second rate novels!! Clarence! Clarence Hadley! Powers of soberness! What are we coming to?

Arthur as a name finally won the day, linked with his mother's family name of Twining. For all his uncle's jesting, the letter reveals the type of intense consideration that Arthur's parents were to give to every incident of his life. James Hadley was thirty-five when his son was born, and Anne Hadley was thirty-nine. They watched over their only child with the oversolicitous care to be expected under the circumstances. Such constant attention may be the ruin of a child unless, as in Arthur's case, he has enough in him to profit by it. Arthur profited in intellectual training, in habits of study and concentration, and in kindred ways. But even at best such a situation leaves some mark on the child, and Arthur had to acquire in adult years that ability for give-and-take with his fellow mortals which less sheltered children learn in the rough-and-tumble of childhood. Certain idiosyncrasies of manner he always retained, but while these would have been a handicap to a lesser man they ultimately served merely to endear him to successive generations of Yale undergraduates. In each college class during the years of his presidency some member would acquire fame for his ability to take off the president, and would be enthusiastically acclaimed as he imitated the nervous walk, the awkward gestures, the characteristic intonation, and the complete absorption in the matter at hand. Years after graduation the act would still be in demand and hailed with nostalgic delight.

It would be easy to exaggerate this aspect of Arthur's childhood. The difference between his childhood and a normal one was a matter of degree only. He had playmates and enjoyed his play. In fact some of the play, perhaps carried on without his parents' knowledge, seems sufficiently hardy. Professor Thomas Thacher had in his yard two huge apple trees, so close together that their branches interlaced. The Thacher children and Arthur used to play tag in these trees, the rules being like those of ordinary tag with one addition: if you fell out of the tree you were "It."

New Haven in the 1860's was a pleasant town for a child, its broad streets lined with great elm trees, and fields and woods never far away. In other quarters of the town factories were springing up and population growing, but the college and its surroundings were a world apart. In later years when Arthur was a grown man it was always a slight shock to his mother that he had acquired some New Haven friends who were not connected with the college and who were not even graduates.

Arthur's home was virtually part of the college. It was a frame house directly across the street from the campus, just above the corner of Elm and College Streets. On this site the Divinity School was later built, to be followed in turn by Calhoun College. Here he grew up in the midst of college life, watching the students on their way to and from their classes, and playing on the campus with the children of other professors. In those days the campus was not shut in by buildings on all sides as it is today. It was instead an open tract, as the adjoining New Haven Green still is, though with more trees than the Green. The college buildings stood well back from College Street in a long row, of which the only one still standing is Connecticut Hall, then called South Middle. The campus was not forbidden ground but a place where a child might easily wander. The low "Yale fence" extending around the block was an invitation rather than an obstacle. It furnished the setting for one of Arthur's earliest recollections, of the president of the college, Theodore Woolsey, hurrying from his home so as not to be late for college prayers and vaulting the fence in his haste.

Other early recollections had the Civil War as a background. The war was very real, even for a child who was barely five when it started. Soldiers drilled on the Green, just outside the front gate of the house. The hospitals were full of wounded soldiers and the children, Arthur among them, used to go with their mothers to help—the mothers to aid in the nursing and the children because it cheered the soldiers to see them. The war one Sunday even trespassed upon the decorum of the college chapel, an event so unexpected that Arthur never forgot it. He was sitting in the pew between his mother and father, when someone slipped through the door and handed Professor Hadley a newspaper just arrived from New York. His father actually read the paper, right in the middle of the sermon, holding it folded and below the top of the pew in front. Then he passed it on to the next member of the faculty, and so it traveled from hand to hand. He leaned over and whispered to Arthur that the *Monitor* had defeated the *Merrimac*.

As Arthur grew older he went further afield than the campus and the Green and the neighboring streets. Two miles from the house was East Rock, a wooded hill with precipitous sides, now a public park but then a tangle of woods and underbrush inhabited only by a hermit who claimed it as his own. Exploring trips to this wilderness were made the more exciting by the risk of being chased by the hermit, who fortunately was not a rapid runner. At such times it was the custom to shout insults at the old man as you ran. Here Arthur reaped an unexpected advantage from his home training. With childish gravity he used to shout an apology for disturbing the hermit before starting his flight, and then flee in silence. Gradually the hermit, while never accepting him as a friend, came to draw a certain distinction between him and other boys, and would leave him undisturbed if he was on East Rock alone.

East Rock became a refuge for Arthur in times when he felt the need of being alone. There were such times in the years when he was around ten, immediately after the close of the Civil War. The period of the war had been a strain to all; in his father's case this strain had culminated with the death of his younger brother Henry, with whom he had been closely associated. James Hadley's health had never been robust, and in 1865 he fell severely ill of an infection which the doctors were unable to diagnose; for three years he was unable to teach, and it looked at though he would never be able to resume work. The small income from his savings and from a little property of his wife's was cut down by postwar inflation and taxation. Every penny had to be counted, and in New England in those days necessities were narrowly construed. There was one particular occasion when all the boys were getting up a baseball team, each chipping in ten cents toward the price of the ball. Arthur could not join the team because he could not contribute. Instead he trudged out to East Rock, climbed to the top, and sat there all afternoon looking out over the city and the harbor.

In lessons, Arthur started at home, and then, until he was twelve, went to a small school attended by the children of the neighborhood. This school was taught by Herr Gottlieb Henness, an eccentric but brilliant teacher. Here Arthur learned excellent German, which was to stand him in good stead in later years.

Through all these years, and until Arthur went to college, James Hadley was the most important influence in his son's education. From earliest childhood Arthur's father treated him as an intellectual equal, and the child responded. The same scientific spirit which James Hadley showed in the college classroom he showed in the training of the boy. Arthur's first reading was under his father's guidance, though he soon read omnivorously on his own account. In mathematics and science, as well as in literature, he learned much from his father's teaching and companionship.

The two shared other interests besides lessons. They made trips together to Buffalo, where Arthur's uncle George Hadley was teaching and where grandfather James Hadley had moved after his retirement from Fairfield. One of these trips was memorable because it was enlivened by a railroad wreck. At home father and son not only worked but played together, even though some of their recreations had a studious flavor. In later years Arthur still could quote common nursery rhymes in doggerel Greek and could count out with Πίθηκος, πίθηκος, φιάλη νέκταρος, in place of "Monkey, monkey, bottle of beer." They played games, notably chess, at which Arthur early became proficient; but they also indulged in less academic pursuits. There still exists a handwritten permit, signed by the Mayor of New Haven, authorizing "Prof. James Hadley and son to fire crackers, squibs and torpedoes" on the fifth of July, 1869, the fourth that year falling on a Sunday.

CHAPTER II

SCHOOL AND COLLEGE
1868—1876

ARTHUR HADLEY entered Hopkins Grammar School in 1868, when he was twelve years old. Going to Hopkins was as much a matter of course for a New Haven boy in those days as going to Yale. The school was even older than the college, having been founded in the earliest days of the New Haven settlement, in 1648, while the college was not founded until 1701. To the school came not only boys from New Haven but also, especially in the later years of the course, boys from other parts of the country who were completing their studies for Yale. Many of these continued as classmates of Arthur's in Yale College. Among those who were his classmates at Hopkins but not at Yale were Edward M. House from Texas, later famous as President Wilson's adviser, and John Hays Hammond from California, the noted mining engineer. House did not enter Yale, and Hammond went to the Sheffield Scientific School instead of to the College. With Hammond in particular Arthur kept up a close friendship all his life.

The curriculum at Hopkins was strictly the normal one of the times: Latin, Greek, and mathematics predominated. It was fortunate for Arthur that he had at home, with his father, contacts with a wider range of interests. The discipline as well as the curriculum reflected the past. The headmaster, Henry N. Johnson, always referred to behind his back as Buck Johnson, tolerated no nonsense, and his method of punishment was to seize the offender by the coat collar, shake him as a terrier shakes a rat, and then slam him back into his seat. The seats were substantial affairs, fixed in place and supported by a central iron pillar, but on one occasion this iron upright snapped under the shock. The seat was replaced, but the fragments were treasured by the admiring pupils, kept in a disused coat closet in the basement, and shown to all new boys as a forecast of what was to come.

Arthur had no trouble with the curriculum, but his health was not good. Though he easily stood among the leaders of his class in studies, he kept up with his fellows in sports with difficulty. Then, and in college, he was a thin, wiry, nervous youth. He was much bothered with colds, and it was at this period that he became partly deaf in one ear. This was never a real handicap to him, as the hearing of his other ear was extremely good. It was only when he was walking with someone that he would have to keep his companion on his right, his "good side." His eyes were a more serious matter, giving him so much trouble, especially in his college years and immediately after, that he feared he might have to give up his studies entirely. Fortunately his fears proved groundless, and though he always had to be careful about glasses and about a proper light when reading, his eyes survived the vast amount of work that he put upon them.

In 1872, at the age of sixteen, Arthur entered Yale as a freshman with the other members of the class of 1876. At the outset of his college course he suffered a great blow. His father had resumed teaching in 1868, but in 1872 he had a return of the symptoms which had marked his previous illness, with fever and much pain; in October he became critically ill, and died on November 14, 1872, at the age of fifty-one. Arthur had always been devoted to his father, and had looked up to him and relied upon him; they had rarely been separated. Now, at sixteen, he found himself without his father who had meant so much to him, and forced to make his own decisions.

Arthur continued his college course, but instead of rooming at college he lived with his mother for the first two years. Fortunately the income from the family savings, though it had seemed so inadequate half a dozen years before, was now increased by better times and lower taxes. It proved sufficient, with care, for the simple life of New Haven and for the modest costs of college in those days.

These costs, as set out in the current college catalogue, are in marked contrast to the costs of today. Tuition was $90 a year. The average figure for "rent and care of a half room in College" was $35 for the year. "Expenses of public rooms, ordinary repairs and incidentals" came to $12 a year, to which was to be added $4 for the use of the gymnasium and $7 for the use of the library and reading room. The library, it may be noted, contained 60,000 volumes, as against the 3,000,000 or more today. Board was figured at from $4 to $7 a week. The total expense, including fuel, laundry, and textbooks, was computed at $340 as a minimum or $568 as a maximum.

The college costs were further reduced in Arthur's case because his high scholastic standing made him eligible for the best scholarships. He led his class for the four years, and was thus valedictorian. He held a Woolsey Scholarship for three years, and in addition a Bristed Scholarship in his junior and senior years and during three years of postgraduate study in New Haven and Germany. The list of prizes he won covered Greek, Latin, English composition, public speaking, mathematics, and astronomy. At the close of his senior year he was elected class secretary, a post he held for many years, editing the triennial and decennial histories of the class.

In spite of his scholastic accomplishments he was not branded by his classmates as a "dig," the then current expression for those absorbed in studies to the exclusion of human interests. He was too obviously interested in his fellow men and all their doings. For him books were simply one means to knowledge. His skill at whist would alone have served to convince his classmates, had proof been needed, that his knowledge was not limited to books.

Arthur Hadley once remarked, contrasting his college days with those of a younger generation, that the undergraduate of the 1870's, compared with his successors forty years later, spent two hours a day less in exercise, and two hours a night less in sleep, the four hours being passed instead partly in the library and partly at cards. Nearly every night saw a game, commencing after studies were over, and lasting until midnight or later in spite of compulsory chapel early the next morning. Some Puritan worries as to wasting his time on cards would trouble Arthur at

ARTHUR HADLEY, 1865

1878

ARTHUR HADLEY   EDWIN WORCESTER
HENRY JAMES   EDWARD ROBBINS

intervals, but he laid them to rest on the score that he was studying as many hours as his eyes would allow, and that cards were no strain on the eyesight.

A contemporary, describing these college days in later years, wrote of Arthur Hadley (*New York Sun*, June 4, 1899):

He liked nothing better than to sit on the fence and chat and joke with his classmates, and he always joined in the singing with an enthusiasm worthy of better results. He was popular, because he was simple, loyal, unaffected, and his mannerisms, in no degree implying superiority, made him attractive and lovable. He was surcharged with the Yale spirit, and stoutly believed that the best fellows in the world comprised the class of '76.

The class of 1876 was like most others in regarding itself as the best class that ever went to Yale. One clear distinction it possessed however; Professor Billy Sumner had termed 1876 a "loud" class, and for some reason this designation was cherished by the members as a compliment.

During his junior and senior years Arthur roomed in college, in Durfee Hall, with Edwin D. Worcester. Both were excellent students, Worcester standing second in the class, and they were in all respects most congenial. Of all his classmates, in later years, Arthur saw most of Worcester and of Otto T. Bannard. Both entered the practice of the law in New York, Worcester continuing in that profession while Bannard went into banking. They were frequent visitors in New Haven throughout their lives, particularly Bannard, who was for many years on the Yale Corporation.

In the 1870's Yale was regarded by teachers and students alike as centering in the four-year academic course. Those taking this four-year course were the members of Yale College. Students taking, say, the scientific course were listed in the catalogue as members not of Yale College but of the Sheffield Scientific School and neither officially nor in the eyes of the undergraduates were they full members of Yale. As an innovation they were being allowed to take part in intercollegiate athletics on Yale teams, but this was a recent development. Arthur saw more of "Sheff" than most, because his Hopkins classmate, John Hays

Hammond, went there. As the two continued to see much of each other, Arthur met and knew many of Hammond's classmates. But even in the case of Hammond, when Arthur was studying in Europe two years after graduation and wrote home about friends he had met in Dresden, listing various Yale classmates he had seen, he refers to him not as a classmate but as "my old grammar school friend, Jack Hammond."

Arthur's breadth of interest not only took in the Sheffield Scientific School but extended even to Harvard. Half a century after the event he described the experience:

In my own student days in the early '70's, I made a visit to Harvard because I wanted to see what Harvard was like; but the announcement of my purpose was regarded by my fellow students in much the same way that they would have regarded a proposed visit to Bolivia or Turkestan. When I got to Harvard—fortified with letters of introduction to the proper seniors—I was received with the same measure of cordial courtesy and half concealed surprise with which we would receive a similar visit from a Grand Lama or a South American general.

Yale in the 1870's was still little affected by educational innovations. Entrance requirements were entirely based on Greek, Latin, and mathematics, with the exception of one added item which appeared on the list of requirements in a separate category: "English Grammar and Geography; a thorough knowledge of which is required."

The curriculum was virtually untouched by the elective system. Instead, in senior year, a medley of brief courses was required of all comers, in the attempt to meet growing demands for diversity. The class was divided, for convenience of teaching, into three divisions, but all three took the same subjects.

In freshman year these subjects were Greek, Latin, and mathematics, with a little Roman history in the second term of the year and some rhetoric in the third term.

In sophomore year Greek, Latin, and mathematics continued, the latter reaching analytic geometry and conic sections. The additional required courses this year were French in the second term and some more rhetoric.

In junior year Greek and Latin continued, but differential and integral calculus could be substituted for part of this requirement in the first two terms, or German in the third term. Everyone had natural philosophy, in the form of Ganot's physics, and one term of astronomy. There was one term of work in logic, and rhetoric continued as before.

In senior year the compulsory variety was so great that there is no alternative but to list the courses as they are given in the catalogue, if they are to be included at all.

In the first term the president, Noah Porter, gave a course in mental philosophy. There was a course in political and social science, and Professor Sumner lectured on political economy. Professor Loomis gave astronomy, Professor Wright chemistry. In history the text was Guizot's *History of Civilization,* in Latin Cicero. Rhetoric and forensic disputation came twice a week. As the only elective element German might be substituted for astronomy or Latin.

In the second term of senior year the president instructed the class in natural theology and evidences of Christianity, as well as in moral philosophy. Professor Dana taught geology. Professor Wheeler lectured on English History in the sixteenth and seventeenth centuries, Professor Sumner on political philosophy, Professor Sanford on anatomy and physiology. Rhetoric and forensic disputation continued.

In the final term of the year came the history of philosophy, and Professor Woolsey lectured on political and social science. Professor Wheeler gave United States Constitutional History, and there were lectures by Professor Baldwin on elements of jurisprudence and on American constitutional law. Professor Whitney lectured on language and the study of language, Professor Eaton on botany.

The uniformity of the curriculum at times held disadvantages for the instructor. In freshman year the three divisions of the class in Greek all had the same professor. When this gentleman announced to the first division that a large part of the annual examination would be sight reading, such a groan went up that he added the passage would be Herodotus, whose Greek was

simple. With the second division, to allay their fears, he incautiously changed his assurance and told them the passage would be
a fable, adding reassuringly that fables were never difficult. Cap-
ping this, he remarked to the third division that the passage
dealt with an incident with which they were all familiar. When
the three divisions began to compare notes it became evident
that the field had been narrowed in a way which offered real
possibilities. Arthur was a member of the committee of three, one
from each division, which was dispatched to the library to go
through Rawlinson's translation of Herodotus and report. The
committee reported three fables in Herodotus as meeting the
requirements, with one of the three easily the favorite. The in-
dustrious members of the class prepared all three, the more
casual merely the favorite. The passage picked as the most likely
one turned out to be the sight passage on the examination paper.
Years later, when Arthur was himself on the Yale faculty, he
enlightened the Greek professor as to what had happened, and
thereby relieved his mind on a subject that had puzzled him for
years. The professor had first suspected the printer who set up
the paper, but inquiry showed that there had been no leak there,
so he had been left completely in the dark as to why all his students could translate Greek they had never seen so much more
accurately than Greek which they had studied throughout the
year.

In the extracurricular life of the college, societies played a
larger part in the '70's then they did by the next century. There
were societies in each year, and the classes of a hundred and
twenty or thirty men were small enough so that the line between
society and nonsociety men was unfortunately noticeable. James
Hadley had always been strenuously opposed to college societies. Perhaps the first decision Arthur ever had to make that went
counter to his father's known wishes was with regard to societies,
but after earnest thought he decided to accept election, and was
always glad that he had done so.

The freshman and sophomore societies have now disappeared
from Yale. Arthur's were Delta Kappa and Delta Beta Xi. With
his junior society, Delta Kappa Epsilon, he always maintained

contact. His senior society, Skull and Bones, remained for him throughout his life a constant inspiration.

There were other, less serious societies, such as Chi Rho, whose name in later years became associated with Omega Lambda Chi, in a song sung annually during a campus springtime Saturnalia of a mild order. In the class of 1876, at least, Chi Rho existed solely for the pleasure derived from initiating people into it, so that by the time all the class had been initiated no more reason for its continuance could be found.

For his freshman society, Delta Kappa, Arthur wrote some doggerel so atrocious that it deserves to be quoted, at least in part, if only to illustrate what appealed to undergraduates then, or perhaps to undergraduates at any period. Its popularity was such that it was printed in an ephemeral college publication of the day, *The Yale Naughty-Gal All-Man-Ax*. The president has convoked the faculty to design the new college chapel. The professor of art has been called upon to produce the most unsightly building possible, and so on with different members of the faculty and different features of the structure. On the question of ventilation, to limit ourselves to one example, the president inquires:

> Now who is he who can produce a draught of winter air
> So cold and yet so copious that each may have his share?
> Then rose a man both old and grave of wondrous knowledge he,
> It was the much respected Prof of Meteorology.
> Said he "The current AQX through CVD will go
> And carry up and down the aisles both rain and hail and snow,
> But when the heat of summer comes the current is reversed
> No breath of air can reach the seats unless the building burst.

Either recollecting such undergraduate verse, or more probably because of his natural objectivity, Arthur Hadley in later years was always tolerant of student criticism and glad to receive it, whether couched in respectful or disrespectful form. While extremely sensitive to criticism, he took it in good part, and gave his critics credit for helpful intentions and not for animus.

By way of contrast with the verse just quoted, the titles of Arthur's articles in the *Yale Literary Magazine* should perhaps at least be listed. This was the serious college publication, and the articles, in order, were entitled: "Molière," "Ulysses," "The Romantic Element in History," "The Earl of Warwick," "The Prodigal Son," "Parnassus."

CHAPTER III

POSTGRADUATE WORK
1876—1879

IN the summer after his graduation Arthur Hadley made a trip to the Great Lakes, stopping to see friends and family on the way; he also traveled to Philadelphia to see the Centennial Exhibition. The following year he spent in postgraduate work at New Haven before going to Germany for two years of further postgraduate work. His college roommate Worcester had also returned to Yale, to study law. A letter from Worcester to another classmate, Charles H. Willcox, describes Arthur's work at Yale and his plans for the future (March 12, 1877):

Hadley, I grieve to say, is not long for this world. He will go to another and better world about the 29th of next May. His conveyance is to be a steamer of the William and Guion Line. The coming summer will be spent in bumming around England and France—if that word can be fitly applied to such gentle enjoyments as we may presume will be sought by Mrs. Hadley and her son.

I am sorry to lose Arthur. His uniformly cheerful ways and his unaffectedly friendly nature have endeared him to me exceedingly. He will be away for several years, and since I too shall leave New Haven in a little more than a year from his departure it may be that I shall, next May, take my last look at our clever, awkward, cheery little valedictorian for a long time.

Hadley's eyes, you will be pleased to hear, are on the upward path. He wears specs all the time now. His oculist has at last hit upon the true fundamental trouble, and declares that he will soon be able to outstudy the veriest Deutscher of them all.

Hadley is greatly troubled to determine a course of study for himself. Now that he is face to face with the task of choosing a life's work, he is perplexed. You remember that he always vowed that, much as he liked mathematics, he would never teach it. He dipped into philology, but Sanskrit quite disgusted him. Philosophy was never attractive to him. This year he has made a wild plunge into history, and last term he had temporarily decided to adopt it for his permanent study. But last Sunday he told me that he was profoundly convinced of the inutility of historical study and of the practical impossibility of reaching firm conclusions. Ergo, exit history. He now has returned to his old love and is nearly persuaded that mathematics is his true sphere. If this resolution holds, he will study, not in Germany, but in Paris. But you may imagine that he is wavering, and he is doing much weighty thinking.

The trip to Europe was aided by the fact that the family house on Elm Street had been sold. The proceeds were invested and the family income correspondingly increased, while there were no expenses for upkeep or taxes during their absence. After detailed budgeting, Arthur and his mother decided that two years in Europe were possible. Berlin as the place for study was selected, but much travel was also planned. It does not seem to have occurred to either of them that Arthur might go alone to pursue his studies, or even that his mother might live with some cousins of hers in England while Arthur studied in Germany. The trip was throughout to be a family affair.

From the description on his passport Arthur Hadley at the age of twenty-one was five feet ten inches in height, eyes grey, nose straight, full lips, chin receding, hair black, complexion dark, and face long. In 1877, and always, he was thin and wiry, weighing around 135 pounds. In later years the receding chin was concealed by a Van Dyke beard.

Mother and son sailed from New York on May 29, 1877, on the steamship *Wisconsin* of the William and Guion Line, landing in Liverpool on June 9. From there they set out to see England. It was the first trip abroad for either of them, and they were stirred by all they saw. In fact Mrs. Hadley, from her vantage point of sixty years to her son's twenty-one, felt that Arthur was throwing himself into the trip with too much enthusiasm. Writing to her sister from Chester a few days after landing, she complained: "Arthur found such intense interest

attached to everything he saw that at the end of the second day
he was worn out with it. He will have to learn to see sights without putting his whole soul into each one of them."

Arthur's exhaustion seems to have been quickly over, or easily
remedied, for two days later he walked up Snowden from
Llanberis, and reported in a letter: "The whole time from the
hotel to the summit was two hours and twenty-five minutes. I
was considerably fatigued when I reached the top, and drank a
whole bottle of ale. Refreshed by this and by three-quarters of
an hour's rest I started on the descent."

The trip through Europe is recounted in detail in letters from
Arthur to his Aunt Mary Twining in New Haven. Starting at
Chester they went through North Wales, part of the way by
post-coach—Arthur included a sketch of the vehicle with the
letter. Next they went to Leamington, and used that as a center
for excursions to Warwick, Stratford, Kenilworth, and Coventry.
After a brief visit to Oxford they went to London, and by the
end of June were installed in lodgings at Mrs. Mogridge's, 13
Charlotte Street, Bedford Square. The towns and the sights are
set out in full in Arthur's letters, from the important monu-
ments, which he found even more impressive than he had expected, down to the unexpected bits of British local color, such
as the handbill posted on the wall in Coventry announcing a
meeting of the "Godiva Bicycle Club."

Later in the summer they took a trip to Scotland, spending a
week in the Lake District on the way north. They went as far
as Iona, and then through the Caledonian Canal to Inverness,
stopping off a week in Edinburgh on the way back. They returned to London after a visit to the Wye Valley and the Isle
of Wight, seeing countless cathedrals along the way, which
Arthur duly noted and commented upon. It apparently rained
daily but without quenching their enthusiasm, except for waterfalls: "There were various lakes and mountains well worth seeing and pretenses of waterfalls, which like all English waterfalls were humbugs. The falls of Lodore in spite of Southey
are insignificant cascades." The particular natural features which
made the greatest impression on Arthur were at each end of the

trip: Fingal's Cave, on the Island of Staffa, and a walk along the coast of the Isle of Wight to Shanklin, "the most beautiful walk that I ever took."

At the start of the trip they had a pleasant stop at Cambridge, and these brief glimpses of Oxford and Cambridge were Arthur's first introduction to a different way of university life, a way that was always to have a great appeal for him. The first paragraph of the following account is taken from a letter to Willcox, the second from one to Worcester, both written on rainy afternoons in Ambleside shortly after the visit to Cambridge.

We went to Oxford, but it was vacation there and almost everyone was away, so that my letters of introduction were of no use. I managed nevertheless to see a great deal. They do make study a most luxurious occupation in these places, surrounding both under-graduates and fellows with everything to make life attractive. When I went to Cambridge two or three weeks later I was still more struck with these things. There they do not shut up everything as in Oxford, but something like half of the men remain in College for a part of the time, so that July does as well as any other month to be there. I was so fortunate as to find Prof. Cowell, the professor of Sanskrit, at Cambridge, and he showed my cousin Kinsley Twining, who was with me, and me a great many things that we could not otherwise have seen. Chief among all we had the pleasure of dining at the fellows' table in the great hall of Corpus Christi College.

There were in the body of the hall some fifty or sixty undergraduates, who had an ordinary good dinner; but at the fellows' table, where we sat as honored guests on each side of the Master, everything was on a scale of regal magnificence. Five or six courses, with wine and ale ad libitum; and when it was all over the fellows, half a dozen of them, went into a smaller room where we sat around a table with strawberries and wine and coffee to which people helped themselves as they liked. We talked about all things under heaven in much the way that a select party of Yale graduates might have done.

After returning to London they spent a relatively quiet month at Mrs. Mogridge's, occasionally going for the day to some neighboring town of interest but making no extended trips. On such brief excursions they saw Windsor, Eton, and Canterbury.

Not all the time was spent on antiquities; Arthur went to see Yorkshire vs. Surrey, and came back with a great admiration for cricket.

In the middle of September they started for the Continent and spent several weeks in Paris, seeing the sights as thoroughly as they had in England, and with almost equal enthusiasm, though the letters home show that by now they regarded themselves as seasoned travelers. Mrs. Hadley spoke virtually no French but Arthur's proved adequate for two; it was accurate and fairly fluent, although then, and always, his accent was terrible. Their energy was unabated, and they seem to have thought nothing of rising and breakfasting in the dark, to take a six o'clock train for a day of arduous sight-seeing. Of one such occasion Arthur wrote bitterly: "The paltry meal with which the French begin the day is not worth anything." They made up for the lack at later meals, and even Mrs. Hadley wrote home: "We take the vin ordinaire with the water always though many of our friends think it unnecessary. We like to be on the safe side, and beside that like the wine itself."

Early in October Mrs. Hadley and Arthur left for Germany. They had been to Chartres while at Paris; now they went to Rheims, and from there to Namur, entering Germany at Aix la Chapelle and going on to Cologne. Arthur's accounts of what he saw are generally too detailed for quotation here, but his eyes were troubling him again at this time, so that his letter to his aunt about Cologne was perforce brief:

At Cologne the chief thing of course was the cathedral, which was magnificent beyond all my expectations. Aside from this the chief object of interest to me was the fortifications. For churches interesting because eleven thousand maidens were traditionally slain by heathen hands, as well as for churches which contain the jaw bone of some saint or apostle, I cherish the most profound contempt.

From Cologne they went up the Rhine, in spite of the lateness of the season; but at Coblenz they found the boat service suspended without notice and so had to miss the upper river. Instead they went to Cassel and from there to Berlin, arriving the middle of October.

At Berlin they started at once on the search for permanent lodgings. They had the advice of friends already there, but none of the places they looked at were satisfactory. At last, when they were in despair, success came unexpectedly and they found an ideal place where they spent the first winter, at In den Zelten, 18. Mrs. Hadley described the event in a letter to her sister (October 18, 1877):

We thought we would try a place mentioned in Baedeker's Guide Book. We found it in the Thiergarten. Here in a beautiful house on one of the streets bounding the park we found on the second floor a delightful parlor and bedroom with the sun all day shining upon them looking out upon this park. The good lady Frau Vorwerk could not give us a third room until the first of November, but as we were in the house twice, once when the family were at dinner, and once when the dinner was cooking, and smelled no onions, we concluded to come.

Our breakfast table is set in our parlor and consists of tea, coffee, bread and butter and eggs. The hours of meals suit Arthur's lectures and although we are some distance from the University (a mile and a quarter) there is a horse railroad about all the way which he can take when he chooses. The price for our board and lodging exclusive of fuel and light while we have the two rooms is for us both $17.50 a week.

We are in the family of a widow lady who was left with seven children to educate and support. They are an intelligent and lively set of young people and beside these there are two young ladies and two young men as boarders, all studying something, and all Germans.

In the following spring Frau Vorwerk moved, and the Hadleys moved with her to Pottsdamer Strasse, 20, liking the new quarters even better than the old. Arthur wrote to Worcester a year later (July 29, 1879):

The trees were in full leaf, and one could hardly realize that he was in a city. For we had the canal in front of us, and by no means such a thing as a canal in America is, but something highly ornamental—banks planted with grass, two or three rows of trees in the streets on either side, and the very canal-boats more like gigantic gondolas than anything else.

Arthur's mother, in more literal but equally enthusiastic vein, had written to her sister (March 19, 1878):

Our rooms will be on the first floor, with only one flight of stairs from the street. Our bedrooms are on the garden, which is large and full of trees. One of the rooms opens upon a large balcony over the garden. Our parlor is a front room commanding the street and a beer garden. I think we shall be comfortable in spite of the latter appurtenance. We pay about 10½ dollars apiece a week. Is that not cheap for these nice rooms and board?

Arthur studied at Berlin for three semesters, or a year and a half, concentrating increasingly on political economy. As a contemporary record, we have his letters to his aunt in New Haven, and his classmates Willcox and Worcester. On October 21, 1877, he wrote his aunt describing his matriculation:

We went up and after signing a great number of papers and having our names and circumstances entered in a great number of different books were pronounced members of the university and received that mystic card which gives the holder exemption from arrest, opens the libraries to him, and gives him seats in the theatres at half-price.

To Worcester he wrote on February 4, 1878, near the end of the first semester, a long letter about his life and plans, from which the following quotations are taken:

I know what I am going to do while in Germany and feel enough confidence in my choice to be able to go at it with my whole heart. I am working and intend to work, in the line of history and political science. I am very much interested in my work, and if my eyes serve me tolerably well, hope to make real and constant progress.

I have about given up the idea of taking a degree in Germany. Berlin and Leipzig are about the only places where the degrees are worth taking—at the other universities (with the possible exception of Strassburg) they are too absurdly easy, so that one would feel really ashamed to carry the title of Ph.D. from Heidelberg, not to speak of Bonn or Jena. As for Berlin (and essentially, also, Leipzig) three years residence in Germany is very strictly required for the degree, and so much time I am not prepared to give. On the whole I think that I lose very little, and gain a great deal, by giving up all intention of trying for a degree.

My lectures for the first semester were chosen quite as much with the purpose of learning good German and hearing distinguished men, as of making progress in my historical studies, but I have had no reason to repent of my choice.

First in interest, perhaps, comes von Treitschke's course on Political Science. Treitschke himself is a queer combination of Enthusiasm, Billy Sumner and the typical Prussian. (I refer to Sumner's manners and modes of thought, not his actual opinions, which are quite at variance with those of Prof. v. T.). Treitschke has been one of the men who have stood by Bismarck in the conflicts of the last fifteen years, and considers it a great admission when he allows that in some minor points the present constitution of Prussia and Germany falls short of absolute perfection. Rev. Joseph Cook would be delighted to see how zealously religious he is. A good protestant, too; he hates the catholics nearly as much as the materialists. He also hates most heartily the French and the English; the Americans come in for a share of abuse, but much less than most other people, and on the whole, I think he is quite favorably disposed toward us. Socially he is a thoroughly pleasant man. I have reason to say so; for the other day he invited me to take dinner with him, although I had had no letter of introduction to him, and had only exchanged a few words with him in the most formal way. It is a little awkward talking with him, as he is almost entirely deaf; but this was made up by the superior ease of talking with Mrs. v. Treitschke, who speaks English perfectly—her mother being English (A young lady of my acquaintance wickedly suggests that that is the reason Treitschke so hates the English.) *

A very different sort of person, both as a man and as a lecturer, is Droysen, whose subject is "Modern History since 1815." If Treitschke is a German Sumner, Droysen is a German Loomis; only his jokes are not quite so good nor his manner so inimitable. But his lectures are thoroughly interesting, and, like Treitschke's, give you the thoroughly German view of things.

Curtius lectures on the history and topography of Athens—not an important course with reference to my present studies—but it is

* Hadley described Treitschke's teaching in an article in the *Yale Review* for January, 1915, called "The Political Teachings of Treitschke."

worthwhile to devote two hours a week to hearing such faultlessly beautiful German as Prof. Curtius speaks.

Herrmann Grimm, with whom Arthur Hadley took a course on the history of German art and culture, is described in a letter of Arthur's to his aunt (November 23, 1877):

Prof. Grimm is in many respects quite a contrast to Prof. Treitschke [whom Arthur had just described as "poetic and pugnacious"], but one whom it is equally important to hear; for if Treitschke is recognized as a leader in German political thought, Grimm is recognized as *the* leader in German art criticism. In his books the style, though flowing, is a model of care; in his lectures it is in the highest degree colloquial and off-hand. Every fourth lecture he holds in the royal museum, where there is a remarkably fine collection of old engravings as well as drawings.

These four professors complete the list of those under whom Arthur studied in the first semester. A picture of his general line of work, and of his life in Berlin, is given in the same long letter to Worcester which has already been quoted in part:

As for my reading, it has thus far been fragmentary, but profitable. What I have been doing thus far has been to try to read up one or two periods of modern political history on which my knowledge has been deficient. I am just now beginning a more comprehensive plan of work of a totally different kind—the history of economic theories —and with them also as far as possible of general economic conditions as they were fixed by laws or by the character of the people. It is a pretty large-sized plan, and one on which I have not advanced far enough to know how well I shall be able to carry it through; but the subject has been well written up for successive periods in essays in innumerable "Zeitschriften," and fortunately there are two good general works on the subject which serve as a capital index and means of reference to these articles.

As for library advantages, they are, on the whole, tolerably good. The University library does not amount to much; but the Royal Library, though not very well managed, is large (900,000 vols.) and generally has the books one wants. It has the advantage over most of the large public libraries in Europe, that under certain restrictions and securities (which the kindness of Prof. Curtius has enabled me to give) one can take books home with them and keep them for weeks. So I am not badly off in this respect; and the two courses of reading I have mentioned (if indeed the first can be called a course) furnish an agreeable variety.

Unfortunately my eyes prevent my carrying out that course uninterruptedly; and then as of old I have recourse to Mathematics, not however in such wise as to go out of my line of study, for the Germans have invented a branch of applied Mathematics which they call the Mathematical Theory of Statistics, wherein by methods varying all the way from elementary geometry to the integral calculus they endeavor to prove—Heaven only knows what! Still it is not by any means without interest, and may have something at the end of it, though to the uneducated, ungermanized mind it seems like a logical circle of the worst kind. But it is something the Germans make a great deal of, and which is on that account well to know; and gives me the opportunity of studying Mathematics by way of diversion without feeling that I am scattering my fires. . . .

Your chum

Arthur T. Hadley

P.S. I see I have not discussed the question of beer. I have tried twenty or thirty kinds, and, on the whole, like none better than Münchener Spätenbräu.

Arthur worked hard at his studies, but there were frequent opportunities for joining in the life of the capital. There were evenings at Bilse's: "where one can sit at a table and drink beer—or anything else he pleases—while listening to music much like that of Theo. Thomas, and only have it cost twenty-five cents, beer and all." At the other extreme of entertainment, Arthur and his mother attended a Court Ball at which the Royal Family were present, and Mrs. Hadley wrote home that "the young people danced to their hearts' content and to the ruin of their dresses and the wilting of their collars."

Arthur and his mother went often to concerts or to the opera. They became good friends of the Americans at our legation, which when they arrived was in charge of the First Secretary, described by Arthur in a letter home as "a thoroughly good fellow—unceremonious, outspoken and kindhearted . . . a son of Edward Everett, 'born in Boston, educated at Harvard etc.'—

but a more un-Bostonian, un-Harvardian, un-Edward-Ever-
ettian man it would be hard to find." Later, after the arrival of
Bayard Taylor as minister, they saw much of his family and Mrs.
Hadley helped Mrs. Taylor in the difficult days after her husband's death.

Among other American activities, Arthur was on the committee of the American church, ultimately becoming its chairman. Here, and elsewhere, he saw much of "two Princeton
graduates named Van Dyke and Marquand [who] are studying
theology here." The three were on many parties together, but
the outside activities of these theological students do not seem
to have weakened the force of their sermons. Near the close of
1877 Arthur, writing home, reported: "I went to church in the
morning and heard a sermon from Mr. Marquand, the other
Princeton Theologue besides Mr. Van Dyke, which had besides
its other excellencies the merit of extraordinary brevity." A
week earlier Mrs. Hadley in describing an evening party wrote
to her sister: "The best dancer was a Theological student, son
of Dr. Vandyke, a Presbyterian minister in Brooklyn. This same
young man preached a fine sermon. He will make a shining
preacher."

Arthur's work went on without interruption in spite of these
outside events. It is true that on one occasion he received a summons to appear before the University Court, which in those days
had jurisdiction over students to the exclusion of the usual police
courts. His friends were delighted, suggested all sorts of crimes
he might have committed, and warned him of the rigors of im-
prisonment in the university jail, where prisoners were limited
to two quarts of beer a day. It turned out to be a matter easily
disposed of. The Germans, not used to American names, had
entered the fees paid by Arthur as paid by Herr Wadley, who
thereafter attended no lectures. This did not trouble the authorities, but Herr Hadley had been haled before the court to explain
why he had been steadily attending lectures without paying any
fees.

Aside from their contacts with Americans, all the life of Arthur and his mother was thoroughly German. Germans to whom

they had letters received them most kindly, and through these friends they met others. As time went on the Hadleys came to take German ways as a matter of course, but in the early part of their stay each evening's entertainment was described in detail by Mrs. Hadley in long letters to her sister at home. Part of one such description may give a glimpse of the background in Berlin in the 1870's. It is dated November 11, 1877, but it would serve equally well for many other evenings:

I will confine myself to a description of a party we attended at Prof. Weber's last evening. As no hour was mentioned in the invitation we were somewhat puzzled to know what time to go, but using the best lights we had we went at ½ past 7. We found no other visitor there, but pretty soon others began to arrive till the company numbered about 30—principally University people, and much the same kind of people as ours. As soon as any person came in a cup of tea with little cakes was offered to them. Very soon all the ladies old and young found themselves seated in the drawing room talking to each other, while the gentlemen were doing the same in the Professor's study.

And here I must give you some idea of the house or rather the apartments which are a fair representative of the dwellings in Berlin. This one is on the fourth (the top) story with very long flights of easy stairs to reach it. When you once get to the top the rooms are very pleasant, being all on the same floor. The house is simply furnished, but like the home of a scholar.

The ladies were some of them in pretty full evening dress but most of them were dressed as we are at home. Occasionally our conversation was interrupted by music which being in Berlin was of course of a high order. Once we were entertained with a recitation by Miss Weber of one of Heine's poems.

All this time the gentlemen and ladies were in separate rooms. But when supper was ready the scene changed. The gentlemen came in to our room and handed us out to supper as appointed. I fell to the lot of an Egyptian scholar and was seated at the head of one of the tables. Arthur was at the other table, at last admitted to the company of the young ladies who were all seated together.

And now began the jolly time. The first thing which was offered to us to eat was green peas, then cauliflower and tongue. The next course was roast veal, potatoes, apples and various preserves. At the end of the course Prof. W. made a neat little speech of welcome to his friends, followed by a universal touching of glasses by all the company. The pastor then followed with a humorous response and proposed a "Hoch" for the Prof. At this the company started up and burst into a hearty song of three stanzas. After this was another speech proposing a "Hoch" for Frau Weber which was given with a will. All this with such a clatter of striking wine glasses, pushing chairs back on the varnished floor, laughing and jollity made such a noise as only people who have been to Germany ever heard.

Then came a richly ornamented large cake, made of rice boiled to a jelly, a little sweetened and baked to a thin crust of something like cake at the bottom. This dispatched was followed by another ornamental flat cake apparently, which proved to be really apple pie. This ended the eating. After a while we rose from the table, each gentleman shaking hands with his lady, and adjourned to the drawing room where everybody shook hands with everybody else. We supposed this was the signal for leave taking and so said our adieus. We found it was not, but as it was late we really left, reaching home at 1 o'clock Sunday morning.

In the second semester Arthur started work in economics with Adolf Wagner. He continued with Treitschke and Droysen in history, and for the rest had Gneist in German constitutional law and Aegidi in German constitutional history. In the third semester he concentrated on work with Wagner, taking his regular courses on finance, and on free trade as exemplified in England, as well as being a member of his seminar. He also studied economics with Meitzen and jurisprudence with Berner.

The only course of a different type that he took in this last half year was Curtius on the sources of Greek history. Of his reasons for taking this Arthur wrote to Worcester (October 17, 1878): "I am reluctant to let go of my classics entirely, inasmuch as I may have to study history or political economy as Pres Woolsey studied jurisprudence (I mean no undue self-appreciation by the comparison)—between the hours of Greek teaching and between the very lines of Greek authors."

This account of Arthur's work at Berlin which began with

extracts from a long letter to E. D. Worcester may well close with extracts from a letter to Charles Willcox, written February 16, 1879:

I am beginning to think that I have stayed here quite long enough. In one year I have heard the best courses in History and Political Science; most of those I now hear are rather second-rate. If I had known as much as I do now about advantages for study I think I should have taken one year in Paris and one in Berlin instead of two in Germany.

The best thing that I am attending now is Wagner's Seminar or discussion class, where we sit round a table and discuss a subject on which an essay has been prepared by some member of the class. Mine was read about a month ago. It treated of "das Englisch-Amerikanische Depositenbanksystem" and was tolerably well received.

Wagner, I am sorry to say, is a socialist. It is astonishing how nearly impossible it is for a German scholar to keep his head straight when he gets hold of such a subject as political economy. But there are more sides to some of these questions than Billy Sumner would have us believe. Nevertheless the man who differs from John Stuart Mill in any point whatever has a strong presumption against himself. So great is my veneration for John Stuart Mill that I am only just beginning to say that I disbelieve the proposition that a demand for commodities is not a demand for labor. Don't be frightened by this avowal; I have not become a protectionist or a socialist or anything of the sort in spite of Prof. Wagner.

Arthur might grieve at Wagner's socialistic leanings but he was objective and admired some of the work of authors who were viewed with alarm in New Haven. While traveling in the summer, after the close of his work in Berlin, he wrote to Worcester (July 29, 1879):

I have lately been much interested in Karl Marx, though I am very far from agreeing with him. His book seems to me to have a higher scientific aim than almost any work on political economy in the last half century. Like Ricardo, he seeks natural laws, not artificial maxims. Much of what he advances is I think a legitimate development of Ricardo's position. Holding some of the worst errors of the socialists, he is singularly free from others.

Years later Thoedore Roosevelt would term Arthur Hadley his fellow anarchist and say that if their true views were known they would be so misunderstood that they both would lose their jobs as president of the United States and president of Yale.

The letter to Willcox went on:

I was present last night at a meeting of the Berlin Political Economy Club, Friederich Kapk in the chair. The subject was the Corn Laws proposed in the new tariff bill, and the discussion waxed very warm. But the speeches were not good. The Germans are not good debaters; . . .

For one thing in particular I have been very sorry. No prize in Political Economy or even modern history has been offered during either of the two years that I have been in Berlin. I do not suppose I should have had much chance of success, but I should have tried very hard. And though I should have been under many disadvantages, my training at home would have given me one tremendous advantage over almost any German that I have met—the power of systematizing my thoughts—and in political economy this can hardly be overestimated. The utter absence of this power of thinking right end foremost is the defect in the German character which is to my mind worse than the tendency to superficiality in our own or to snobbishness in the English. Of the essays that have been read this winter in Wagner's seminar there has not been a single one which I could not have improved infinitely by a little transposition in the arrangement. We have a great deal to learn from the Germans; but it would be lucky for them if they tried to learn a little from us in return.

In an earlier letter (February 4, 1878, to Worcester) Arthur had given a page of specific instances of German educational failures, saying:

As for the system of education here (I mean secondary, gymnasium education) anybody must be foolish to look upon it with admiration. It is mentally a school of classical pedantry, whose end and aim is to teach boys an absolutely correct use of the Greek Particles. . . . But I will not scold at their system of education, it is enough for me that the university here furnishes me with what I want for my present purposes.

Criticism from another angle is found in one of the Lowell Institute Lectures which Arthur Hadley delivered a quarter century later in 1902. These lectures were printed in part in the *Atlantic Monthly* for February and March, 1903, but the following portion was not included:

With the teaching of physical science, the German government does not ordinarily interfere. It has the same reason for tolerating physics that the Catholic church had for tolerating the scholastic philosophy. It believes that it has nothing to fear from it. But when it comes to the teaching of political science the case is much altered. Here the way of the innovator is often made very hard. If he is content to teach his new doctrines without salary the government does not indeed refuse him the use of its lecture halls, as long as he is not absolutely revolutionary in his utterances. But such a man teaching without salary is dependent upon his fees, and if the examiners do not look with favor upon the results of his teaching they can affect his fees most adversely by rendering his courses useless for the purposes of the final examination.

For any position which gives influence upon this examination or which confers an independent salary, the government exercises the appointing power; and while it does not often interfere with a man's teaching after he is appointed to such a position, it exercises in advance a pretty close preventive scrutiny upon what he is likely to do. It indeed allows the faculties the right of nomination; but the university statutes ordinarily provide that the names of three nominees, instead of one, shall be sent to the government, which is thus enabled to exercise a wide range of influence upon the opinion of the permanent teaching force. Not until a man has reached the highest goal of his ambition in university circles can he be said to become free from this restraint; . . .

The professors, for other reasons as well, came in for criticism, as evidenced by a letter from Arthur to his aunt written on December 12, 1877:

My vacation began Saturday, and lasts two weeks. Technically there is no vacation at all, but the German professors are a lazy lot, and glad to get off from all the work they can. My professors are better than most of the others, and content themselves with only two weeks—most of those that Henry Farnam hears take a much longer time. I am sorry to say that the students are quite as lazy as the professors and most of them hurried off before the lectures were over. On last Friday the audiences were only about a third of the usual size.

The students themselves were of all sorts. Some Arthur liked, but in general he compared them with American students to the advantage of the latter. There was great variety; in one of Treitschke's courses, for example, Arthur sat next an "old officer" who wore the Iron Cross of the first class, and who seemed to have inside knowledge of all the latest political news. Arthur's critical attitude toward his fellow students did not prevent him from having a good time with them. On the occasion of the celebrations on the Emperor's return to Berlin in 1878 the students all marched (the Americans in a group and carrying American flags) and then spent the night at a "Commers," or beer-drinking celebration:

It was held in a large hall with room for some two thousand fellows to sit and drink beer. We Americans . . . had had a table reserved for us; but there were so many of us that there was not quite room for all at this one table, and Frank Eastlake and I found places somewhere else among one of the German Students' Societies. Of course we enjoyed it all the better here, especially as our neighbors, finding out that we were Americans, introduced themselves to us and were very polite indeed. . . . The exercises consisted of singing and speeches—the latter partly by professors. Among those who spoke were Zeller, the Rector of the University; Wagner; the celebrated surgeon Langenbeck; and the Anatomist du Bois-Reymond. Some of the songs were magnificently sung. I left at about 1 A.M.; how much longer the thing continued I have no idea.

The February letter to Willcox quoted earlier outlined the plans that Arthur and his mother had for six months of travel before returning to the United States, and then discussed his prospects after his return. He planned to be back in New Haven in September, 1879:

Not that I am likely to have at that time anything in particular to do; I have no prospects for an appointment as tutor, and shall have to spend my time studying with Sumner, Walker and others, writing essays if I can get anybody to read them, and taking private pupils if I can get anybody to coach. It is a rather slim outlook for anybody who is tired of intellectual bumming, but it is the best prospect that I see for myself starting life as an embryo political economist.

At any rate I know I should work better, if I knew in what direction my ultimate work was to be, and how far each particular piece of work was likely to tell. If I have some particular motive for a piece of work, I can work at it harder and faster, for a short time at any rate, than most men I know. If the object is no more definite than mental improvement which I owe to myself, I can be, and am, a miracle of laziness.

In the spring vacation in 1878 Arthur and his mother had spent three weeks in Dresden, mostly in the art galleries. There, also, they ordered the Meissen dinner set that was to do constant service for the Hadley family for over half a century and which still is in current use. In the summer vacation Arthur went on a month's walking trip in the Alps, which will be described in a later chapter. He then joined his mother and they traveled together for two months. Starting in Switzerland, they visited Savoy and then went down the Rhine, seeing sights indefatigably all the way. They arrived in Paris early in September. It was the year of the Exhibition and much of their time was spent there, with the balance in the Louvre. The first of October they left for Amiens and Brussels, where Arthur spent a day at Waterloo. From Brussels they went to Antwerp, getting back to Berlin in time for the opening of the term in the middle of that month. With them on this summer trip and during the following year was Arthur's first cousin, Mary Hadley, a girl about his own age, whose father had died the year before.

After the close of Arthur's work at Berlin early in March, 1879, he carried out his plans for six months' travel with his mother and his cousin. They spent the three months of spring in Italy, and then worked back by way of Vienna to Holland, and thence to England for the steamer home. After two years of residence and study in Europe Arthur was the better able to appreciate what he saw. In the cities where they stayed much of his time was spent in the galleries but a good deal also went into getting his ideas about political economy in order or studying in libraries that had collections of particular value. His enthusiasm for what he saw was unabated but he was more discriminating, although he laments of his views on art that "my taste is just correct enough to be commonplace, and not correct enough to stamp me as a devotee of high art." He was less hurried and no longer attempted to cover all the sights: "I have lost all belief in 'second-class lions' and positively enjoy not looking at them." Over sights about which he was enthusiastic his letters are as exuberant as ever. Rome, where they spent five weeks, was above all a delight to him.

At one time they planned to include Greece in their trip but they decided against trying to crowd too much into the months at their disposal. Another objection to travel in the Mediterranean countries they brushed away more easily: "I do not imagine that the plague is likely to make any difference with our movements. I do not believe that the disease in Salonika is anything but ordinary malignant typhus." Other rumors proved equally groundless. They made the trip to Paestum, something of an undertaking in those days, and were amply rewarded. Arthur wrote: "We had been more or less warned against the excursion on account of danger from brigands; judging from our experience the only danger is from starvation. If any of your friends design going there, tell them to take provisions with them; there are no good provisions to be had south of Salerno."

As the time for return to America drew near, Arthur looked forward eagerly to getting home. He loved Europe, and returned there in later life as often as he could; but he always remained at heart thoroughly American. His expressions of this in letters home went to a length that would have surprised his cosmopolitan friends, and were of a type that we associate today with those who have traveled little. In his case they sprang not from ignorance of Europe but from ardent affection for America. For example, in describing the royal wedding at Berlin he had written of the flags of all nations that filled the streets, including "last but not least, the stars and stripes which floated over the American legation and consulate and looked the proudest and handsomest of them all." Or again, in describing a Thanksgiving Day sermon preached by Dr. Thompson in Berlin: "It was pitched in quite a gloriously patriotic strain, and tended still further to exalt the national pride which travel in Europe anyway tends to foster in the heart of a right minded American."

On August 30, 1879, the Hadleys sailed from England on the *Algeria*. They landed on September 10 in New York and went straight to New Haven.

CHAPTER IV

EARLY TEACHING
1879—1883

I SHALL work primarily on political science, with more or less philosophy on the one hand and jurisprudence and constitutional history on the other. How I am to make a living with it I do not know; for that I must wait and see."

So Hadley wrote to E. D. Worcester on June 24, 1879, after his studies in Berlin were over and he was traveling on the Continent. The statement reflected his hopes; reality was to be very different. In July, 1879, his first offer of work arrived, as described in a letter of the 29th to Worcester:

It was about two weeks ago that I received a letter from Mr. Dexter [the Secretary of the Yale Corporation] announcing my appointment as tutor. It was not unexpected to me, as I had already heard of the fact indirectly. But I was much surprised to learn that my services were wanted next term for Freshman Greek, Mr. Beckwith having unexpectedly resigned. Had I known a month earlier, I could have arranged to take it, but at the time I received the letter my arrangements were so far made that I could not well change them and they brought me home too late for me to think of entering upon the tutorship next term. I could not think of undertaking classical teaching without much special preparation. It will be much better to wait some months and take the chance of making a success, than to step half-prepared and altogether hurried from the steamer to the recitation-room, with great prospect of a lamentable failure. And it does not do for a tutor to make a failure in the beginning. When the next vacancy occurs, I wish it might be in Mathematics; but I think I should take whatever might come. Anything better than to grow rusty.

Actually, Hadley took the Greek teaching in spite of his misgivings, and did well at it. His notebook for the course shows

that he started the year with a series of informal talks on Greek
history by way of background for what the class was to read. The
next year he went from Greek to Latin. In fact, the difficulty
was that he was continually shifted from one subject to another
as need arose. His appointment was as tutor, in those days the
designation of the initial grade in the faculty hierarchy, corresponding to that of instructor today, and the tutors were used to
teach whatever subject might be called for. In the four college
years from the fall of 1879 to the summer of 1883 he taught
Greek, Latin, Roman law, logic, and German. In addition to
his modest salary as tutor he received his room free in return for
serving as proctor, first in the North Entry of South Middle
(now Connecticut Hall) and then in Farnam.

His spare time was spent in the ordinary manner of a young
instructor in a college town, and here the last century seems
much like the present one. On January 4, 1880, he wrote
Worcester:

I am in New Haven society somewhat—about as much as I have
time for. The chief bond of connection is the Hier-wird-Deutsch-
Gesprochen Verein—a club organized by the indefatigable Delia
Lyman. The members are of all ages from Prof. Fisher down. The
club meets once every two weeks at the house of some one of the
members. The entertainment, in the way of eating, is restricted.
Beer and Pretzels are the proper thing, though in consideration of
the taste of some of the ladies we have coffee and cake as well. We
play games in German, and there is generally some special entertainment besides. At the last meeting [Frank Bigelow] Tarbell
and I acted in the play of "Einer muss heirathen."

As for the rest, my social life is limited to making calls, and receiving semi-occasional invitations to whist parties. On the whole my
most vigorous social feat has been the making of fifty-one New-
Year's calls—a very tolerable number for New Haven.

He resumed his devotion to whist, and wrote Worcester a
year later that he had formed a thousand-point whist club with
Alfred Ripley, Charles C. Camp, and William M. Hall, all
fellow tutors, the score on that date, February 27, 1881, standing Ripley and Hall 920, Camp and Hadley 937.

One casual association started in those days was to last for half a century. A group mainly composed of young instructors took to dining together once a month and called themselves the Colby Club after one of the number. At first the membership was somewhat indefinite but it soon became fixed. In the early years a few new members were taken in as others moved away, but no attempt was ever made to expand it to younger men and so keep it alive. Hadley, one of the earliest members, was at the same time the youngest, the college classes represented running from 1869 to his class of 1876. The roster, as it stood at the close of the nineteenth century, was: Thomas Hooker and Eli Whitney of the class of '69, Samuel A. Galpin and Morris F. Tyler of '70, Thomas G. Bennett and Charles S. Hastings of '70 Sheff, Henry B. Sargent of '71 Sheff, Clarence Deming, Edward H. Jenkins, Edwin S. Lines, and Theodore S. Woolsey of '72, William Beebe and Samuel T. Dutton of '73, Henry W. Farnam and George L. Fox of '74, and Arthur T. Hadley of '76. Earlier members had been James F. Colby, Edwin S. Wheeler, Thomas R. Bacon, and Frank B. Tarbell.

For over fifty years the club met monthly, and the members would miss almost any other engagement rather than a meeting of the Colby Club. There would be a dinner, followed by a paper written by one of the members, followed by much talk, tobacco smoke, and beer. The club was locally famous for its supposed enormous consumption of the latter, as well as for the lateness of the hour at which it adjourned. So far as I know there were no archives, and such of Hadley's papers as are extant have come down by a process of haphazard survival in his files. They bear testimony to the diverse character of the papers presented by the members, a diversity more than substantiated by occasional references to the contributions of others. Hadley's own papers include two on European trips and one each on a trip to the Pacific Coast, the novels of Walter Scott, the New York, Westchester, and Boston Railroad, the Chinese written language, western railroading methods, the abolition of legislative assemblies, Darwinian ethics, military maneuvers, and a history of the club itself. Missing papers, to which only incidental references remain, included one on a trip to an international congress of statisticians entitled "Statistics Grave and Gay."

During these early days in New Haven the Hadleys built the house in which Arthur was to live the rest of his life, spending $6,000 for the lot and $14,000 for the building. It was conveniently located within easy walking distance of the college, only a few blocks from the nearest of the university buildings, and about half a mile from the campus. They moved in during the spring of 1881, and Arthur no longer lived in college as a proctor. Writing to Worcester while the house was still being planned he said (January 4, 1880):

We (i.e. Mother) have bought the lot on the N.E. Corner of Whitney Ave and Trumbull St, and expect to begin building early in the spring. I go to the architect's office almost every day to work over plans. We have the interior pretty much arranged, and are hard at work trying to get a satisfactory exterior. I do not want you to infer from all this that we are likely to do anything startling; the money we can spend is so limited that we have the much harder problem of making a simple house which shall look well. The worst of it is that the city fire laws require us to build of brick, and a given amount of money will of course not give nearly as much scope for attempts at architectural effect as if the house were of wood.

In view of what was achieved even in brick, we must be thankful for the New Haven fire laws. The interior of the house was well planned and comfortable but the exterior was extravagantly variegated, with projecting bays, the whole surmounted by a towering roof of red tile, with a wooden third-floor balcony squeezed in for good measure. Architecturally terrible, it was a delightful house for the children who grew up there in later years, with its many nooks and corners, and above all with its enormous attic under the sloping roof, an attic fifty feet long and twenty feet high, lighted by little windows that looked out over the roofs and tree tops of the city.

Aside from its height the plan of the house was a customary one for those days. From a high porch you entered a hall, with the seldom used parlor on the left, and on the right the con-

stantly used living room, called the library. This last was
lined with books from floor to ceiling. In one corner was a fireplace, where a fire burned daily all winter. This living room was
on the southwest corner, so the sun came in nearly all day long
through the tall, narrow windows. Beyond the living room,
and reached either through it or from the hall, was the dining
room, again a sunny room, as it was the southeast corner room
and got the morning sun. For all that, in New Haven winters
breakfast at quarter past seven was eaten by the light of the gas
jets overhead. Parlor, living room, and dining room all opened
into each other or the hall with no doors to open or close, a fact
of great utility when the house, in later years, was crowded at
official receptions. The three rooms described account for three
corners, the fourth was occupied by the pantry and the kitchen
on the first floor and by a servant's room above. In later years a
small wing was added for a servants' sitting room downstairs
and two servants' rooms and bath above.

The second floor was reached by stairs at right angles to the
hall, beyond the parlor. These were narrow and steep. In fact,
the ceilings were so high that as Arthur's wife remarked in later
years the house would have been much roomier if laid on its side.
On the second floor there were three corner rooms, one over
each of the living rooms on the first floor, with a dressing room
in the space over the front hall. To the original bathroom on
this floor a second was later added. After Arthur was married,
he and his wife slept in a big double bed in the southwest corner
room. Their daughter had the southeast room, and the third
room, originally occupied by Arthur's mother, became a guest
room.

Up again, by high and narrow stairs as before, much given to
creaking if you were returning after the household was in bed,
you reached the third floor. Parts of the roof began at this level,
so the rooms no longer had windows on two sides. On this floor
were two bedrooms, a bathroom, and a big study where Arthur
worked, once more with well-filled book shelves. One of these
bedrooms, in later years, was occupied by the two sons, the other
was a guest room.

Up once more, and you came to the attic previously described. It held under the eaves a miscellany of old trunks and old household articles. The spacious center was clear of obstructions, except as children filled the floor with toy railroads. At one end was a large billiard table, placed here because it was the only unoccupied spot in the house with sufficient room.

This description, lengthy as it is, has yet to take in the cellar. This was well lighted because of the height of the first floor above the ground, so that the laundry, on the south side, was one of the sunniest rooms in the house.

Like any house, no matter how comfortable and how livable, that is used for half a century, it acquired idiosyncrasies. For example, it seemed impossible to clean the living room chimney often enough, and every few years it would take fire, always at the most inopportune moment, say on a cold winter's evening as guests were sitting down to dinner. The second floor guest room had its own bath, but this was in the nature of a hazard for inexperienced guests. The bath had been added some years after the house was built, and the pipes were unduly exposed, so that they froze on cold winter nights unless you left a little water running. When this happened the family were always most careful to assure the guest at breakfast that the room and not its occupant was to blame; but sensitive guests at times felt some embarrassment, nonetheless.

The house stood on its corner lot, with grass plots between it and Whitney Avenue, and a little yard behind with shrubs and flower beds. Whitney Avenue in 1881 was still unpaved, but a few years later it was given a paving of macadam as far as Sachem Street, two blocks beyond Trumbull Street. From that point on for years it remained little affected by the growth of the city. Then, in the next century, came trolleys, and interurban trolleys, and automobiles. The corner of Whitney and Trumbull was to pass, during Hadley's lifetime, from a quiet spot in a college town to a busy traffic intersection well characterized by one visitor. Asked in the morning whether he had passed a good night, he replied: "I don't wish to appear critical, but if the Hadley family had any commerical sense they would tear down this house and put up a filling station."

After four years of work as tutor Hadley felt compelled to make a change. His attempts to be allowed to give a course in political economy were unavailing. He had continued his studies in that field on the side, but found that the work of teaching other subjects left him little time for economic research and none for publication. Some of the courses which he taught he enjoyed, particularly that on Justinian, but teaching elementary German he found drudgery of the weariest sort. At last he took a drastic step, gave up his position in the college, and struck out on his own as a free-lance writer.

He summed up his reasons for the change in two sentences of a letter to C. H. Willcox (April 26, 1883):

"The faculty would be glad to have me stay, but cannot or at any rate do not offer any opportunities for teaching in my own line, and I feel as if I had worked in their line about long enough. Until I do something tangible and distinctive by which I can command a place elsewhere, I can never command a place here such as I want."

The Yale faculty had always been conservative, and although Arthur worried as to whether or not the fault lay in his teaching, the real reason why he could not get the work he wanted was the unwillingness of the older professors to give such importance to a new subject. An earlier example of this resistance to innovation, this time in another field, is given by an entry in the diary Arthur's father, James Hadley, kept when he was a professor at Yale. Under date of July 7, 1851, he wrote, describing a faculty meeting at which it was decided not to establish a professorship of history:

To the president's at 7½. Talk on some overtures in regard to a Professorship of History— . . . The questions discussed were whether it is worthwhile to have a Prof. of History, whether it is best to abridge so much the instruction given by the President, whether it is well to have a Professor of such limited range, whether it is desirable to give so much importance to the department of history. The discussion was rather rambling, but the conclusion was unanimous . . .

Not consoled by such precedents, Arthur unburdened himself in a long letter to Worcester, who was then in Europe (July 10, 1883):

I felt the winter more from being so entirely in the dark—and somewhat in the dumps—about my own plans. When I took up the German two years ago, I intended, and said, that it was to be only temporary on my part; and a year ago I said that I did not wish to take it longer than this year—that is than till now. I had supposed that by the end of that time there would be something given me more in my own line, in return for my temporarily tiding them over their German vacancy. I had some tolerably distinct reasons for thinking so, but I was disappointed. At a meeting of the professors (from which the assistant professors were excluded) held in January, they decided that they could not offer me any such position as I wanted, but asked me to take an ordinary tutorship. This was under the circumstances adding insult to injury in connection with the way it was offered, but I did not feel independent enough to stand on my dignity, and said that I would consider the matter. The more I considered it, the more I felt that to accept an ordinary tutorship on those terms would be to say goodbye to all ambition or prospect of rising. The work, to be decently done, takes so much time and strength as to leave one little freedom to make an impression on the outside world; and I did not want to be dependent for the chance of getting to work in my own line on the time when the Professors might choose to promote me from a tutorship. So I said "no."

I felt pretty blue about that time, for one reason why they went back on me was that I had not been as successful in teaching elementary German as they thought I might have been. This was harder to bear because there was an element of truth in it; I had not been satisfied with my own success as a drill master in that subject. At the same time I had made no failure as compared with what others had done in the same line; and I felt that it was unfair to me to be judged by this, while what I had done in logic and other things was entirely forgotten. But that was not the main thing that occupied my thoughts; I had the uncomfortable sense of being stranded, seven years after graduation, "without visible means of support";

and I was anxious as to whether, in the absence of routine work I had the moral strength to do myself justice, or the tenacity of purpose to make an impression on the world.

However, I made a vigorous strike for work, and got some. You probably know the name of J. J. Lalor of Chicago; and perhaps you know of his Cyclopaedia of Political Science of which two volumes have been published, and the third is to appear at the beginning of next year. After some correspondence, and some indication of what I could do, he gave me considerable work for that, so that I write a number of articles in his third volume—Overproduction, Profits, Reciprocity, Speculation, Subsidies, Transportation, and probably two or three others. This will keep me pretty well occupied till October, for I shall do a great deal of investigation in connection with this writing. I may as well tell you, what I of course have not told about here—the thing that has gratified me most of all, that after receiving my article on Overproduction (the only one I have thus far written) which embodied a great deal of such looking up of figures and facts, Mr. Lalor wrote that he would pay me for such work at the same rate as he was paying General Walker and David A. Wells. It is to be sure by no means a rate to grow rich on; but it is a gratifying fact, and an incentive to hard work.

Of course as this took shape my spirits rose. I can only look four months ahead; but I have the feeling that my getting this work now means getting some other work then; and the hope that there is a demand for trained economists, and that specialists' work here is likely to be appreciated. My plan is now to write all I can, both in things like this and for newspapers and reviews, until I can make such an impression on the public as to command some first-rate place as professor of pol. economy, pol. science or history. Of course I had much rather such a place would be in New Haven than anywhere else; but if it were a choice between the right kind of work somewhere else and the wrong kind of work here, I should choose the former. However "the morrow shall take thought for the things of itself."

You can imagine that with this work on my hands, I do not take very much vacation this year. I expect to take a walk in the White Mountains that may occupy two weeks; and I shall probably try to get to Buffalo for a short visit. The month of August I shall spend almost entirely in New Haven. At that time the library is closed—most of the week—to the general public, and therefore all the more useful to those who can get in and have everything all to themselves.

CHAPTER V

AN ECONOMIC FREE LANCE
1883—1891

ARTHUR HADLEY started without delay on his research and writing, spending the summer of 1883 alone in the house on Whitney Avenue while his mother went to Waterville in the White Mountains. His routine during these summers of work was to start by getting his own breakfast. The resultant meal does not sound appetizing; he found he could save himself trouble by putting tea leaves in a glass of tap water the night before, drinking the liquid the next morning as accompaniment to slices of bread and butter. In the morning he worked in the college library. He lunched at some restaurant, usually Traeger's, and nearly always with one or more men who like himself were spending the summer in studies at New Haven. In the afternoon came more work, but he usually left off in time for a few sets of tennis before dinner.

Sometimes he dined with friends, or, if he was working in the evening, would get himself a meal in the empty house. He lists such a meal in a letter: three large slices of bread and butter, Stilton cheese, and seven peaches. "Those desiring variety," he adds, "can substitute bananas for peaches and pilot crackers for bread." Minor amenities were handled in a manner that distressed his mother. "The only thing wanting as yet is a good napkin and that I shall doubtless find as soon as I really set to work. What I am now using is the thing you put under the tea cups. It is clean, and equally absorbent with a napkin, but is oblong instead of square."

It is perhaps misleading to use the term routine in connection with Hadley's schedule of work. There was nothing fixed about it, and when he became particularly interested in a problem he would work for long hours and at high pressure. E. D. Worcester, an orderly soul, rightly objected to such lack of regularity and would write urging him to mend his ways. In one letter (November 8, 1884) Worcester admonished him:

You certainly have your full share of intellectual curiosity and enthusiasm, and you ought to cultivate phlegm; else we shall see you the victim of excessive indulgence in intellectual pleasures. The waters of the Pierian spring are to be drunk deeply, but regularly. The ill-guided mortal who drinks to bursting whenever thirst takes him, shatters a constitution that would have been built up to colossal strength had he confined himself to one glassful after each meal.

Worcester heartily approved, however, of Arthur's new line of work, though he poked fun at him (September 12, 1883):

What lends so mysterious a grandeur to one's reputation for scholarship as the report that one has written for a cyclopaedia? It far surpasses the mere writing of a book. Any fool can write a book; but it is only the giants of the intellectual world, the 'prodigies of mentality,' who contribute to cyclopaedias. And again, you will doubtless some day have the sweet pleasure, tasted by so few, of saying to the impertinent pupil who tries to trump you with a quotation from that sacred cyclopaedia: "Yes, I know the article to which you refer; I wrote it myself, twenty years ago."

In this summer of 1883 Hadley wrote the articles for Lalor's *Cyclopaedia,* as planned. Magazine articles followed soon after, among the earliest being one in the *Andover Review,* which invited him to choose his own subject, "only we are unhappily debarred from attacking a protective tariff." As time went on he became a regular contributor to the *Independent,* doing most of its articles on economic subjects during the later 1880's. He also wrote for the *Financial Chronicle.*

Among the various publications for which he wrote in early years the *Railroad Gazette* was the one to which Hadley devoted most time. He was particularly interested in railroad history and management, so writing for the *Gazette* fell directly in his field. Beginning in 1884 he was engaged on a permanent basis to write the notes on foreign railroad matters. Ultimately he came to be an assistant editor. In those days the managing editor was S. Wright Dunning, and the *Railroad Gazette* under his leadership not only was the leading railroad weekly but reached out in many directions.

In later years it was a standing joke with the Hadley children that you could mention no famous man of the previous generation without being told that "he used to be one of the men who hung around the Railroad Gazette office." That there was some foundation for this is indicated by a paragraph in Hadley's memorial article on Dunning in the *Railway Age* for June 7, 1924:

The Railroad Gazette office became a gathering place for men who were interested in the future of transportation. Men like Wellington or Chanute found welcome opportunities for discussing their theories. If Prince Hilkoss came from Siberia or Colonel Prout from Central Africa, they were drawn to the Railroad Gazette office even more by Dunning's personality than by the facts which they expected to learn.

For a dozen years Hadley worked in these surroundings, making frequent trips to New York. Even after pressure of academic work forced him to drop railroad writing, he maintained many of these early contacts, and always with pleasure.

At first Hadley's earnings as a free-lance writer were modest in the extreme. In a good week he might make twenty-five dollars, but there would be other weeks spent largely in research. Nevertheless he had the stimulus of knowing that his work was published, and he was able to earn enough to meet his personal expenses and his share of household expenses. After a few years, as his reputation became established, his earnings grew, and he was able to save a substantial amount each year; substantial, at least, by academic standards.

The family accounts were kept in a chunky notebook five by three inches, started by James Hadley thirty years before, in the first year of his marriage. The pages held out for forty years, until in 1892 Arthur had to start a new one. In 1884, the first full year of Arthur's free-lance venture, the book shows that his mother had an income of about $2,500, her original holdings of securities having been augmented by securities received from the

estate of a sister, Julia Twining, who had died a few years before. Arthur had an income from securities, left him by his father, of $400, and from his writings of $870; so the combined
family income in 1884 was about $3,800. By 1888 the family
total was $8,200, with Mrs. Hadley's income furnishing the
same amount as before, but Arthur's risen: his investments
brought in $1,170, college salary $1,775, the *Railroad Gazette*
$1,272, and other writing and royalties $1,537.

Hadley combined an ability to save with an ability to invest
wisely. During all the subsequent years, when he was first a professor at Yale and then president, his expenses exceeded the
salary that went with the post. He was able to supplement this
salary, however, in part by income from past savings and in part
by outside writing. This writing was always so in line with his
college work that it added to his value to the college instead of
representing a diversion of effort. This let him meet expenses,
be in a position to give modestly to causes in which he was interested, and have something over to add to his savings, the
figure at which he aimed for this last being $2,000 a year.

This self-imposed saving was intended, at least in the early
years of his married life, to meet anticipated higher expenses
when his children were going to school and college. When that
day came, however, the income from his growing list of investments was able to take up the slack. At his death in 1930 he left
an estate of half a million dollars. Obviously the greater part of
this was due to judicious investment; it was not a case of the
principal growing by compounding the interest, as in a savings
bank, because the greater part of the income was spent each year.
On the other hand the increase was not due to speculation; his
list of investments was always conservative and he never bought
on margin.

It would be pleasant if some simple rule could be derived
from Hadley's practice which would let others attain the same
result. Actually, the increase was produced by careful consideration of the risks and advantages in each particular situation.
Many of his investments were in local enterprises where he knew
himself that the management was efficient. He had losses as well

as profits, but the profits predominated. He believed that if a careful and intelligent man bought and sold with an eye to long-term investment he usually came out ahead in the long run, while the attempt to buy and sell with an eye to quick turnover and quick profits usually resulted in loss, the few alluring exceptions to the contrary notwithstanding.

Hadley gave up teaching because Yale would not let him teach political economy. Paradoxically the immediate result was that Yale offered him an opportunity to teach in his chosen field. In the long letter to Worcester of July 10, 1883, already quoted there is a final paragraph, added later:

Since I began my letter I have had an appointment as instructor in Pol. Science, in the Graduate Department. Whether I get any pupils remains to be seen. I get no salary, apart from the possibility of meagre fees. So it is not a very brilliant position; but for all that I am rather glad of the place. I shall try to get together a class on the Industrial History of Recent Times, or something of the sort. Until I see whether anybody wants to study with me, I am saying as little about my appointment as possible. Luckily the newspapers did not get hold of the fact at all.

The actual title adopted for the new course was "Railroads and their Industrial Effects," although it was listed in the college catalogue as "Industrial Problems of the Day." Not only did it attract good students, both graduate and undergraduate, but its title caught the fancy of the press and it received much outside attention. A year later the *New York Sun* wrote (October 2, 1884):

At Yale College a series of lectures has just been begun on the problems of railway management, the laws natural and political that the development of the railway systems of the country have created, and it is announced that nearly all the students are eager to attend these lectures. Into the banks, the manufactories, and the railway offices the young men are now going who formerly would have looked for a career only at the bar and in politics.

Writing to Worcester at about the same date (November 2, 1884) Arthur said:

It makes a great difference whether one is actually on the academic faculty in active interior contact with the students as students, or whether it is only the exterior contact that one gets meeting them as a sort of free lance. I have gained twenty times more than I have lost by the change; but it would be useless to deny that this is a real and serious loss as far as it goes.

Another thing which I feel is the absence of routine. I have work to do, too much rather than too little; but unfortunately not of a kind with which I dare to occupy my whole disposable time, or anything like the whole of it. It is too exciting, there is too little about it that is purely mechanical. If I work too long one day, I am sure to feel the reaction the next day, and sometimes—what I object to a great deal more—it impairs the soundness of my sleep.

Lately, I am getting some easy routine work of a rather peculiar character. The papers have advertised my lecture course so extensively that I have a letter about it from somebody almost every day. Not in general from men who have even a remote idea of joining the class; but men whom I am glad to help all I can. They must sometimes wonder how I get time to write them as long letters as I do. Really it is a relief to have routine business of this kind, which I feel is business, but which involves little intellectual effort.

My class is not unlike what it was last year. The attendance averages a little larger; but I have not so many first rate men, at least among the graduates. In my advanced class, one hour a week, I have only two men, and I have a great deal of trouble in the way of preparation. Luckily I can use a great deal of my material for those lectures as material for newspaper articles.

Hadley's lecture notebook shows that he planned his lecture course as follows:

Introduction. Outline of the Subject and the Questions at Issue. 2 lectures.

I. History of Transportation System of the United States. 8 lectures.

II. Organization and Business Methods Today. 15 lectures.

III. Railroads and Railroad Legislation in Foreign Countries. 7 lectures.

IV. Railroad Legislation in the United States. 7 lectures.

V. Economic Grounds and Limitations of State Interference (whatever is left) say 18 lectures.

The whole approach of the course was facts first and theories only after the facts were known. Thus, before taking up theories as to the regulation of profits there was an exposition of book-keeping and accounting methods generally. This was followed by a description of current practices in railroad accounting and the methods used in determining costs, real or nominal, in a variety of situations, for example where freight cars are in use on other lines. Working through the yellowed sheets of the notebooks and going over the penciled notes, one is impressed with the mass of practical knowledge that Hadley made his own before adventuring on the course. The lectures themselves are only given in outline, but from the accounts of those who took them they were interesting as well as thorough. Even in the bare bones of the notes this is indicated at times:

How shall we determine what sum is available for the payment of a dividend?

Or, a dividend having been paid, how shall we know whether it was earned?

If original entries were cooked up we cannot usually detect it.

If it is a mere trick of bookkeeping we can usually make something out of it.

The subject matter of Hadley's courses at Yale developed as the decade passed, and while railroad practice always played a prominent part, he came more and more to treat of industry generally and of economic problems as a whole. Another course he gave in those years was on industrial history. By 1888 he was also lecturing on industrial legislation; because of its subject matter this particular course drew a substantial part of its attendance from students at the Yale Law School.

In the spring of 1885 Hadley delivered a series of lectures on railroad problems at the Massachusetts Institute of Technology in Boston. He lectured daily for a period of two weeks to a group of about thirty. Before the course started he was extremely nervous and he hardly slept the night before the opening lecture. This initial nervousness was to stay with him all his life, in spite of his constant speaking. Thirty years later, when an undergraduate debater was apprehensively getting ready for an intercollegiate debate, Hadley said to him: "I can give you a real piece of encouragement; after years of experience I have discovered that no one else can see my knees shaking."

Once the lectures were under way Hadley's apprehension departed. He enjoyed giving the course and felt that he had done creditably. He wrote home to his mother daily, telling how each lecture had gone and appraising it with considerable objectivity. Thus on April 5, 1885, he wrote:

"Saturday morning Mr. Atkinson came in to my lecture. He said he had an engagement which would require him to leave in the middle of it, but he stayed all through. From this I conclude that he liked it. I was not in a particularly fluent mood verbally; luckily my matter was uncommonly strong."

This trip to Boston was only the first of many in the years to come. Hadley always enjoyed the city and the friends that he made there. General Francis A. Walker was then president of M.I.T. and was most kind to his young visiting lecturer. At his house Hadley met Charles Francis Adams, Jr., for many years the head of the Massachusetts Railroad Commission, and John Codman Ropes, the military historian.

The talk, at the first meeting with Ropes, turned on some obscure battle in the wars of Frederick the Great. Hadley advanced his view as to the engagement. Ropes differed. Hadley tried again, whereupon Ropes demolished his position so completely and convincingly that Hadley apologized for his temerity in expressing an opinion. Ropes replied: "You wouldn't dream of apologizing if you only knew what a pleasure it is to me to meet a man who has any views on that battle, no matter how erroneous." After the dinner Ropes carried Hadley off with him and the two sat till all hours of the night talking military history. Ropes did much of his work at night, and Hadley received a standing invitation to come in whenever he might be passing by and see the light in the Beacon Street study. Of this invitation he frequently availed himself, on this trip and in later years. Sometimes there would be other visitors; on one occasion Hadley wrote home about meeting "Oliver Wendell Holmes, Jr., the author of a brilliant work on jurisprudence."

More often Ropes and Hadley were alone, and their talk would be of military history, generally our Civil War or the campaigns of Frederick the Great, but with excursions into other subjects. One of these other topics was the hexameters of Horace; the two men agreed that these were worth all the rest of Latin literature together, and they would strengthen each other in this heretical belief.

Hadley's first book, *Railroad Transportation*, which embodied the material he had developed in his lectures and articles, was published by Putnam in the autumn of 1885. It had an immediate success, abroad as well as at home. A Russian translation was published in 1886 and a French translation in 1887.

All over the world railroads were a leading problem of the day, and all over the world this little book became an authority. In less than three hundred small octavo pages it dealt with the whole field, in a style that was concise and eminently quotable. Hadley said in later years that he had been fortunate in selecting a subject which was of real importance but where the literature, although growing fast, did not yet exceed in volume what one man could read. He believed that he had studied everything written on the subject, not only in book form, which was an easy task, but in periodicals and technical reports and statistical sources, in foreign languages as well as in English. In this he was aided by the fact that, partly by nature and partly by training, he was a phenomenally rapid and retentive reader. He could go through a book, turning the leaves so rapidly that he would appear to be merely skimming over them, and at the end not only retain the gist of the book but be able to quote, or at least paraphrase, long passages from it.

The full title of the book was *Railroad Transportation, Its History and Its Laws*. Starting with an account of developments in transportation, it next explained the way in which railroads were financed and rates set. It described the interplay of legitimate financing and speculation, of competition and combination, of industrial initiative and governmental regulation. The book closed with a comparative study of the same subjects in other countries: England, France, Italy and Central Europe.

The conclusions reached were stated with an accuracy that appealed to experts and a simplicity that appealed to practical railroad men who ordinarily had no use for experts. Thus Sir Thomas Farrer in England and James J. Hill in the United States alike rated the book as the leading authority. One quotation from the text will serve as an illustration (p. 261):

The difficulty with most theories of railroad rates is that they are not based on actual practice, but upon somebody's preconceived notion of what that practice ought to be.

The practical railroad manager has one general principle in this matter. He lowers rates whenever he thinks it will increase net earnings—in other words, as long as it will increase gross earnings faster than it increases operating expenses. Any theory which shall correctly represent American railroad practice, must be based on this principle.

In 1885 Hadley appeared before the Senate Committee on Interstate Commerce, when that body was engaged in hearings leading up to the Interstate Commerce Act. He presented a statement and answered many questions that were asked by the Committee. He followed Commissioner Fink as a witness, and an account of the occasion was given in a current newspaper (the date and name of the paper are missing from the clipping):

The gentleman who followed him had no practical experience whatever in railroads. He was Arthur T. Hadley, son of the old Greek Professor, whose name and works are familiar to collegians everywhere. The Anglo-Saxon bluntness of the German expert gave way to a broadening of the A's and a whirring of R's that were for a time painful to everyone in the room. Mr. Hadley's Yale mannerisms, however, were soon forgotten in the matter which he thoughtfully presented to the committee. A Senator said to me afterward: "That paper will read better, contains really a clearer analysis of the railroad situation than anything that has been presented to us. It is an example of what pure mind culture will do. Mr. Hadley's mind has been drilled in analytical studies. He has taken up railroads, I

understand, as worthy of a life study. He has gone at them as his
father did before him at the Greek language—to separate, dismem-
ber, critically and judicially examine them, not in specific cases but
as a great whole. It has resulted in his ability to discuss railroads
from every point of view, with a facility surpassing even a trained
experience such as Mr. Fink is known and acknowledged to possess."

Three years later, in 1888, Hadley was asked by the Interstate Commerce Commission to supervise the arrangement of
the statistics which they were collecting, but was compelled to
decline because of press of other work. For the same reason, in
1889 he was forced to say that he could not take charge of the
statistics on transportation in connection with the Eleventh Census of the United States.

Hadley had a chance at practical applications of economic
theories when, in 1885, he was appointed Commissioner of Labor Statistics of the State of Connecticut, a position that he held
for two years. It carried a salary of $2,000 a year and called for
only part-time work. The salary was a welcome addition to his
earnings but at the same time increased the vehemence of the
attacks made upon him by the practical party politicians, who
were out to get this plum for one of themselves. Hadley, on the
contrary, had not been a candidate for the post, and at first was
inclined to refuse it, partly because he was skeptical of what
could be accomplished under the legislation which had just created the Bureau of Labor Statistics. As he phrased it in the first
report issued by the bureau: "It was specially provided that no
persons should be required to leave their residences or places of
business to communicate with the commissioner, and the provision for traveling expenses was stricken out of the act—thus arranging that the facts should not come to the commissioner, and
hinting that the commissioner should not go to the facts."

The work itself he enjoyed greatly, though it meant constant
traveling to and from the State Capitol at Harford, where his
office was located. This was an hour by train from New Haven.
On days when he worked at the Capitol he would take the 7:45
train in the morning to Hartford, spend the forenoon, and return
to New Haven in time for work there in the afternoon. The train

to New Haven was often late in going through Hartford, but
this occasioned him no loss of time. The State Capitol Building
was separated from the railroad line by an open park, and Hadley's office was on the ground floor. He could see the train as it
came in, and by climbing out of the window and hurrying across
the park he would arrive in time to swing aboard as it was pulling
out of the station.

The two annual reports issued during his term of office are
interesting reading. They won the respect of the public but were
not popular with extremists in the ranks of either capital or labor.
He had been appointed by Governor Harrison but was not re-
appointed by the next governor, Lounsbury. The change brought
an outcry in the press, but the new governor was firm and appointed (to quote a contemporary newspaper) "an obscure gentleman of good character engaged in the manufacture of paper
barrels in Hartford."

The reports show vividly the labor conditions existing in the
1880's. Many plants paid wages only monthly, and employees
were continually in debt to the company store. As for the living
quarters in some of the towns, when Hadley a few years later
went through San Francisco's notoriously ill-housed Chinatown,
his comment was: "The Chinese lodging houses are not so bad
as I expected—not so bad for instance as medium grade tene-
ment houses for workers of the corresponding class in the
east."

The six-day week, with at least a ten-hour day, was the rule.
Only one employee out of every twenty worked as little as fifty-
four hours a week. In spite of a law to the contrary, children under ten were working sixty or sixty-six hours a week in the textile
mills. The reports not only give the statistics, they set out the
comments of employers, workingmen, and third parties.

They reflect the situation in an industrial state, passing from
native American labor to increasing reliance on foreign labor
(1885 *Report*, p. 42):

"Instead of the American, who wants to rely on himself and
be let alone, as well as let other people alone, there is coming in
an element of foreign labor that prefers to rely on others; does

not specially care to be let alone, and greatly enjoys regulating somebody else."

This labor group felt that the commissioner did not go far enough in advocating legislation to cure existing conditions. Instead he urged only modest legislative reforms, believing that it would be hard enough to enforce even these and out of the question to enforce more sweeping ones. On the other hand, employers were not pleased with some aspects of the frank portrayal of existing practices, nor with comments such as (*Idem*, p. 97):

In the case of an actual strike, the sympathy of constituted authorities usually seems to be against the strikers. The employer, in such cases, takes care to keep within his technical rights, and society must support him, just as society must support officers when soldiers mutiny; but in each case the ultimate blame for the trouble is likely to rest more with the employer than with the employee; more with the officers than with the men.

The office of labor commissioner was Hadley's first government appointment but it was not to be his last. In the United States any man with an established position in his field and a willingness to serve is apt to be called upon at frequent intervals. He served on the Connecticut Board of Mediation and Arbitration in 1895 and two years later on the Connecticut Charter Commission. In 1910 he was to serve as chairman of the Railroad Securities Commission appointed by President Taft.

As class secretary Hadley had the work of arranging for the decennial reunion of his classmates in 1886, and he put in much time editing a record of their careers. Fifty-one came back, or nearly half the class, and all lunched with the Hadleys on Whitney Avenue, the first of many such events.

A month before the reunion Hadley had received an appointment which was, to him, a vindication of the course he had taken in striking out for himself. Yale, which three years before had refused to do more than continue him as tutor in elementary German, now created a professorship of political science and appointed him as the first incumbent. It was true that the letter of notification from the Yale Corporation cautiously added: "The Corporation is not at present able to make themselves responsible for any permanent salary in connection with this chair." Nevertheless a part-time salary of $1,600 a year for five years was made available by a gift from Henry Farnam.

The fact that his teaching duties would be only part time was an advantage rather than a disadvantage, for it gave him time for his existing commitments on the *Railroad Gazette* and elsewhere. Until 1891, when he became full-time professor of political economy, Hadley regarded himself as a free-lance writer doing some teaching on the side, rather than as a college professor. His initial teaching schedule, in the fall of 1886, came early in the day and early in the week. He had a class of seniors from 8:30 to 9:30 from Monday through Thursday, and a class of graduate students from 10:00 to 11:00 on Tuesdays and Wednesdays. He could, and frequently did, go to New York Thursday morning after class, getting to the office of the *Railroad Gazette* before lunch and with time for two and a half days of work in New York before returning to New Haven on Saturday evening.

As Hadley became better known through his teaching and writing, he was increasingly called on for outside lectures. Following his 1885 lectures at the Massachusetts Institute of Technology, he gave another course of lectures, this time at Harvard, in 1887. In addition to various other lectures in the East he was invited in 1890 to give a series of four lectures in Minneapolis on railroads, with particular reference to rates and legislation. This proved an interesting experience. A local paper, in describing one lecture, said (December 28, 1890):

Prof. Hadley presented last evening to another appreciative audience his second lecture on railroads. . . . The professor showed himself a thorough master of the subject, and easily answered or parried the numerous questions which at the conclusion of the lecture prominent railroaders like President Hill, Paymaster Wright and others propounded, and manfully withstood even the onslaught of C. J. Buell.

Hadley wrote to his mother on this trip (December 26):

"I have heard of Western hospitality; I am now experiencing what it is. If I may trust from the first day's experience it will be limited only by my physical endurance."

And again, at the close of the trip:

"I had intended to go home to Minneapolis that evening, but the Nushka Club of St. Paul had been kind enough to invite me to the great social event of the season, their New Year's Eve masquerade ball. It proved to be a fine thing, well worth going to, about the pleasantest party I ever attended."

During these years Mrs. Hadley lived in the house on Whitney Avenue, except in the summer when she went to Waterville, New Hampshire, in the southern part of the White Mountains. Arthur would usually spend two weeks with her there and occasional week ends, but it was too long a journey to be taken frequently. Connections, too, were poor. On one occasion, when he was traveling up on Saturday afternoon, the train got later and later, until it was evident it would miss its connection at Lowell with the through train from Boston to Canada. This meant spending a night in Lowell and most of the week end ruined. The conductor would not wire ahead to hold the train but he told Hadley he could send a wire over the railroad line if he wished. Banking on the fact that there would be no one on duty at Lowell on a Saturday night with sufficient authority to disregard a peremptory telegram signed by an unknown name, Hadley got the train numbers from the conductor and wired Lowell: "Hold number seven up to one hour to await arrival number eighty-nine." Number eighty-nine was a little over one hour late by the time it got to Lowell but number seven was still there, Hadley was rushed across to it, and the train pulled out. Not only was he received with open arms but he was ushered by the conductor and the brakeman to an empty private car at the end of the train. After the train was well under way and he was at no risk of being thrown off, Hadley asked: "Who am I supposed to be?" The conductor and brakeman said in surprise that when the telegram came they figured he must be connected with the president of the road, whose empty private car they were taking north. Hadley disillusioned them with some mis-givings, but they bore no malice and the three of them spent the evening sitting in the presidential chairs on the rear platform of the car, swapping stories.

Even on commonplace trips to and from Waterville Hadley never suffered for want of interest. In a letter written to his mother on July 20, 1886, he reports on his trip back to New Haven:

The journey passed off quite without adventure. I left Mr. Elliott in Compton Village and walked to the station, where I spent some time in examining the rail-joints of the B.C. & M. which are peculiar. When I fully understood them, I explained to an old farmer who came along how it was that they secured lateral stiffness but not vertical strength. The old fellow was a trifle dazed at first, but be-came quite delighted before we had finished. He was particularly pleased with the exposition of the theory of shearing strains. I also read quite a good deal of the freight tariff of the Boston & Lowell RR which was lying on the ticket agent's table; and had an excellent time altogether.

During a few summers Hadley went further afield. In 1889 he took his first trip to the Pacific Coast, spending six weeks, partly in company with Theodore Woolsey and partly with Henry Farnam. They went to Toronto, and thence by rail and steamer to Port Arthur on Lake Superior. From there they went to Vancouver over the Canadian Pacific, which had been opened a few years before, stopping off for a week's walking in the Canadian Rockies. They worked down the coast as far as San Francisco, where they stayed at Berkeley with Tom Bacon, a fellow member of the Colby Club who had moved to the University of California. They broke the trip home with a week's walking around Lake Tahoe and then returned by way of Salt Lake City and Denver. In Hadley's case this was followed by an interesting week in out-of-the-way parts of Missouri, looking up real estate belonging to some of his Twining cousins.

The West was a new world, and Hadley's letters give his experiences in detail and with delight. There was the express train on which they rode that "had to make some stops not on the schedule, and there was one hill which it could not get up at all. The engine had to take on the baggage car and smoker to the nearest siding and then come back for the rest of the train. I have seen that happen to freight trains, but never to an express." There was the Grand Pacific Hotel at Kamloops which, a railroad official had told them, "belied its name. We were frightened, for we thought that he meant it was not pacific; but he only intended to say that it was not grand. He was quite right." They left Kamloops, incidentally, on a freight train, the better to see the country; but it turned out to be a most comfortable trip, as they made friends with the division superintendent and he had his car hitched to the rear end for them.

They were in Seattle a few months after the fire which wiped out much of the town. Hadley described the scene (August 26, 1889):

The business on the main street is done almost wholly in tents. The throng of buyers and the variety of wares contrast strangely with the primitive arrangements for accommodating them. It is Broadway in an Arab framework—"the voice is the voice of Jacob but the skin is the skin of Esau." Some of the signs on the business tents are worth preserving; I give a few, taken from various restaurants:
   "Coffee like your Mother made"
   "Waffle foundry"
   "The New Delmonico: the only three for a quarter place in the city."
   The last is puzzling; but inappropriate in any event, for the old Delmonico is not a place where you can get three of anything for a quarter.

Customs and signs in San Francisco he found no less strange to his eastern eyes, and he wrote on August 30:

Just outside of Oakland there is quite a large cemetery with an elaborate gateway. Immediately *inside* the gate, instead of a chapel like that in New Haven, are the headquarters of the Republican County Committee, with a sign to that effect twenty feet long. To the right of the entrance is a smaller, but hardly less conspicuous sign, "No shooting allowed in these grounds." Finally, one section of the ground bears the suggestive inscription: *"Thermal Vale Nursery on this side."*

There are pages of description of the Rockies in Hadley's letters, or of the cities where he stayed, or of railroad matters. There is even a detailed description of an "instrument of the Zither sort" on which a Chinese cook played. Hadley examined it carefully afterward, tried it out, and set forth his views as to the relation of the intervals and tones to those on Western musical scales.

Hadley on several occasions planned trips to Europe but was prevented by pressure of work from going except in three years. In 1882 he took a walking trip in Norway and in 1887 and 1890 in Switzerland. The account of his walks and climbs is better reserved for a later chapter, but on all these trips he took time for work in his field of economics. This was particularly true of the 1890 trip, on which he attended the meetings of the British Association for the Advancement of Science, held at Leeds and lasting the better part of a week. Many of the British economists Hadley already knew, but the meetings gave him a chance to make the acquaintance of others, both British and foreign.

On September 4 Arthur wrote from Leeds to his mother:

The first evening was occupied with the address of the president, Sir F. Abel. The Invited Guests sat on the platform, where I had the pleasure of seeing Mr. Marsh. This morning I read my paper to an audience which seemed to enjoy it and which engaged in an active discussion. I met Mr. and Mrs. Marshall—not met in discussion but socially—Mr. Innis Palgrave, Prof. Brentano, Mr. Ashley, Prof. Sidgwick, and a number of others whose names you would be less likely to know. I have been put on the section committee, which gives me more opportunities for meeting all these men, and is something of an honor. But Mr. Marsh is vice-president of his section, which is a much larger honor.

The letter written the following day comments on various members present:

Professor Marshall is a charming man, but only too obviously an invalid. I was a good deal worried lest the strain of presiding over the section should be too much for him; but I understand he has more reserve strength than would appear at first sight.

Edgeworth I like exceedingly. He is a man not much older than I, straightforward, affable and attentive. Brentano is a wonderfully agreeable man, seeming almost as much English as German in his way of thought. John B. Martin I like, but he suffers from deafness so much as to interfere with conversation. Ashley I have as yet seen little of; the same may be said of Sidgwick. The last-mentioned stammers fearfully. He yesterday proposed a vote of thanks to Mama—Mama—Mama—Mama—Marshall, in such a way that I had some difficulty in keeping my face straight. This was however not quite so bad as the performance of Sir F. Bramwell, who in moving a vote of thanks to the President of the Association for his great public address (which was unconscionably long) said "I cannot at this late hour do the subject justice. I should have been glad to embrace an opportunity of properly supporting this motion *earlier in the evening.*"

There is an account of extracurricular activities in a letter of September 9:

On Sunday I took a longer walk, though perhaps in a more leisurely manner, with a party made up as follows:—Mr. F. Y. Edgeworth, who invited me, and of whom I have already given my favorable impression; Mr. Wycherley,—if that is the way he spells his name, —a geographer who is not much at talking, but jolly and efficient; Mrs. Bryant, a distinguished graduate of London University, who looks it, all over, but is not half so bad as she looks—in fact, who is first rate company; Miss Collins, a girl of about twenty-five, with an international reputation for her work among the London poor, and not at all bad looking, but with an amount of aggressiveness about her which might ultimately become fatiguing; Miss Childs, a graduate of London University now teaching in one of the northern suburbs, apparently quite humble because she has no such exalted claims to distinction as her two companions, but extremely good looking and attractive, after a type more common in America than in England. Altogether, it was an uncommonly nice party. They are going to take a walking trip in Yorkshire after they get through here, in company with the distinguished young psychologist Alfred Sully. They were kind enough to urge me to join them for any part of the time which I could arrange; and it was with extreme regret that I found myself unable to do so.

Following the meeting at Leeds, Hadley visited various British economists, spending three days with Acworth in Dulwich, then stopping with Alfred Marshall in Cambridge, and finally with Sir Thomas Farrer in Northumberland.

From London he wrote to his mother on September 13:

I have been having a glorious time for the last twenty-four hours. Last evening I went out to Mr. Acworth's at Dulwich. He has a nice wife and a charming home. At dinner we had Tom Farrer's company; his father is confined in Northumberland with a sprained ankle, which he takes philosophically. Tom Farrer has invited me to spend next Wednesday night with him, and I think I shall be able to do so.

This morning I have been looking over the handling of the London passenger traffic and have visited the signal towers at Herne Hill, London Bridge and Waterloo, besides making the acquaintance of many of the station and yard men and a few higher officials. At Waterloo I had a specially good time, the foreman of the signal tower being one of the brightest men I ever met, and some of his appliances most ingenious. The people in the passing trains stared to see a man without any uniform walking across the tracks and poking his nose into the interlocking apparatus.

CHAPTER VI

COLLEGE PROFESSOR

1891–1899

IN 1891 Arthur Hadley became a full-time professor and a regular member of the faculty. Far more important for his course of action, then and in the future, he married.

It is difficult for a son to write objectively of the home life of his parents, but it is my belief that it would be impossible to find a happier marriage. Helen Hadley was a perfect partner for her husband in every conventional way, but the most important fact is that the two were so completely happy together for the forty years of their married life.

Helen Harrison Morris was born in New Haven on May 12, 1863. Her father was Luzon Burritt Morris, judge of the Probate Court in New Haven. He had been born on a farm near Newtown, Connecticut, in 1827. Working first as a blacksmith's helper and then as a machinist, he had saved enough money to put himself through Yale, graduating in 1854. He went into the practice of the law, and became not only a leading lawyer but a leading citizen of New Haven. In 1892 he was elected governor of Connecticut, being the first Democrat to hold that office since the Civil War.

In 1856 Luzon Morris had married Eugenia Laura Tuttle, the daughter of Lucius Tuttle, a resident of the little town of Wolcott, just outside Waterbury, Connecticut. Luzon Morris and his wife had six children, all of whom led long and full lives. The eldest, Robert Tuttle Morris, the surgeon, had been in Hopkins with Arthur Hadley. They used to go to each other's houses to play, but boys at that age have little use for baby sisters and Arthur did not meet Helen, so far as either could remember. The next three children after Robert were daughters: Mary, who married Charles M. Pratt, Helen, and Emily. Next came two sons. Charles followed in his father's footsteps and became a lawyer in New Haven. Ray went to New York, becoming a banker and a partner in Brown Brothers.

Helen attended New Haven High School and then went to Vassar, from which she graduated in 1883. She returned to New Haven, where she and Arthur were in the same group that saw much of each other. They became good friends but for years neither regarded the other in any different light. In 1890 Arthur suddenly decided that he had been in love with Helen for years without realizing it, and rushed over to her home to acquaint her with his discovery. It took her some months to arrive at a similar conclusion on her own part, but in January of 1891 they became engaged, and were married on June 30 of that year. They went on a honeymoon, first to the Berkshires and then to Europe, returning to America the last of August.

Arthur Hadley could not have found a wife who helped him more or made him happier, yet in many ways they were most unlike. He was an only child, nervous, brilliant, and impulsive. She had grown up in a large family, and had a calm and orderly mind. In the multifarious duties of the wife of a college president, to say nothing of running a house and raising a family at the same time, Helen Hadley was a miracle of quiet efficiency. This efficiency was achieved with so little fuss that it went almost unnoticed, except by her grateful and adoring husband. She, on her part, very wisely did not try to convert her husband into a normal, routine citizen, though she gradually succeeded in modifying some of his extreme eccentricities of manner. Thus she prevailed upon him to remember to face his audience when lecturing; he used to become so interested in his subject that he would forget he had an audience and stride about the platform, at times with his back to his hearers. She limited herself to a few points of this sort, where she felt that his eccentricities were really a hindrance to him.

Helen Hadley's outstanding quality was her sympathy. She truly loved her fellow men and women, unconsciously and as a matter of course. Of some particularly trying person, with whom no one else could get on, Helen Hadley would say, and say sincerely, "She must be terribly shy, to try to cover it up by acting in that way. I know just how she must feel, because I have always been tormented by shyness myself." With this sympathy went a great interest in people; she was a mine of information, freely given, about generations of her neighbors, their lives, their relatives, and their doings. But here again, though facts were facts and spades were spades, she always gave the characters the benefit of every possible doubt, and sometimes of rather impossible ones as well.

Her sympathy went out to all, but she devoted herself particularly to the college community. When young wives of new faculty members came to New Haven, they were apt to find Helen Hadley soon coming in to see them, and they quickly learned that it was no official call from the president's wife but a visit from a helpful friend. How she managed to make so many calls is a mystery, and at that she always reproached herself for not seeing as much of the younger faculty as she intended. Her friendship was appreciated and returned, and nowhere is her memory held in higher regard than by that whole generation who came to teach at Yale while her husband was president.

Amid all these official duties, Helen Hadley was running her home, receiving a constant stream of guests, and bringing up a family. There were three children, Morris, born March 21, 1894; Hamilton, January 13, 1896; and Laura, March 31, 1899. In spite of official duties, both parents managed to see more of their children than do most parents. For one thing, the family all breakfasted together, and normally all lunched together as well, though often Arthur had other engagements and could not get home. Sundays were spent together, at church in the morning and on walks in the afternoon. But principally they had a life in common because both parents, from the earliest days, treated their children as friends and intellectual equals. Arthur had been brought up this way himself, and it never occurred to him to do otherwise; Helen fell easily into the same fashion.

To give a personal illustration, one of my earliest recollections is when I was five and my father was elected president of Yale.

HELEN HADLEY

ARTHUR HADLEY AND MORRIS

I do not remember the students crowding in front of the house for a speech, though I must have seen it and enjoyed it. What I do remember is my father sitting with me on a bearskin rug that used to lie in the front hall in the days before my younger brother gave it an all-too-efficacious haircut with the library shears. My father explained to me that he was going to be president of Yale, that one thing that bothered him about it was that he might not have time to see as much of me and my brother and sister as before, but that he thought he would be able to arrange it all right, and he hoped I would be patient with him while he was getting it worked out. I too was distressed at the prospect of seeing less of him, which is why the conversation stuck in my memory, but I think I assured him stoutly that it would be all right.

One further illustration may be included of Arthur Hadley's unconscious use of methods that nowadays are to be learned in books on child guidance. This once more involves me, although I have no memory of the incident. On the back of one of the sheets of my mother's engagement calendar for 1901 is an entry scribbled down at the time. This calendar was always crowded with detailed entries as to formal engagements, with an added hodgepodge of additional notes on every conceivable subject, and even accounts of household incidents like the following:

Morris came in in early morning to A.T.H.

M. "I had bad dreams all night."

A. "What about?"

M. "The devil was trying to get me."

A. "What did you eat last night?"

M. "Bread and milk. Did that do it?"

A. "No. What did you read last evening?"

M. "Pilgrim's Progress. But I had a worse time than Christian, for the devil kept coming back to me."

A. "But he didn't get you."

M. "No."

A. "That's right—the Bible says 'Resist the devil and he will flee from you.' "

M. "Why?"

A. "Because he finds other people he can get easier."

M. "Really?"
A. "Yes."
M. "Good thing to know."

This has taken us long past the day in the summer of 1891 when Helen Hadley's diary reads: "Came to 93 Whitney Avenue 'for keeps.'" It was not easy to move into the same house with a strong-minded mother-in-law of seventy-five, who had lived there for years with her only child. Old Mrs. Hadley liked and approved of her daughter-in-law, but the situation was difficult nonetheless, and the difficulties grew during the six years until the elder's death in 1897. Fortunately in the summers all parties could have a holiday. The house at 93 Whitney Avenue would be closed, and Mrs. James Hadley would spend the summer with her Twining cousins. In the summers of 1892 and 1893 Arthur and Helen Hadley went to Europe; in 1894 and thereafter they went to Newtown, in near-by Connecticut.

Hadley was now a regular professor, not merely a part-time one, and was joining in all the activities of the faculty. He was again experiencing the administrative duties that are part of the lot of the faculty, duties that are burdensome and time consuming, yet without which no one can really feel himself a full-fledged member of the college world. In a letter of November 2, 1884, to E. D. Worcester Hadley had lamented the absence of "active interior contact with the students as students"; now he was having this again and was enjoying it.

The amount of work that Hadley was able to accomplish in this decade, day after day, was prodigious. He had a full teaching schedule. With many of his students he had contacts outside the classroom, and helped them with their problems, scholastic or otherwise. On top of this he was carrying a heavy burden of work with students in the graduate school, where he gave advanced courses. In 1892 he was appointed dean of the courses of graduate instruction in all fields, with a consequent burden of administrative work. And in addition he was one of the original editors of the *Yale Review*, founded in 1892, and wrote for it frequently.

Any or all of these activities might have to be carried out after a night spent in helping look after an ailing baby, for the children had their share of childhood illnesses. Yet in spite of all this he found it possible to keep up his outside activities. He lectured in other cities. He wrote many articles which appeared in magazines or the proceedings of learned societies. He wrote a textbook in economics. He was active in the American Economic Association, of which he became president in 1899. These varied activities are grouped together here to show the amount of work in which he was engaged, and to correct the picture of a professor's life that is held by many who have never shared it, a picture of a peaceful existence, with easy hours spent in libraries or other untroubled spots.

Hadley's undergraduate course in Political Economy was open to juniors and seniors, and was taken by more men than any other course in the college; 253 in 1899. A large class enrollment may be due to various causes, but in Hadley's case it was due to the teacher's ability and force, for the course was a difficult one, calling for hard work and for independent thinking.

The idiosyncrasies of the lecturer must at times have distracted the attention of his class but they seem to have aroused liking rather than ridicule. Later generations of college students who knew him as president regarded his mannerisms as sufficiently marked, but they were as nothing to those of his youth. Sometimes he would lecture at length with his back to the class; at other times he would rock back and forth in his chair, at imminent risk of crashing over entirely. On at least one historic occasion, as he was lecturing while seated, he put both feet in the wastebasket, where they stuck fast. Not noticing this consciously, he continued to talk, all the while thrashing the wastebasket from side to side as his legs struggled to free themselves.

It was at this period that Hadley began to acquire his almost legendary fame as a college figure. Most of the stories about him are inventions, but the most improbable ones are sometimes the true ones. Thus, on the subject of his absentmindedness, there is no foundation in fact, so far as I know, for the inherently plausible story that once, on entering a street car, he shook hands with the conductor and tendered a nickel to one of his friends. But it is a fact that when my brother and I were undergraduates we came upon him once near the campus deep in conversation with our uncle Charles Morris. We stopped beside them, and our father turned to us abstractedly and said politely: "Good afternoon; I don't know whether or not either of you gentlemen already know my brother-in-law, Charles Morris, of the class of 1895."

Similarly, with tales of his intellectual ability in varied lines, I can vouch for the accuracy of at least one incident from my own college days. The paper for the Barge Mathematics Prize in calculus included one problem which was too much for all the contestants, although most of us devoted considerable time to it, in my case the better part of an hour. In the evening after the examination I was at home, talking with my father, and rashly instanced this particular problem as one which even he could not have solved. "I am afraid you are right, my calculus is very rusty," he said. "Let me see, how did that question go?" I repeated it. My father was smoking his pipe; he puffed at it a couple of times and said: "That doesn't sound as if it ought to be difficult." Two more quick puffs and then, with a delighted smile: "Why yes, that's easy—" and he outlined the solution. I incredulously rushed for paper and pencil—but he was right.

The many stories of Hadley's intellectual ability in the most diverse fields are all simply varied instances of the fundamental fact that he had an extraordinary mind, exceptional alike in its quickness, its power of discrimination, and its memory. The whole was admirably summed up by a later president of Yale, Charles Seymour, who had been a young member of the faculty when Hadley was president. Seymour in his memorial address on Hadley spoke of

the celerity of apprehension, which enabled him to master a subject in a new field with uncanny speed; . . . the depth of understanding which made him authority in the field he chose to call his own; the ingenuity and adaptability manifest alike in a closely reasoned discussion or in a game of chess; the natural wit, scintillating and snapping like sparks. . . . But the great fact of his life is not so much that he possessed these qualities and was able to utilize them, as that he had the intelligence and character never to be mastered by them. . . . It would have been easy for him to trust to his wit, for Hadley unprepared could give a lecture on any namable subject that would meet the most exacting standard; instead he devoted himself to the task at hand with a seriousness and a capacity of application that matched his genius for understanding.

Hadley's qualities were appreciated by the undergraduates as well as by his colleagues on the faculty. Helen Hadley was always particularly delighted by one instance when a freshman guest at Sunday dinner, after some illuminating remark by the president, turned to her and said admiringly: "How true it is that there is no one from whom you can't learn something."

One undergraduate course with which Hadley experimented and in which he was much interested was in economic debates. There was one debate each week, certain members of the class taking part, the rest listening and criticizing. All were supposed to prepare themselves by an investigation of the authorities, and the speakers further constructed briefs of their arguments. Subjects were taken from a list worked out by teacher and class together and embracing economic subjects of current importance. The subjects ranged from self-government for Cuba to the eight-hour day and from government ownership of telegraphs to bimetallism. Criticism by the teacher was not only on the subject matter but was practical as well. Hadley's notebook for the course is full of scribbled notes on the various speeches, jotted down while the debates were in progress for use in later criticism. One such note reads: "With the kind of argument you have (which is sound) you want to avoid the appearance of flippancy. People distrust truth when thrown at them in a superficially clever manner."

In his courses Hadley tried to put into effect his ideas as to what education should mean. These ideas were not novel but in some respects they went counter to the popular ideas of the time, as when he once said: "Ten hours of training in civics is not

the equivalent of one minute of training in order and obedience."
This was in an address delivered in 1900 on "Fundamental Requirements in School Education" [printed as one of the chapters
in *The Education of the American Citizen*]. While this dealt
directly with secondary education, he felt that the same principles held true at the college level as well. He believed that
education should combine the imparting of knowledge and the
evoking of power. Both were necessary, but he felt that the current emphasis was far too much on the former:

We are in the presence of a combination of causes which produce a
real danger that our teachers will lay too much stress on knowledge
and too little on power.

In the first place, the pupils, with few exceptions, enjoy being
taught knowledge, and do not enjoy being taught power. The teaching of knowledge satisfies their curiosity; and anything which satisfies curiosity is a pleasure to the average child no less than to the
average adult. The teaching of power fatigues the mind; and the
average child dislikes mental fatigue almost as much as the average
grown person. . . .

In the next place, the teacher likes to see tangible results; and the
imparting of knowledge gives those results. When a pupil has mastered a fact this can be made evident immediately; while it takes
days and weeks to be sure that he has mastered a principle . . .

Not until the value of studies is tested by their effects upon working efficiency does the public find how imperfectly it has measured
the relative importance of different kinds of education.

Hadley's contacts with his students were not limited to the
classroom. He coached undergraduates in such diverse fields
as tennis on the one hand and debating on the other. In tennis he
played a very accurate game. Anyone seeing him lecturing or
talking would have thought from his awkward and unrelated
gestures that he had no muscular coordination, but when his
mind was on a game and not on intellectual matters his movements were as accurate as before they had been erratic. In coaching tennis his principal specialty was imitating the style of the
Harvard or Princeton opponent against whom the Yale player
was likely to come.

In coaching debating he seems to have followed the same method, to judge by a letter written to the *New York Herald Tribune* by one of his former debating pupils, John Kirkland Clark of the class of 1899. Hadley had participated in training all of the Yale debating teams against Harvard and Princeton from 1895 through 1899, years when Harvard was trained by George Pierce Baker and Princeton by Woodrow Wilson. Clark went on to say:

In no activity of his life were his splendid mental range and trained imaginative power more clearly and helpfully engaged. It was Mr. Hadley's regular course to analyze the various arguments to be developed by the opponents in the light of the personality of the debating coach on the other team. His ability . . . through his insight into the personality of Woodrow Wilson in the one instance, and of George Baker in the other, was almost uncanny in its accuracy.

Most men in the college had but one course with Hadley— the general one in economics. From 1886 on, when he became a part-time professor of political science, certain of his courses are listed as open to seniors—which really involved little change, as qualified seniors had always been admitted to his courses by special permission. But all these other courses, even that in economic debates, were relatively small and largely made up of graduate students. These smaller courses, however, are the most significant in tracing the development of his economic interests.

In 1883–84 the one course he gave was listed in the catalogue as "Industrial Problems of the Day." In 1884–85 the title of his single course was "Railroads, their history, their business methods, and the social problems connected with them." He offered it again the first term of the next year, and in the second term one entitled "Relations between political economy and legislation, in connection with the work of the State Bureau of Labor Statistics."

Hadley experimented with a variety of courses during the fifteen years of his active teaching, and there was equal variety in attendance, some being popular and some having only a student or two. Aside from his general course on the principles of political economy, there was only one subject on which he invariably lectured and that was corporations. Even here the emphasis varied. He would always deal with the history of corporate development and the effects of corporations upon labor, prices, profits, and the like; but in some years the stress would be on industrial legislation and "the grounds and limits of state interference with industry," while in others he would stress the economic problems of corporations. In the early years of his teaching there was one other course which he always offered—on railroad administration.

On economic theories, Hadley usually gave one fairly general course, with another advanced one open to specially qualified students. Here again the emphasis varied. In 1886–87 the title was "Socialism—an account of recent movements." In the following years it was called "Modern economic theories." For a few years the course in this field was omitted, but by the end of the period he was again offering "The history of political and economic theories."

On economic history, as distinct from economic theory, he originally gave a special course. From 1887 to 1891 this was on the industrial history of the United States since 1850, and was open to both undergraduates and graduate students. After 1891 much of this material was included in his general undergraduate course in political economy, though he continued to offer a separate advanced course for graduate students.

During the first half dozen years of his teaching, the courses offered by Arthur Hadley fell in one or another of the fields listed above. From 1890 on he continued to teach in these fields but presented additional courses of a highly varied character. That of 1890–91 for instance was entitled "Methods of studying political events, an account of the chief sources of contemporary historical information and the methods of using them for scientific work." There were two in 1892–93, "Relations Between Economics and Law" and "Ethics as a Political Science." The substance of the latter is included in *The Education of the American Citizen* (pp. 100–134). In 1893–94 his additional course was on the problems of modern law and modern commercial ethics.

From 1894–95 till the close of his teaching in 1899 this was listed as "The relations between economics and ethics—an historical study of the development of moral and legal standards in their relations to one another, followed by criticisms of various schemes of social policy and legislation." This was a graduate course. For undergraduates as well beginning in 1895 he gave a course in conjunction with Professor Schwab known as "Economic policy." Hadley's part in this is described as lectures "on the growth of the modern industrial system and the legislative problems connected with it."

For three years Hadley was Dean of the Graduate School, although he himself held no earned graduate degree. In the 1890's positions and titles in the Graduate School were somewhat hit-and-miss. Hadley is listed in the Yale official catalogue as "Dean Graduate School 1892–1895," but on January 19, 1895, he himself wrote E. D. Worcester:

"I am not dean of the Faculty as you carelessly credit the catalogue with stating, but of the courses of graduate instruction. A dean, in my case, is a man who answers all the stray correspondence which anybody puts to him. I am going to get out of the office next year. I have had it since 1888 or '89, but it grows worse and worse."

Economics: An Account of the Relations between Private Property and Public Welfare, was issued by Putnam in 1896, eleven years after the publication of Hadley's *Railroad Transportation.* Max Lerner says of the book: * "Although a text book in form this work was in reality as intelligent an apologia and as judicious a defense of the economic institutions of the day as the American literature contains." It was not so regarded at the time by some of Hadley's more conservative friends, themselves pillars of those economic institutions. They felt that some of his remarks verged on the radical, and wrote him so. Nevertheless, viewing the book from the perspective of half

* In his excellent biographical article on Hadley in the *Encyclopedia of Social Sciences* (VII, 239–240).

a century, Max Lerner's characterization seems sound. Hadley did believe that the economic institutions of the day, with all their faults, were a better basis for future development than any of the rival schemes proposed by socialists or others. The very fact that he was not blind to the faults, and realized the need for change, lent strength to his position, however much it may have distressed a few conservatives at the moment.

Beyond a general description of his approach, I shall not attempt a summary of his economic theories here, or a condensation of the book. Irving Fisher, who when a young instructor had worked as Hadley's assistant, selected one point for special emphasis in reviewing his colleague's work: *

He [Hadley] was one of the first economists to point out the fallacy in Ricardo's formula, that, under free competition, the value of different kinds of goods will tend to be proportional to their cost of production. . . . "It is not true," he said, "that when the price falls below cost of production people always find it for their interest to refuse to produce at a disadvantage. It very often involves worse loss to stop production than to produce below cost." (Railroad Transportation, page 70) . . . So far as I can learn, Professor Hadley was the first to enunciate this principle, that it often pays to run at a loss—a principle which today is widely recognized as fundamental in economic theory.

Economics embodied his early findings but now applied them in relation to the whole field. The book is a model of clear exposition but it is not easy reading in the popular sense. Hadley recognized this himself, and wrote in the introduction (p. iv):

I have put things as plainly as I could; but there are some parts of economics where no amount of effort by an author will relieve the reader of the necessity of doing independent thinking on his own account. There are many problems of business life which are so complicated in reality that it is unwise to treat them as if they were simple. There is no foundation for the popular belief that questions of money, of the tariff, or of the relations between labor and capital, are easy to understand if properly presented. The sim-

* Obituary in the *Economic Journal*, September, 1930, p. 530.

plicity obtained by looking at them from one side only is apt to be secured at the expense of thoroughness and too often of candor.

In spite of this warning of difficulties to come, Hadley at times cuts through a difficult explanation by a telling phrase. Thus, on Ricardo's theory of rent, he says (*Idem*, p. 290):

"Although Ricardo combined the experience of a landlord with that of a banker his theory of rent represents essentially a banker's view of farming, which like a farmer's view of banking, takes much more account of the profits than of the losses."

Reference has already been made to Hadley's recognition of the seamy side of the institutions of the day. In *Railroad Transportation*, for example, after discussing combinations by capital in self-protection, he wrote (p. 77):

There is another aspect of our subject, still more serious than any we have yet treated, which we can do little more than touch upon,— the competition and combination of labor. Labor is in the market, like any commodity; its price is largely determined by competition, and this too often takes the form of cut-throat competition. A workman working for starvation wages is like a factory or a railroad running for operating expenses. In flush times the workman gets comparatively good wages; he marries, and is able to support a family in reasonable comfort. The family becomes a fixed charge upon him; and it is of the utmost importance to society that he should be able to meet his fixed charges in this respect. But a commercial crisis comes, and the demand for labor diminishes. Men who have no family to support come into direct competition with him. He can better afford to work for what will keep body and soul together than not to work at all, even though his wages are brought so low that his children perish for lack of the food which should give them strength to resist disease. And so wages are brought down to the starvation minimum, to rise above it only after long years of waiting and misery. The workman seeks relief in combination; but combination is far harder for him than for the capitalist. Where there are ten factories to combine, there may be ten thousand workmen to be held together,—not to speak of the almost unlimited floating labor supply which may be brought in at any point. . . . It is beyond our purpose to discuss what general improvement is practicable in this field. We only call attention to the close relation between the two problems of starvation wages and bankrupt competition. If capitalists and workmen can but see this analogy, it may help them to an understanding of one another's position.

The socialists, in spite of their unpractical proposals, have the merit of seeing the close relation between these two problems.

The reference in the preceding sentence to the unpractical proposals of the socialists sums up Hadley's principal objection to the members of that school. As he said two decades later: * "I have known a great many socialists, but I never knew a single one who was really careful in his arithmetic." While he paid tribute to the socialists' hearts, it was at the expense of their heads: †

They are, as a rule, men who see clearly the existence of evils in modern industrial society which some economists have overlooked, and others have deplored as inevitable. . . . They claim for themselves, more or less consciously, a superior moral purpose because they are trying to right visible wrongs by direct state activity. . . .

Of course it will not do to undervalue the emotional element in dealing with economic matters, as men of the more purely intellectual type are sometimes prone to do. Reasoning about human conduct is full of chances of error; and if the outcome of such reasoning is to leave a considerable number of human beings in hopeless misery, society is justified in demanding that every premise and every inference in the chain of reasoning be tested, and every rational experiment be made to see whether such a consequence is really inevitable. Instances have not been wanting when the conclusions of the economists have been proved wrong, and the emotions of the critics have been warranted by the event. The factory legislation of England furnishes an historic example. The economists, as a rule, condemned this legislation as wrong in principle and likely to do harm; but the results showed that these economists had overlooked certain factors of importance with regard to public health and public morals which vitiated their conclusions and justified public opinion in disregarding them.

* *Baccalaureate Addresses*, p. 200.

† "Socialism and Social Reform," *The Forum*, October, 1894. Reprinted in *The Education of the American Citizen*, p. 51. The passage is used in part in *Economics*, p. 17.

But while the men of emotion may sometimes be right and the men of reason wrong, the chances in matters of legislation are most decidedly the other way. It is safe to say that the harm which has been done by laws based on unemotional reasoning is but a drop in the bucket compared with that which has been done by laws based on unreasoning emotion.

Hadley believed that there was no royal road to the solution of many of these problems but that the community and individuals would all have to do their part. Laws could not take the place of public consciousness or of responsible behavior. Thus, on the subject of compulsory arbitration in labor disputes, which is still being urged as a panacea, he said: *

As matters stand at present, a strike begun on trivial grounds may be allowed to interrupt the whole business of a community. The natural alternative would seem to be compulsory arbitration, but this in practice has not worked nearly as well as could be desired. . . . Whatever can or cannot be done by legal enactment, society must at any rate recognize that those whom it has placed in charge of large industrial enterprises are not simply handling their own money or other people's money, but are above all things leaders of men; and it must judge the financier who has through his negligence allowed the business of the community to be interrupted by strikes, as it would judge the general who, in his anxiety to secure the emoluments of his office, had allowed his country to be invaded and his armies paralyzed.

It was his conviction that the economist should work matters out from the standpoint of the community as a whole and not as the representative of one pressure group or another. He saw the utility of spokesmen for particular interests but thought that this utility was a narrow one. Above all, he thought that there was a surplus of such spokesmen, while the number of those who could view matters as a whole was limited and their contribution particularly valuable.

He appreciated that this type of work would not meet the approval of extremists on either side, but he had faith in the ulti-

* "The Formation and Control of Trusts," *Scribner's Magazine*, November, 1899.

mate acceptance of such work by people in general. Speaking of "those who have more money than votes, who will desire to extend the sphere of commercial activity, and those who have more votes than money, who will desire to extend the sphere of political activity," he went on to pin his hopes on "the great majority of people, who have one vote and just money enough to support their families." *

Hadley's *Economics* was widely used as a textbook. Pressure of work as president of Yale made it impossible for him to revise it and keep it up to date, but it continued in use to some extent for a quarter century. From time to time revision was discussed by the publishers but it was never carried out. Many years after publication, in answer to a letter from George Haven Putnam, Hadley wrote (March 13, 1920):

I appreciate your feeling regarding my book on Economics, and if the right man were in sight I should consider seriously the question of a revision of the kind you have in mind. At present the right man does not appear to be in sight. For a number of years preceding the war the development of economic thinking has been away from certain habits of analysis which were characteristic of the English school. I was brought up in this school by Professor Sumner; and while I differ from him regarding a good many of the data from which he started, I hope that I have kept something of his method. I very much doubt whether a man trained in another method can revise one of my books without taking the life out of it. Raper was a nice fellow; but his handling of Railroad Transportation made an unrecognizably different book out of what I had written, and I somewhat fear that a similar result would be felt here.

I see a strong reaction toward English methods, and I think that ten years hence we shall have younger men who could work in the style that Sumner and Charles Francis Adams and I did—if I may be allowed to be a "third among such intelligences." But ten years is too long to wait. May I make an alternative suggestion?

As you probably know, I expect to retire from the presidency a year from next summer. I think I could myself at that time take up the revision of my Economics. I should (1) shorten the book to about three-quarters of its present length; (2) make some rear-

* *Ibid.*

rangements in the order of material; and (3) make the illustrative discussions come from present-day questions rather than from those of twenty-five years ago. This last will be the part that will involve the most labor; but I think I have kept up sufficiently with my economic reading to do it without great delay, so that the whole thing could be done and out of my hands a year or so after my resignation. How does this strike you?

Please answer as frankly as I have written. If you think that a revision by a younger man would suit your purposes better I will try and see whether anything can be done in that line, but I would rather keep the book my own if I possibly can.

Actually, the revision never took place. It developed that unknown to George Haven Putnam and Hadley alike the book had been allowed by Putnam to go out of print, so that for a year orders for it as a textbook had been perforce turned down and the colleges still using it had shifted to other texts. Under these circumstances it seemed unprofitable to attempt to revive the book.

In addition to working on *Economics*, Hadley during the 'nineties was writing for various periodicals. A bibliography is printed as an appendix to this book. In the early years the bulk of his work was in the *Railroad Gazette* and the *Independent*. By the end of his service as professor this had changed, and the bulk of his writing was in the *Yale Review*, with some articles in such publications as the *Quarterly Journal of Economics*, the *Economic Journal*, and the *Political Science Quarterly*, not to mention more popular periodicals such as the *Nation* and the *Forum*.

During these years Hadley took a leading part in the American Economic Association, and became its president in 1899. He was a charter member of the International Institute of Statistics, founded in 1886, and also contributed to the publications of the American Statistical Association.

Hadley always had much work in New York, and during this period he became a member of the Century Club, where for the next forty-five years he was a familiar figure. Meetings in other parts of the country took him still further afield. Some of these trips were in connection with the Economic Association or other organizations, but more were due to lecture engagements or calls to speak at gatherings of Yale graduates.

His speaking gave him practice that was to stand him in good stead as president of Yale. He learned to address audiences effectively and to deal with hostile critics. One incident with an objector was recounted in the *Yale Alumni Weekly* (July 20, 1899):

After the New York speech in the winter of 1898, in which Professor Hadley took up attacks upon Yale in the alleged cause of temperance . . . H. A. Hull, of New London, wrote a letter to the New Haven Register, in which he put the following questions:

"Suppose a young man, having or desiring to have a sound body, a clear mind and a pure heart, should ask these questions:

"1. Where should a Christian gentleman drink rum?

"2. When should a Christian gentleman drink rum?

"3. How should a Christian gentleman drink rum?

"4. Why should a Christian gentleman drink rum?

"I use the word 'rum' generically. In His name what answer do you think should be given?"

Professor Hadley did not reply through the newspaper, but sent a letter to Mr. Hull, which the latter gave out. It contained as his answer the following:

"If a young man asked me these questions for his own guidance, I should say that the gospels obviously prescribed no fixed rule; but that he had better not drink in doubtful cases. If he asked the questions not as a guide for his action, but as a basis for judging others, I should tell him frankly that the gospel was far more explicit in urging abstinence from sweeping judgments than abstinence from alcoholic drink."

There were relatively few such interludes, however, and most of the lecture engagements were plain hard work. Some of the trips are described in letters home, but more are simply recorded in a line-a-day diary kept by his wife, in which the most incongruous entries are run together.

One series of entries in 1894, starting on February 14, reads: "A wrote my valentine and read examination papers." The reading continued through the 19th, when he finished the papers,

147 of them. On the 20th there was a *Yale Review* meeting, on the 22nd "A addressed the High School and then went to Chicago at 1:30." The afternoon of the 26th he returned to New Haven, and the entry for the 27th is "A had college lectures again as usual."

As to the valentine, this was a practice that continued throughout Hadley's life, and for each St. Valentine's Day he would write his wife a valentine in verse, sometimes humorous, sometimes serious.

CHAPTER VII

VACATIONS

IN COLLEGE towns, at least until recent times, the "year"
was nine months long. Then at the end of June came the
three-month "vacation." You might stay in town and work,
in fact you generally did at least part of the time, but it was
known as vacation just the same. These three months were so
apart from the other nine that they call for a chapter to themselves.

The departure of the undergraduates changed the campus
from a busy spot to a deserted place of peace and quiet under the
great elm trees. By some unconscious convention vacation was
received in the same spirit by all connected with the college, even
though they might live half a mile away, where the absence of
students made little visible difference. In the Hadley house on
the corner of Whitney Avenue and Trumbull Street, as soon as
Commencement Week was over, it was the custom of summer
evenings to sit on the wooden steps of the front porch, close by
the sidewalk. This was a thing undreamed of in term time, no
matter how hot the evenings might be in early June. But in
vacation it was the custom, which lingered well into the twentieth
century.

Cushions were brought out, and the whole family disposed
themselves comfortably, though the children's stay was brief
before they had to go up to bed. Neighbors strolling by stopped
for a chat. As it grew dark, the fireflies came out, and a man came
by and lighted the gas lamp on the corner, then continued up the
street lighting the others. Farther off, on the opposite corner,
a big arc light would go on with a click and splutter, sending out
a glaring light from which the porch was sheltered by the thick
summer foliage of the trees. The night was warm and dark and
friendly, the passers-by unhurried, especially the large police-

man, who would pause to ask how long it had been since the police sergeant had been by. This question puzzled the children,
until their father explained that the policeman had to know what
sort of an excuse to make up, and that it helped him to know
how much time he had to account for.

Mornings too were pleasant in vacation. Throughout the college year there were early classes to be met. After Hadley was
president he did not have to hold classes but, worse yet, he had
to preside at morning chapel at ten minutes past eight each day.
Relieved of this early morning duty, the family rose in vacations
at seven instead of at quarter of. Work started a little later, that
was all; but there were fewer interruptions and more could be
accomplished than in term time. With luck the day's stint would
be finished by four in the afternoon, leaving time for tennis at
the Lawn Club before supper at half past six.

In his early years as a teacher Hadley usually spent the greater
part of the vacation working in New Haven, and this was true
of most of the younger men. The Colby Club in those days held
its monthly meetings right through the summer, and the attendance seems to have been good. In 1885, for example, at the
meeting held in the last week of July, ten of the fourteen members were present. In later years Hadley was more often able
to get a summer off and go to Europe, but it remained true that
in most summers the whole family remained in New Haven
till at least the middle of July, and even during the rest of the
summer Hadley himself had to spend several days of nearly
every week in New Haven.

The womenfolk and children usually went away for a month
or two, the men joining them on occasional week ends, or for
longer stays. After Hadley married, the place where his family
went was Zoar, in Newtown Township, twenty-odd miles northwest of New Haven, in the hills bordering the valley of the
Housatonic River. This was his summer home for the rest of
his life. It was the part of Connecticut from which Helen Hadley's family came, and the house where she and Arthur spent
their summers was one she and her sister Mary had often visited
as children. This sister married Charles M. Pratt, of Brooklyn,

who later bought the house. The Pratts never lived there, and gradually turned it over to the Hadleys for the summers. Finally, in 1916, Charles Pratt deeded it to Helen Hadley as a present on her twenty-fifth wedding anniversary.

The house was on an abandoned sixty-acre farm. It had been built, and well built, around 1730, with a great stone central chimney which served two fireplaces in the cellar, three on the ground floor, two on the second floor, and a smokehouse in the attic. A kitchen wing had been added a century later. The new owners added first one, and later several, bathrooms. For years, however, the bathrooms relied on a water supply furnished inadequately by a hydraulic ram on a little stream that ran through the place, so that baths were perforce shallow during summer droughts. To get satisfyingly wet all over you walked three miles to the Housatonic. In those days, before the Housatonic dam at Stevenson, the river ran through unspoiled and almost uninhabited country, stretches of swift water alternating with long, still reaches.

Now the house can be reached from New Haven by motor over a through road that goes to Danbury. In those days you went by train; a local on a branch line, making all stops, and taking an hour for the trip. You arrived at Botsford Junction covered with cinders, and then drove three miles from the station to the house. As the road was a country one, and the farm horse phlegmatic, this added at least another half hour to the trip. After some attempts at daily commuting Hadley gave it up. While he was working in New Haven he would come out to Zoar for a long week end, from Friday evening to Monday morning, and if work was light he might also come out once in the middle of the week.

Work in New Haven in most years took up the greater part of the summer, and in some years he hardly got to Zoar at all. In the summer of 1914, for example, Hadley's engagement calendar shows that the family went to Zoar on June 28, and he spent the first week with them. He got off for one more week in August, and had planned a third week off for September but didn't get it. For the rest he had only week ends in Zoar.

During the summer, in addition to his day-to-day work in New Haven, he notes: "Work to be done: Oxford Lectures for publication. September Sermon. President's Report."

Outside activities at Zoar did not exist, which was one reason Hadley so enjoyed it; no better place for a complete rest could be imagined. After breakfast he would go to the closet where the hammock was stored at night, take it out, and swing it in its appointed place under a maple tree by the corner of the house. Then he would light his pipe, and sit pleasantly in the shade. His wife would work all day in her garden with equal pleasure. To a critical child, who probably regarded his father's laziness as unchivalrous, Arthur Hadley explained, between puffs at his pipe: "When your mother and I were first married, I thought if I helped her in the garden it would let her get through sooner so that she could come and sit in the shade with me. Instead, I found it only encouraged her to work even longer."

As the children grew older a tennis court was added, and, when the valley of the Housatonic became built up, a swimming pool was installed beside a brook in the valley below the house. In the early days the only exercise was tramping through the countryside, but that was an unending delight. For years, on Sunday mornings Helen Hadley would drive to church, while the men would go off for an all-day walk. By way of a contemporary account, here is an entry from a son's diary in 1911:

Every walk is different, but they're all good fun, so I'll tell about the one into the Shepaug Valley.

Uncle Charlie [who lived a quarter of a mile away] comes down armed with chops, frying pan, butter, and corn-meal mixture. Father and I (Hamilton has a sore foot) come with oranges, meat, gingerbread and cheese. I take the haversack with the oranges, the corn-meal and the butter, and off we go. Beyond Berkshire we pick up Messrs. Wheeler and Hooker with their food, and the walk is fairly started.

Three miles down to the Housatonic River, then across Bennett's bridge, and up the Housatonic to Deacon Mitchell's. We turn off the river road and climb steep hills by an enticing but not-to-be-drunken brook. Then level walking above a wonderful gorge. Then just plain walking, followed by a cross road where another farm road crosses ours. Discussion of the maps (which I fish out very wet with perspiration from a hip pocket). Walk resumed. Increasing thirst. A brook. Small but fairly cold. All drink except Father. Hills, with more discussion of map, followed by more hills and more discussion. It is now one o'clock.

Then twenty minutes drop via a disused wood road, into the Shepaug Valley. March resumed down the Shepaug River. Heat, weariness, thirst, hunger, no drinkable water to be found.

1:40 P.M. A spring. Rejoicing. A fireplace of three stones is built, the fire started, egg and water added to the corn-meal, spits are cut. Hooker and I wash our weary feet. Spirits, already revived by water, further revived by food. Corn bread delicious as usual. No mushrooms to be cooked because the drought had killed them all, so we had picked none as we went along. Food. Peace. Tranquility. Everyone else smokes and I try to get a peaceful rest on a slippery bank.

3:20. Frying pan cleaned, refuse burned, fire extinguished. 3:30, walk resumed. Swift arrival at Housatonic. Five miles or so to Sandy Hook bridge, and then on to Bennett's bridge, where some turn off for a swim, while the rest go home. Swim in the Housatonic, then three miles home. Distance twenty-four miles.

Walks were of all lengths, from day-long tramps of the sort described down to walks with some young child up the farm lane to the woods behind the barn and on to the hilltop pastures beyond the woods. The children enjoyed the walks whatever the length, but in some ways the shorter, leisurely ones were the best fun, for there was ample chance for talking and the talk ranged over every subject under the sun.

Hadley believed that vacations should be times of complete rest, and the children never had any vacation work. They early found that if their father laid in the books for summer reading the assortment contained more light literature and detective stories than if their mother made the selection. But Hadley's mind, at work or at rest, was never dull, and to talk with him was a constant delight. There was continual give-and-take, and the children at times would advance their side of a discussion so emphatically that visitors were a little aghast at their lack of respect.

Their father never gave the matter a thought but met their points as seriously—and as successfully—as though he were debating with his contemporaries.

Occasionally, on a walk, the subjects under discussion would call for more than words, and then father and child would stop, while the father would mark out on the roadside with broken twigs the positions of the opposing forces at Waterloo, or the relative distances of the planets from the sun, or whatever the topic might be. One childhood inquiry of my own fortunately came just as we were approaching a sandy stretch of the untraveled country road. This was before the days of automobiles, so we smoothed out a nice patch in the middle of the road, under some shady trees, and my father took a stick and drew diagrams in the sand to show the nature of calculus, and how Leibnitz had approached the problem, and how Newton, and how we worked today. I was fascinated, but not until years later in college did I realize how thorough a grounding in calculus I had received in that one summer afternoon; not as to details, of course, but as a way of looking at the world in general and variable quantities in particular.

Each summer Hadley tried to go still farther away than Zoar for at least two weeks of complete change. In his later years this often meant staying with the William K. Townsends at their camp in the Adirondacks. In earlier years it took the form of walking trips, usually in the White Mountains but sometimes in the Catskills or the Finger Lake district of New York or elsewhere. Two or three friends would set out for a week or more, carrying light rucksacks. They would tramp all day and spend the nights at country inns or at farm houses.

Climbing instead of walking was sometimes possible, especially on two trips to the Canadian Rockies, the one with Henry Farnam in 1889 and another in 1897. Hadley and Farnam tramped through part of the Canadian Rockies and the Selkirks, a district that was just being opened by the Canadian Pacific. They had both become experienced in this sort of climbing in the Alps, and when they struck off to view some "unnamed and unexplored" mountains, Hadley wrote home of the glacier work required: ". . . it presented no difficulty and at that time of day no suspicion of danger to anyone at all familiar with that kind of work—I really knew more about such things than the guide, and took the lead near the top."

Europe, to Hadley's way of thinking, was the ideal place for a complete vacation, preferably in the form of a walking trip with some mountain climbing thrown in. His first experience of such a trip had been in 1878, as a student in Germany, and he had other enjoyable trips of the same sort in later years. All his life, even when he was no longer young enough for difficult ascents, he still listed mountain climbing as his favorite recreation in *Who's Who*. His office was decorated with photographs of mountain peaks, although they had to share the honors with English cathedrals.

A 1906 trip in Switzerland was the subject of a paper for the Colby Club, parts of which apply equally well to the 1878 trip or any of the others in the intervening years.

Between the Ormonts and the Gemmi there is a mountain region of which the Wildstrubel is the centre—a sort of continuation of the main chain of the Bernese Alps, little known to Baedeker and less to Cook. Here the primitive simplicity of manners and morals is preserved. Here there are no carpets on the floor. Here the landlord stands in deep and usually well deserved awe of the headwaitress. Here the little grandchild of the shoemaker to whom you go to have your boots mended refuses to go to bed until the stranger superintends the operation. Here—rarest of all, they deem it robbery and extortion to charge even the casual tourist more than a dollar a day for everything, including wine.

This Arcadia may be entered from several directions. The four of us entered it from Spiez. Thirty years ago, when I first knew Spiez, it was a charming little steamboat station on the lake, with one shady restaurant and a delightful view. Now it has become a railroad centre; where instead of one good restaurant there are many bad ones, with inadequate shade and intolerably numerous yellow jackets; where English is spoken by everybody, and the manners and charges are correspondingly objectionable. But there

is a road that goes from Spiez—the narrow gauge line which leads
you up the Simmenthal, through places called Esshi and Wimmis
and other names that savor of the old fashioned Swiss cottages that
we used to play with as little children; a line that is taken by Swiss
tourists only, and as a rule not by many of them. The Simmenthal
is a lovely valley, with green pastures and steep precipices; but
the mountains are less than ten thousand feet high, and therefore
they do not come up to the standard set by Thomas Cook as a re-
spectable basis for exploration. After an hour or two you leave the
cars at a place which rejoices in the impossible name of Gstaad—it
appears to be a philological rule of these regions that all the vowels
occur in one part of the word and all the consonants in another—
and walk up the valley to Lauenen, which is the objective point of
the first day's journey.

Greatly to be praised is the hotel Wildhorn at Lauenen. It is an
admirable type of little Swiss inn which was beginning to grow rare
even in my days as a German university student, when I first made
the acquaintance of the Alps; a type of inn where the duty of hospitality appeared to be a pleasure, and where the primitiveness of
the arrangements was more than atoned for by the extreme of cleanliness, liberality and friendly spirit. Not but what the landlord had
his weaknesses, of which his subordinates were fully aware. When
a good dinner was set before us we asked advice of the waitress about
the drink—whether the red wine or the white wine was better. She
replied that both were equally good. "But one," we said, "is probably better than the other." "If it is," she said with dignity, "I am
not aware of the fact." "What does Mr. Landlord drink himself?"
we ventured to ask by way of an indication. "Oh, Mr. Landlord
will drink anything he can lay his hands on!" However, she ultimately condescended to remember that Mr. Landlord, when he had
the choice between several kinds, did seem to drink Waadtlaender
by preference. So we followed his example, and found it a good one.

It was one of the opening days of August—the Swiss Fourth of
July. We were first made aware of this fact by bonfires that were
appearing on the hills all round. "What are those fires for?" we
asked the waitress. She replied that she didn't know enough to be
able to tell it in German. I asked if she could tell it in French; but
that appeared more impossible still; and I unfortunately did not
understand the local *patois* of three quarters bad German and one
quarter bad French. Finally she said "They celebrate three men

that swore." Visions of Captain Kidd or of the army in Flanders swept before my mind for a moment, but I then made a lucky guess, and said, "The three confederates?" She was overjoyed, and said, "The same." After that a common understanding was established and we helped set off the fireworks—which were not of remarkable quality, but with care a fair percentage of them could be made to go.

The next morning we had the unique experience of going over a pass with beautiful views of the Bernese Oberland on which for four hours and a half we met no trace of a tourist. We arrived at the village of Lenk in time to win the admiration of the village by our prowess in taking charge of its fire department. I say *our prowess*— my own personal part in the fire was a somewhat inglorious one, as I was at the village shoemaker's with both boots off for repairs when the fire alarm came, and the shoemaker rushed at once to the fire without telling me where my boots were. I found one of them, but not the other; and this, besides wasting valuable time, prevented my services when they did come from being as efficient as they should have been. But two of the party went into the burning building and covered themselves with glory. To my eye the most picturesque feature of the fire was a broad shouldered Swiss, who had an astonishing talent for catching bureaus when they were thrown down to him from third story windows. The two athletic members of the party kept feeding them to him as fast as he could take them; but at the end of fifteen minutes he appeared as fresh as at the beginning, and cried for more bureaus and wash stands to catch.

The next morning took us over another pass to the town of Adelboden. This is an abode of fashion, which we had intended to leave on our left and go up a desolate valley, with the intent to come down upon the Gemmi Pass from the west. But just as we reached the mouth of this desolate valley it began to rain—and the prospect of a three hours' wetting, with no clothes to change to, does not appeal to me as forcibly now as it did twenty-five years ago. The only noteworthy thing that occurred at Adelboden was the remark of an English lady of fashion on the appearance of our party as it strode into the town: "And *do* the natives carry their clothes on their back like that? How picturesque! But it must be very heavy!"

Fortunately the rain was only temporary; and two days later found us above the Gemmi Pass, ascending the highest peak of the region, the Balmhorn. We started at 1:30 A.M. by lantern light. It was daylight when we got to the glacier. The glacier was steep—abominably steep—and involved a good deal of step cutting. It is strange how much steeper a glacier seems at the age of fifty than it does at the age of twenty-five. But it was good interesting going.

In an earlier Colby Club paper there is a reference to another innkeeper who met with Hadley's hearty approval. He was in Germany, at the little walled town of Ochsenfurt: "We lunched at an inn known as the Snail. I asked the man why it was called the Snail, and he said it was on account of the sign over his front door. When I asked why the sign was put there he said he didn't know; they put it there in 1510; they probably had reasons."

Hadley's letters discussed not only mountains but incidental moral problems. Thus he wrote from the Hotel Jungfrau, Wengernalp, on Sunday, July 21, 1878:

My dear mother: I have to begin this letter with a confession, or rather a statement of what I have done, which I took a long time to make up my mind to, but which I venture to hope you will not really disapprove. If you do feel doubtful about it,—and I own I did myself when the matter was first spoken of—you have only to write to me to prevent a repetition of anything of the kind. We spent last night at Lauterbrunnen, and it was proposed to take advantage of the pleasant weather to walk on to Grindelwald. Worcester seemed to feel no doubt in his mind about the propriety of this course. I was at first strongly inclined to dissent—but when I considered that the exigencies of the weather would force us to take one day of rest in seven very certainly, I contented myself with stipulating that the day's work should be so laid out that we should find it a day of real, if not formal rest. This the others consented to do; and as I sit here, right in the face of the Jungfrau and the snow mountains on either side of it, I cannot say that I repent of what I have done.

His companions on this 1878 trip were three college friends, Edwin D. Worcester, Henry A. James, and Edward D. Robbins. Some of their days were certainly far from restful, though they made no unusually difficult ascents. On one day, starting from Macugnaga at 2 A.M. with Franz Andermatten and another native as guides, they crossed the Weissthor Pass, and felt so fresh that they ascended the Cima de Jazi before descending by the Gorner Grat to the Riffel Inn above Zermatt. The next day they started at 1 A.M. and climbed Monte Rosa.

Hadley was next able to go to Europe in 1882, for two months with H. C. White and E. C. Bigelow. One month was to have been spent in walking through Norway, and the group did the first half of this as planned. Unfortunately, just as they reached Jotunheim, where their climbing was to begin, White was taken critically ill. Bigelow went on with the trip alone, but Hadley felt that someone must stay with White and sacrificed the balance of his trip. White recovered too late to allow time for more travels in Norway.

Hadley did not make another trip until 1887 but when it came it was a good one. With Alfred L. Ripley, J. B. Gleason, and Bernadotte Perrin, he sailed the end of June and was away for nearly three months. Ripley and Hadley were together nearly all the trip, the others from time to time. The month of July and half of August was spent tramping, mostly in Switzerland; the balance of the summer was divided between Paris and London. A letter of July 26, 1887, from Poschiavo is illustrated with a charming little pencil sketch of the Campanile in view from the window, and reports:

"Our life is, all things considered, a pretty regular one. We rise at 4:30, breakfast at 5, walk three or four hours, lunch at 10 or 11 and then walk some more, dine at about 2, rest through most of the afternoon, and in the evening take perhaps a little more walking and pretty certainly a little more to eat."

In 1890 Hadley had ten weeks in Europe. The last part of this trip was spent in England working and attending the meeting of the British Association already described. But before this there had been a month of walking with John Bristol and James F. Colby, as well as some mountain climbing in Switzerland. Two quotations from letters written on this trip will show a further reason why Hadley liked going to Europe: he was an excellent sailor and enjoyed every minute spent at sea. From motives of preference and economy combined he was apt to travel on slow boats, and each added day was an added pleasure. He would walk the deck by the hour or sit in the smoking room talking with interesting strangers. In the nineteenth century intellectual games were still indulged in as a means of entertainment on ocean voyages. In a letter (July 18, 1890) written as the steamer was approaching the Lizard, Arthur sent his mother a copy of some verses of his which had won first place in a contest to make the best rhymes with "Lizard":

> On the summit of the Lizard
> Dwelt a high and haughty wizard;
> Fierce and bold he was, and arrogantly rash,
> When he donned war's frowning vizard
> All his enemies he scissored
> Into pieces of the size of chicken hash.
>
> All the way from A to Izzard
> This astute and cunning wizard
> Every secret of the magic art did know,
> Not a fear disturbed his gizzard
> Till "Old Rob" once raised a blizzard
> And consigned him to the place where wizards go.

Six weeks later (August 28, 1890) he wrote describing a rough channel crossing on a small steamer:

When I came down upon the steward with a demand for breakfast, he was astonished and said he had none ready; but the captain invited me to breakfast with the officers of the boat. The mate was the most companionable, in fact he was more than half an American, having served as a volunteer in our navy during the war. He let me go up on the bridge with him and otherwise broke rules in my favor; fearing no evil from the bad example as most of the other passengers were physically incapable of profiting by it.

In 1891 the Hadleys went to Europe on their honeymoon, and they went again the two succeeding years. There were some professional engagements involved in 1892, for Hadley attended the International Congress for Internal Navigation, held in Paris. This trip lasted longer than intended, as they were held in New York harbor for several days on their return; that was the year of the cholera, with quarantine for returning ships.

For the next nine years, while the three children were being born or were too young to travel, there were no trips abroad; but in 1903 they went, taking their eldest son with them. In 1906 the Hadleys accompanied Helen's sister and brother-in-law, the Pratts, on a European trip, taking all five Pratt children and the three Hadley children. In the winter of 1907–08 Hadley was Theodore Roosevelt Exchange Professor at the University of Berlin, and his wife and the two boys were with him. In the years 1910, 1912, and 1914 the Hadleys with one or more children traveled to England or the Continent. The war prevented their going again until 1922, the year after his retirement as president of Yale. From then on he and his wife went abroad almost yearly.

Hadley found traveling as a married man very different from traveling as a bachelor. Helen was a conscientious and indefatigable sight-seer. "Europe gets properly appreciated," her husband once wrote, "when she is around." She on her part complained that Arthur's idea of a perfect day in Europe was to sit on a boulder in the country, smoking his pipe and watching cattle graze—which could be done equally well in Connecticut. He succeeded, however, in securing some such days, or would occasionally get away with friends on brief and relatively easy walking excursions.

CHAPTER VIII

EARLY YEARS AS PRESIDENT OF YALE

1899–1901

IN 1899 Arthur Hadley was elected president of Yale, a position he was to hold for twenty-two years. It was with the greatest reluctance that he gave up research and teaching for the labors of administration. He always hoped that after retirement as president he could once more return to research. In spite of the prospect of being able to influence the development of Yale along lines that he thought essential, he probably would not have made the change except for his wife. He had grave doubts as to whether he could be of more service as president than as teacher; she had none at all, but was confident that as the head of the university his influence would be immeasurably increased.

From his own standpoint the strongest motive for taking the post was his conviction that Yale had fallen out of touch with the times and that a change was necessary if it was to fulfill its possibilities. The situation was one that had been developing for many years and cannot be understood without a brief digression into Yale history.

Yale had been founded in 1701. For a century it struggled on with varying success. In 1795 it called to the presidency a graduate, Timothy Dwight, who was a born leader and an educator with views far in advance of his time. He took a college which had been disorganized by the years of the American Revolution, and brought it to a position in the forefront of the intellecutal life of the day. The tradition started by Timothy Dwight was maintained by his successor, Jeremiah Day (1817–46), and was brilliantly carried forward by the next president, Theodore Dwight

Woolsey (1846–71). During all these years Yale men could take pride in Yale's position among American colleges, whether measured by the quality of the students who were drawn to New Haven from all over the country, or by the instruction they received, or by their services throughout the nation in later life. Yale men felt that their college could lay claim to leadership, and while such claims never go unchallenged, study of contemporary records affords this one much support.

The very excellence of the traditions established by Timothy Dwight made it the harder to effect a change as the world outside the campus moved away from the world of 1795. The difficulty did not come to a head for many years. President Woolsey was a man of such ability that he was able to move with the times and yet retain the support of the conservative element who were anxious to avoid a break with the past.

This conservative element was strong at Yale. The governing body, or Corporation, which selected the president and held the ultimate authority, consisted of eleven Fellows. To these there had been added, in 1792, the governor of Connecticut, the lieutenant governor, and the six senior senators, but the attendance of these ex-officio members was largely nominal. The eleven, like all their predecessors before them, were Connecticut Congregational ministers. The original charter in 1701 had provided that Fellows must be "ministers of the gospel inhabiting within this Colony & above the Age of forty years," and though the legal restriction had been dropped in 1745, the eleven were a self-perpetuating body and adhered to the tradition in choosing their successors.

It was this group of Connecticut Congregational ministers who had the choice of Theodore Woolsey's successor in 1871. There were two outstanding candidates for the position, Noah Porter and Daniel Coit Gilman, typifying in their persons and their careers the choice between an ultraconservative Yale or a Yale that would look to the future. The same problem was faced by many colleges in those years. At Harvard, to take an outstanding example, the new order won the day with the election of Charles W. Eliot in 1869. The Yale Corporation in 1871 made the opposite choice and selected the conservative candidate.

That Arthur Hadley, at fifteen, knew much of the heated discussions preceding the election is doubtful. What he told me in later years was probably largely made up of what he learned subsequently. College communities are much given to discussing such matters, and the Hadley family would have been particularly interested, not only because Arthur's father was a professor but because Arthur's uncle, Alexander Catlin Twining, had been President Woolsey's college roommate and was his close friend. Whether or not Arthur's picture of the Yale history of the 1870's was accurate, the important fact for his later life was that he believed it to be so.

The successful candidate in 1871, Noah Porter, was a graduate of the class of 1831. He represented all that was best in the Yale of the past. Like all his predecessors in office, he was a Congregational minister. Sixty years old when elected president, he had served for many years at Yale as professor of mental and moral philosophy, and also as acting professor of didactic theology. He was the author of *The Human Intellect, with an Introduction upon Psychology and the Human Soul.* Granted the premises upon which the Corporation selected the president, a better man could not have been found. The difficulty for Arthur Hadley was that he felt certain the premises were no longer correct.

The unsuccessful candidate, Daniel Coit Gilman, was forty years old, a graduate of the class of 1852, twenty-one years after Noah Porter's class. Gilman was also a Yale professor, but his subject was physical and political geography. He was, in spite of his comparative youth, one of the Governing Board of the Sheffield Scientific School. The younger graduates and younger members of the faculty had hoped ardently for his election. In the year after he was passed over by Yale, he became president of the University of California, and soon thereafter went to Johns Hopkins as its first president, where he amply justified the judgment of his Yale admirers. For a quarter of a century, as president of Johns Hopkins, he was active in shaping the course of higher education for all the country. Hadley always felt that under the guidance of Gilman Yale would have taken the lead in American education.

Many of the younger graduates believed that Yale had made a mistake, and that more liberal influences were necessary on the Corporation. In response to the popular pressure, in 1872 six representatives elected by the alumni were substituted for the six senior Connecticut senators who for eighty years had nominally met with the eleven self-perpetuating Fellows. This change, however, still left the ministers in the majority, and these continued to maintain the clerical tradition in choosing their successors. They would even select Connecticut Congregational ministers who had never been to Yale rather than take Yale men who were not Connecticut Congregational ministers.

In 1886 the Corporation, in choosing Porter's successor, again elected a president to meet the standards of the clerical tradition. It was once again not a case of the Corporation choosing an inferior candidate as against a better one, for the new president was an outstanding man of great ability. It was a case of a choice between two different futures for Yale. The new president was Timothy Dwight, Yale 1849, grandson of the Timothy Dwight who had built so wisely in 1795. Nearly sixty when elected, he had been professor of New Testament criticism and interpretation. Like his grandfather, he was a Congregational minister. He worthily carried on the traditions established by that grandfather, but the direction which Yale took was once more determined by the wisdom of the past rather than by the possibilities of the future. This is not to say that Yale was not well run, or that it failed to prosper under Timothy Dwight's able guidance. Timothy Dwight wrote justly when he described the work of his own administration in his closing report as president, in 1899:

The Commencement Day of 1899 will close the thirteenth year of the present President's official term. It may also, in a certain sense, be regarded as closing the present century of the history of the institution, as the first President Dwight, whose accession to his office was a turning point in its development, entered upon his duties in 1795. . . . The great plan of these hundred years, which was formed so largely, and so wisely, in the mind of the one who became the chief administrator and leader at their beginning, has been carried forward in its development during their whole progress.

Even in 1899, when Timothy Dwight retired, it was not easy for the Yale Corporation to bring itself to entrust a forty-three-year-old professor of political economy with the charge of a college that had been governed by venerable clergymen. Hadley's lack of any earned graduate degree seems to have occasioned little comment, but his lay status occasioned a great deal. He was the first layman to hold the presidency, and it was not offered to him until the Corporation had considered several ministers, none of whom was willing to stand. The process began in 1898, and many meetings of the Corporation were held. Meanwhile pressure from graduates, faculty, and students for Hadley was growing.

The *Yale Alumni Weekly* summed up the course of the election: *

President Dwight's resignation was hardly announced before the name of Professor Hadley was on men's tongues and in the newspapers as his possible and probable successor. Like every early boom, if the word may be used of what was merely the expression of a very common opinion and a very earnest hope, a reaction followed this condition, and for two or three months the situation looked extremely uncertain. . . .

The attitude of Yale men toward his candidacy was one of the controlling features in the final crystallization of opinion in his favor in the Corporation. The interviews and letters by which the *Weekly* sought to gauge Yale sentiment in this matter showed, according to a careful estimate in this office, that it would be safe to say that three-fourths of the Yale men in the country who had seriously considered the problem were more in favor of Professor Hadley as the best possible choice than of any other man. Besides all this, a representation was made to one or more individual members of the Corporation by no less than fifty full professors in Yale, giving it as their opinion that Professor Hadley had eminent qualities for this high office. This combination of graduate and Faculty sentiment, together with the strikingly unanimous feeling of undergrad-

* June 7, 1899.

uate Yale, was perhaps the final force which removed all doubt as to his choice.

Hadley had welcomed the good wishes of his friends but had sought to restrain them from urging his claims unduly. On April 8, 1899, he wrote to his classmate Rufus Smith of Cincinnati, thanking him for his own efforts and William Howard Taft's on his behalf, but adding: "The place is so difficult a one to occupy, that no man can afford to undertake its duties unless he has the hearty support of all the conflicting interests represented; and there would seem to be far more chance of this unification of sentiment, if the discussion is allowed to go on as quietly as possible."

The eleven Connecticut Congregational ministers, who made up the successors of the original Fellows and were still a majority of the Corporation, had been genuinely troubled about the religious and educational views of the candidate. Writing two weeks before the meeting at which Hadley was elected, one of the ministers addressed him directly, in a letter which gives the attitude of the group so clearly that it is worth quoting at length, especially when we consider that it was with this group that Hadley was to work in governing the college in the years to come. The writer, incidentally, was one of the non-Yale members of the Corporation.

May 11, 1899.

My dear Sir:

My only, and I hope sufficient excuse for writing you this letter is, that I am a member of the Yale Corporation, and desire light upon the questions that present themselves at this present crisis. I first thought of a personal interview with you, but, on the whole, think it prudent to take my present course, by letter.

At the outset, let me assure you that the points concerning which I solicit some information from you, *are not points of personal* anxiety or even of dubiety, on my part: but rather such as I would have cleared a little for the benefit of others.

Let me therefore suppose that you are a gentleman on somewhat intimate terms of acquaintance with Prof. Hadley; and let me proceed to enquire of you, as such, what is your opinion, judgment, or testimony concerning the said Prof. Hadley, as regards the following points of interest:

(I) His Christian faith and standing. Is he, broadly speaking, a Christian believer? Is he, for instance, a member of the Christian Church? It is not a question of "orthodoxy," old or new, but rather a question of personal and (I may add) vital relation to the essential and the historic Christ.

For instance (again) do you think he would accept or does accept, substantially, that symbol known as *The Apostles' Creed?*

. . . . .

(II) His attitude towards what I may generalize as *classical studies* in the Academic Department. This is not a question of improvements or changes to be made; but rather a question whether or no, in your opinion, Prof. Hadley would be inclined or disposed to *revolutionize* and "rip up" things in that department, and to act the part of a *radical reformer* in the *College,* to the undoing of its distinctive character.

In your judgment is there any ground for apprehension that he would be so far progressive as to lay aside a wise conservatism in respect of such matters?

My putting of this matter is somewhat vague, but I think you will readily perceive what I mean to ask. Is it not a question of development by *evolution* or *revolution?* I am well aware, my dear and honored Sir, of my boldness in thus writing to you, but perhaps the directest way is the best. . . . I will strictly hold whatever you may be willing to say, as *confidential;* unless, perchance, you permit me to share the confidence with Mr. [Joseph Hopkins] Twichell.

In that case I shall simply say to others of my associates (if I had anything to say) that I speak from the testimony of *one most intimately* acquainted with Prof. Hadley. . . .

I am yours most sincerely,

Edwin P. Parker.

An undated pencil draft of Hadley's answer, in his handwriting, was in the files clipped to Dr. Parker's letter:

Dr. Edwin P. Parker
My dear Sir—

Far from requiring any apology, your letter puts me under obligation by its courtesy and kindness. I am quite ready to say to you, or to Dr. Twichell, as I should say to anyone who asked me, that I am a member of the Church of Christ in Yale College, and that I believe it to be of fundamental importance for Yale to keep its essentially Christian character; also that I am conservative on the question of classical study and am emphatic in the belief that in this as in other matters our progress must be through evolution rather than revolution.

But I feel grave reluctance to have these words of mine quoted, even in the third person, as a means of convincing those who have asked [about] me. I would much prefer that the members of the Corporation should as far as possible get their information from other sources; on the first question, from the serious minded students who have come under my instruction, on the second from my associates on the faculty. Any man who understands how trying are the duties and responsibilities of the Yale Presidency, and what qualifications are required to meet them, must, I believe, shrink from being in any wise an advocate of his own candidacy. Trusting that my reluctance on this point may not seem to you overstrained, I am,

Most sincerely yours

It may best be said at this point, to forestall any misapprehensions, that these same clerical members of the Yale Corporation gave Hadley splendid support, once he was elected. They were relieved to find that though they had chosen a layman, this layman was as devoted to Christian ideals, and as eloquent in their behalf, as any ordained minister. He on his part respected their point of view and worked with them patiently. He realized that they sincerely believed that if Yale was to be impartially administered it must be administered by Connecticut Congregational ministers.

In later years Hadley greeted with delight President Lowell's tale of the parallel situation at Harvard. When a boy, Lowell had asked his father why all the members of the Harvard Corporation were Unitarians, and his father had replied: "If we were to admit a member of any other denomination, there would at once be the risk that the college would become sectarian."

The clerical Fellows at Yale were equally convinced of their own impartial infallibility, but were nonetheless open to judicious approach. On one occasion, in connection with a proposed honorary degree to an engineer of distinction, the award was blocked by the clerical group, until one of their number incautiously said: "Yale was founded to promote service to church and state, and what has this man ever done but build a big bridge?" Hadley saw his chance and shamelessly made the most of the derivation of "pontifex" as meaning "bridgebuilder." He carried the day and secured the grant of the degree by saying: "The highest title in ancient Rome, in either church or state, was Pontifex Maximus."

The ministers not only approved the new administration but during Hadley's term of office voluntarily abandoned the "ministerial tradition," and as vacancies occurred in their number they sometimes elected laymen and sometimes ministers. By the end of Hadley's administration, in 1921, seven of the eleven were laymen. The change was in large part due to Hadley's tactful handling of the situation, though he himself gave the full credit to the ministers, saying in his last presidential report that the growth of new university problems had made the continuance of a clerical majority an anomaly and that "to the credit of the ministers be it said that they recognized this fact and abandoned an old usage, not as a reluctant concession to public opinion, but as a result of their own personal judgment as to what was right."

The Yale Corporation elected Hadley president on May 25, 1899, and on the same day a committee of three waited on him at his home with the formal notification. The news spread rapidly, and that evening the undergraduates marched to the house, with torches and much shouting, to cheer and to call for a speech. Hadley came out on the porch and spoke to them. As president he was to make many hundreds of such impromptu speeches during the succeeding years to eager groups of undergraduates or graduates. Almost never is there any record of what he said, but this occasion was an exception. A reporter from the *Waterbury American* was in the crowd, and took down the beginning of the speech, as well as he could in the torchlight and the shouting:

Gentlemen: I thank you sincerely for your prompt readiness to share with me the responsibilities of making Yale at the beginning of her third century equal to the promise of her first and second centuries. And I realize that what has made that development possible has been the earnest and whole-souled cooperation of students and president—and I add the alumni. But I am at a loss for words. The occasion bewilders me. I think the occasion is too serious and meaningful for a light speech, and too light for serious address.

From all over the country poured in the messages, congratulatory and hortatory, that greet a newly elected college president. The personal interest of the graduates is a potent force in American colleges, and in none more so than in Yale. Many messages came from men unconnected with Yale, and here and there were letters from economists who lamented Hadley's loss to them even while they sent their congratulations on his new work. Alfred Marshall wrote from the Tyrol: "My dear Hadley—for I can't call you President, that sounds too awful. . . ." A long letter from W. M. Acworth in London, after the congratulations, went on: "I can only grieve that you will have to give up to things in general the time and energy which I could have wished—largely from personal reasons, as I could then have pilfered from you—devoted to railway economics."

The summer of 1899 was spent in making plans and in securing a treasurer and a secretary for the university. The former incumbents, both good friends of the new president, felt that he should be free to select his own immediate assistants. Moreover the treasurer, William D. Farnam, had served through nearly all of President Dwight's administration, while the secretary, Franklin Bowditch Dexter, had started in 1869 under President Woolsey and served throughout the administrations of President Porter and President Dwight. For the new treasurer Hadley secured Morris F. Tyler, president of the Southern New England Telephone Company, who served for five years until ill-health forced his retirement. The new secretary was Anson Phelps Stokes, of the class of 1896, who held office throughout Hadley's administration, and whose abilities were responsible for enlarging the scope of the office and giving it the position it now occupies not only at Yale but at many American universities.

Any spare moments in this first summer were filled with the other activities that fall to the lot of new college presidents. There were dinners given by alumni associations. There were honorary degrees from other universities. There were trips to talk with members of the Corporation or with others about particular university projects.

In September the college year began under the new president, but the inauguration ceremonies were not held until October 18. They started with an impressive academic procession in the afternoon and ended with an enthusiastic undergraduate torchlight parade in the evening.

The academic procession was led by some fifty university and college presidents, marching two by two in order of precedence determined by the date of the founding of their institutions. President Eliot of Harvard and Provost Harrison of Pennsylvania headed the group, followed by President Patton of Princeton and President Low of Columbia, and so on through the roster of American universities. After them marched other college delegates, the principals of high schools and preparatory schools, then governors and government representatives. Finally came, to quote the official list, "graduates in the order of graduation and the Faculties of the University in the order of seniority."

The inaugural address delivered to this audience was a straightforward presentation of the situation at Yale and of the plans of the president. It was well received, not only by the immediate audience but in editorial comment all over the country. Hadley outlined his line of approach:

"We may best understand the work which Yale has to do if we study the problems in their general form, as they come before the whole brotherhood of educators as a body; and then try to solve them in the particular form which is fixed by the special circumstances, past and present, which have made Yale University what it is."

After dealing successively with the problems raised by increasing differences in wealth on the one hand and increasing differentiation in courses and professional schools on the other, he stated the central problem as he saw it:

"How shall we make our educational system meet the world's demands for progress on the intellectual side, without endangering the growth of that which has proved most valuable on the moral side?"

On the purely intellectual side he felt that the individual professors, under the keen competition between universities, might be trusted to see to the excellence of instruction in their several departments. For all else, and especially for the balanced growth of the university as a whole, he believed that the burden rested on the administration in general and on the president in particular.

The rest of the address was devoted to a consideration of certain specific problems. The suggested shortening of college courses to three years, then much under discussion, he believed unwise. He dealt with the perpetual problem of keeping student expenses low enough so that the college could draw from as wide a group as possible, and with the allied problem of providing scholarship aid in forms which would be helpful rather than demoralizing. After a discussion of other general questions, he went on to Yale's peculiar problem:

Yale's organization differs somewhat fundamentally from that of most other American universities. It is a group of colleges whose property is held in the name of a single corporation, but whose management is, by tradition and in some slight degree by legal authority, located in the hands of the separate Faculties. . . . This form of organization has advantages and disadvantages. To reduce the latter, while retaining the former, can only be the result of unconstrained discussion and independent negotiation. The effort to impose a prearranged policy is likely to prove futile.

The best means of securing workable organization, in Hadley's opinion, was by the use of general university funds. This would put the administration in a position to assist men in the different departments to cooperate at those points where the absence of such cooperation did most harm.

The address was significant, but only the future could show whether its aspirations would have actual influence on Yale development. The inauguration ceremony was itself significant, however, in giving tangible evidence of change. For the first time in two hundred years the emphasis was on Yale in its relation to the outside world rather than on Yale as a world in itself. The large number of distinguished guests was one aspect of this, guests not only from the world of education but from other fields as well. Another aspect, which evoked a surprising degree of comment, was that for the first time Latin orations were omitted. In the words of one newspaper account: "The inauguration ceremonies were simple in themselves. They were conducted in English, the traditional Latin pronouncements having been abandoned at Dr. Hadley's request."

The undergraduates had their real share in the celebrations after nightfall. A jubilant torchlight procession wound through the streets, headed by a dummy railroad train built out of slats and canvas. The train was realistically painted; its locomotive poured out clouds of smoke, and its cars were labeled in large letters "Hadley R. R. Transportation Co." The marchers wore academic costume as far as the cut of their robes was concerned, but the gowns were of brilliant hue, each class having its own color. Military bands competed as best they could with the shouts of the paraders. As each section of the parade passed the president's house, the cheering reached a climax, and there would be a halt with cheers for Hadley and then more cheers for Eliot of Harvard, as the two presidents stood side by side on the porch reviewing the parade.

The inauguration over, Hadley settled once more into the work of his office. He had been a little worried over his youth, since he was only forty-three and many of his faculty were twenty years or more his seniors. He soon discovered the truth of a friend's comment, that "a college president is, ex officio, the oldest person in the college."

Another piece of advice proved equally consoling. Early in his administration, he and President Eliot were attending the inauguration of another college president. Eliot said to the new incumbent: "Now that you are president you are fair game for all newspapers. They will take something you say today, dig up something to the contrary you said in the past, and claim that you are a liar." Hadley asked: "Why, President Eliot, have they claimed that with you?" "Claimed it?" said Eliot, "they've proved it."

In general the press treated the new president very well indeed, but there were occasions when Eliot's remark was a great consolation. In fact, even before the inauguration Hadley had discovered that words spoken in New Haven might be picked up by the press all over the country and handled severely. In the course of an address to the New Haven High School soon after his election he said, referring to the war with Spain: "In the Army the scramble for commissions wrought much havoc." A storm of protest arose in the press. The remark was undoubtedly injudicious, and in later years Hadley would have been more cautious in his phrasing. At this distance some of the newspaper rejoinders make interesting reading. The *New York Sun* (June 25, 1899), after upbraiding him for his "ignorance and misconception," assured him that "from beginning to end there was no instance of weakness or breakdown in the Army or its supply departments. . . . In the history of war there has been nothing more heroic or skillful than its record."

The inauguration was in 1899. In 1901 the Bicentennial of the founding of Yale was to be celebrated. Much of the intervening year was taken up with plans for the occasion, and with trips to meetings of Yale graduates all over the country. A Bicentennial Fund of $2,000,000 was being raised. Plans for a Bicentennial building program were being worked out. Over and above these special tasks, Hadley was busily employed in developing his ideas on university policy and in explaining his plans to graduates at alumni meetings in many cities.

The trips to alumni meetings were time-consuming and exhausting, but Hadley enjoyed every minute of them. In the eighteen months between his inauguration and the spring of 1901, in addition to numerous speeches in New York City and in the cities of Connecticut, he made frequent journeys to more distant points. There were separate trips to Washington and to

Pittsburgh. After trips to non-alumni gatherings at Brunswick and Ithaca, there was a Western trip to Cleveland, Chicago, St. Paul, Minneapolis, Omaha, Denver, Colorado Springs, Kansas City, St. Louis, Louisville, Cincinnati. Following this there were separate trips to Philadelphia and Boston. Then came a week's trip with meetings at Baltimore, Washington, Rochester, Buffalo and Scranton. A trip to the Far West took him to Berkeley, San Francisco, Leland Stanford, Santa Barbara, Los Angeles. Another trip on which he had started was cut short by the serious illness of his year-old daughter, and it was not until a later year that he took his first trip as president to the deep South, speaking at Charleston, Savannah, Birmingham, New Orleans, and Dallas.

Hard work in New Haven accounted for most of the time of the new president, but there is little of interest to record in discharging the routine duties of an office. One particular challenge which was out of the ordinary he met successfully, and so patiently and at the same time so decisively that the memory of the incident made his task easier in later years. The old sophomore societies of Hadley's undergraduate days had long since been abolished. New and more secret ones had grown up in their place, which included in their combined membership only about one sixth of each class. Feeling ran high between society and non-society men, and the problem became so serious that the intervention of the faculty was invoked by the undergraduates themselves. Hadley made every effort to work out a satisfactory solution. The demand was for abolition of the societies, but Hadley refrained from such drastic action, even though a majority of the students and graduates appeared in favor of it. At the same time the president and the faculty made it clear to the representatives of the sophomore societies that they must themselves mend their ways if they were to be allowed to continue at Yale.

This the societies failed to do. They decided that the administration would not venture to abolish them, particularly in view of the importance of some of their graduate members among the alumni. Hadley bore with them until they had exhausted the patience of what outside supporters they originally had. Finally the societies held a joint party in New York in violation of a college regulation to which their attention had been called in advance. A day or two later Hadley sent for the officers of the societies, who came expecting a stormy session but nothing more. The president showed them a newspaper reference to the event and asked them whether it was erroneous in any way. They admitted the correctness and awaited an explosion. Instead, the president quietly requested them to inform their fellow members that the societies had been abolished and that thereafter membership in any of these societies would mean expulsion from the university.

In place of the popular outcry against abolition on which the societies had counted, there was almost complete acceptance of the change. The members made furtive attempts to keep the organizations alive, but they vanished from the college life with hardly a trace. All that was left was an arrangement, of the sort dear to the heart of the undergraduate, whereby one man in each successive class with much secrecy selected a member of the next class and passed on the torch to him. This supposedly secret arrangement was called to the president's attention by a zealous informer who wanted even this remnant rooted out. Hadley disappointed him by saying that one man didn't make enough of a society to require action, quoting the Latin maxim: "Tres faciunt collegium."

As the first year of Hadley's presidency drew to a close and the graduation of the class of 1900 approached, the new president was faced by a problem of an entirely different sort. All his predecessors had been ministers, and had preached a baccalaureate sermon to the graduating class on the Sunday of Commencement Week. There was considerable feeling, in those days, that it would not be proper for a layman to stand in the pulpit and deliver what would be to all intents and purposes a sermon. Hadley went ahead and did it, with almost universal approval. He was careful to call the talk a baccalaureate address and not a baccalaureate sermon. Also, although he started with a Bible text, he introduced it with circumlocution, saying: "Were we to choose a text for this morning's talk it might well be: 'Followers of them who through faith and patience inherit the promises.' " This was in 1900. In later years he dropped the circumlocution, though he continued to call the talks addresses and not sermons. In all but name they were sermons, and often most moving ones, leading up to the close when he would say, "Gentlemen of the graduating class," and the seniors would rise and stand while their president addressed his final words to them.

These baccalaureate addresses, together with the matriculation addresses on the opening Sundays of the college year, were from time to time collected and printed in book form. *Baccalaureate Addresses,* published in 1907, covered the addresses through 1906.* *The Moral Basis of Democracy* includes most of those from that date through 1919. The remainder, through his retirement in 1921, are in *Education and Government.*

Charles Seymour, in his memorial address on Hadley, said of these baccalaureate addresses and of the man who delivered them:

His position in the country, an historian has pointed out, was not unlike that of Lord Rosebery in England, although Hadley never held political office. At least once a year he delivered an address or sermon to which the entire nation listened. He caught and held universal attention, partly through perfection of phrase, partly through the innate common sense of his conclusions, partly through the vital quality of the topics he discussed: Belief in Men; The Honor of the Service; The Duty of Independent Thinking; The Man Who Was Prepared; The Price of Greatness; The Good Fight of Faith; The Compelling Power of Ideals.

The Bicentennial Celebration was the culmination of many months of hard work. The preparation had been divided into three parts. One group had been busy for two years in raising the much needed $2,000,000 endowment, a large sum for those days. Another group had been in charge of the site and plans

---

* This volume also includes three addresses not made in New Haven, which would have been termed sermons had Hadley been a minister. These were delivered in the Old South Church in Boston, the Second Presbyterian Church in Philadelphia, and the Broadway Tabernacle in New York.

for the Bicentennial buildings: the Dining Hall, Memorial Hall, Woolsey Hall, and Woodbridge Hall. A third group prepared for the celebration itself. In all this work the president had a part, though the heaviest burden in the work of the third group was carried by Prof. John Christopher Schwab, ably assisted by Anson Stokes.

The scope of the celebration is well illustrated by the diversity of the committees into which the third group was ultimately divided. One committee was charged with state and municipal participation. A committee on decoration inspired thousands of citizens to decorate their homes and then guided them on the decorative scheme, so that the whole center of the city was part of the pageant. A committee on guests saw to it that the hundreds of official delegates were housed with faculty or hospitable residents. The thousands of returning graduates were looked after by another committee and given sleeping quarters and meals. A committee on printing and publishing brought out for the occasion a distinguished series of volumes by faculty authors. There were committees on exhibitions, on undergraduate participation and on graduate participation. Even the weather was taken in hand. Study of the New Haven weather records showed that the chances of rain were least in the last half of October, and the celebration was set for October 20–23. This arrangement was no less successful than the others, and perfect weather prevailed throughout.

This was just as well, for the attendance surpassed all expectations and far exceeded the capacity of any buildings, so that only the open-air events could be attended by all. Nearly half of Yale's total graduate body returned, or about 5,000 out of the 10,000 living graduates. The number was swelled by men who had attended college but who had not graduated, as well as by the numerous delegates from other institutions, and above all by the undergraduates. The official figures gave a total attendance of just under 9,000, with the probability that still more were present who had omitted to register.

The opening day, Sunday, October 20, was marked by special services in the churches of the city in the morning. In the afternoon there was an address on Yale in its relation to Christian theology and missions. On Monday and Tuesday mornings there were further addresses on Yale's relation to various fields of endeavor: law, medicine, science and letters, the development of the country. Monday afternoon there was an address of welcome by the president, with responses from representative delegates, followed by a reception.

The popular highlights were a grand torchlight procession of students and graduates on Monday night, and on Tuesday night a student dramatic performance on the campus, depicting the history of Yale. Stands had been built on the campus, and the whole 9,000 were able to be present in a body. To these two events should perhaps be added a third, a football game at Yale Field on Tuesday afternoon in which the graduates defeated the undergraduates. The captain of the graduate team was Walter Camp. The players ranged from Thompson of the class of 1879, who had played on the first Yale team to meet Harvard under the Rugby rules, through Gordon Brown, the captain of the Yale team in 1900. Camp, Thompson, and some of the veterans were soon replaced by substitutes, but the substitutes in turn were men of might. Corbin at center was flanked by Heffelfinger and Brown, with Fred Murphy and Chamberlin at tackle, Greenway and Hartwell at end. Behind the line were McCormick, Lee McClung, Brinck Thorne and Butterworth.

After all the preliminaries and interludes, the great event of the celebration came with the commemoration exercises on Wednesday morning. The long academic procession proceeded from the campus across the Green, back to the campus, and so to the Hyperion Theater, which was used perforce as the one building which could come nearest to seating the multitude. Here, after a commemorative address by Mr. Justice Brewer of the United States Supreme Court, honorary degrees were conferred upon sixty-two recipients. The final recipient of the Doctorate of Laws was the President of the United States, Theodore Roosevelt.

Mr. Roosevelt's invitation to receive the degree had been given while he was still a private citizen, after the end of his term as governor of New York and before his inauguration as vice-president. He had accepted, and in the meantime had become president on McKinley's assassination in September. This had complicated the academic plans, for the Secret Service insisted on the most elaborate precautions to forestall another assassination. President Roosevelt and President Hadley marched side by side at the head of the academic procession flanked by numerous police. At the reception on Wednesday afternoon, which closed the celebration, the guests were not allowed to come within fifteen feet of the receiving line.

Throughout the celebration Hadley subordinated himself to the occasion. His address of welcome on Monday was admirable but far shorter than any of the principal addresses by others. At the commemoration exercises on Wednesday his only words were the brief sentences which accompanied the conferring of honorary degrees; but these caught the popular fancy, perhaps because of their very brevity. In the newspaper accounts of the occasion they were stressed time and again. In place of the usual formal account of the career of each candidate, Arthur Hadley addressed one short sentence to each man as the degree was conferred. Although he had carefully worked out the exact words to be used in each case, he spoke without notes, and the briefness and spontaneity relieved the length of the ceremony.

Hadley was quick to deviate from his prepared remarks when occasion offered. Mark Twain, sitting in the row of candidates and listening to the president's remarks to earlier recipients, entered into a whispered bet with his neighbor as to which episode of Twain's career Hadley would single out. The bet had to be called off because when Mark Twain was presented such a roar of applause went up that Hadley said: "For whom the universal acclaim renders any assignment of reasons a work of supererogation."

One particular feat of the president's fascinated the graduates. At the reception for delegates greetings were presented from universities at home and abroad. The foreign universities usually presented their greetings in English, but arrangements had been made to respond to greetings in French or German should need arise. The delegate from Upsala, in Sweden, presented his address in Latin. Unperturbed, Arthur Hadley responded in Latin. When congratulated afterward on his flowing response, he explained: "Fortunately the vocabulary of compliment in any language is small. As soon as he began I realized what I was in for, so I coiled down his remarks as he made them, and when my turn came, paid them out again in reverse order, with appropriate changes in construction." Another view of the feat was furnished by Chauncey Depew, who as a member of the Corporation was close at hand when Arthur Hadley received the delegate and delivered his response. Depew leaned over to his neighbor and said: "I never realized before that Hadley knew Swedish."

CHAPTER IX

THE DAILY LIFE OF A UNIVERSITY PRESIDENT

ARTHUR HADLEY was by now growing familiar with the work of a university president, so far as it is possible to become familiar with anything so constantly changing. He described the life in a paper read to the Colby Club in 1902. The paper is unfortunately missing, but he seems to have worked over part of it for an article in the *Youth's Companion* for June 4, 1903, on "The Task of a College President." It would appear that he drew on it again for an article in the Yale Alumni Weekly of November 28, 1906. The first of these published articles was cast in general terms, the second went to the opposite extreme and assumed that the readers were familiar with much about Yale. The two articles between them give a picture of Hadley's work in his own words. For lack of the missing Colby Club paper I have combined quotations from the two articles in the following pages. In order not to break the continuity I have not labeled the various paragraphs as to source, nor have I indicated where words have been omitted or changes made in fitting the two together.

In his charming little book on The Ways of Yale in the Consulship of Plancus, Professor Beers has described the college of yesterday for the graduate of today. The counter-part of the picture is still wanting. No one has properly described the Yale of today for the graduate of yesterday. To do this in an adequate manner would be the work of genius. I shall only attempt the much more limited task of describing the one part of the life in which I am particularly engaged.

In the middle of the nineteenth century there was hardly a college in the country which had a thousand names on its catalogue or a million dollars in its invested funds. Now, fifty years later, there are many institutions which have three or four times that number of students, and scarcely a month passes without the announcement of a million-dollar gift to some educational endowment. With this enlargement of scope, the character of the president's work has altered. He has become less of a professor and more of a business man.

The traditional college president of the last generation was a scholar of venerable aspect and character—almost always a clergy-man. He taught his classes exactly like any other member of the faculty of the institution.

The visitors to his office—or his study, as it was then more appropriately called—were chiefly students or parents of students, who sought his advice and counsel regarding conduct. They found him seated amid his classical dictionaries or his commentaries on the gospel, his face wreathed in a smile which was kindly or sarcastic, as the occasion demanded. They left his presence helped equally by the inspiration of his personality and by the shrewdness with which in a long experience of teaching or preaching he had learned to read human nature and meet its wants.

This was his daily life, broken by no emergencies greater than some student prank at the expense of the faculty, some rebellion against the quality of the food furnished in the college commons, or some fight which had arisen from the misdirected zeal of the sophomores on the one side and the members of the local constabulary on the other. In such emergencies the figure of the president was seen appearing, like the god in the old Greek plays, to calm the troubled elements by his presence—and it is truly surprising to find how often he succeeded.

The type was a noble and sometimes a magnificent one; but like many other noble types of former days, it is fast disappearing. The modern university is too large for any one man to be acquainted with all its members and to do justice to all their complaints.

Even the anxious mother recognizes that in a community of three thousand students it is useless to send the president a letter like that which was written to one of my predecessors:

"Sir. I rely upon you to see personally that my dear boy takes a bath at seven o'clock every morning."

The minute supervision of the daily details of student life, which in former generations did some good and much harm, is a thing of the past. The duties of personal advice and counsel which still remain now fall upon the shoulders of the officers known as deans, rather than upon those of the president himself.

The dividing point between the new and the old at Yale comes at the beginning of the administration of my immediate predecessor, President Dwight, in 1886. Down to that time Yale, though it possessed many of the attributes of a university, did not possess the university spirit. The undergraduates taking the academic course made up the College, and the College was regarded as the metropolis of learning, and other departments as outlying districts. The construction of a few new buildings had not greatly impaired the integrity of the Old Brick Row; nor had the development of a few modern improvements in the curriculum seriously affected the simplicity of the old course of study. The College Fence still stood outside the grounds instead of inside; those grounds were still a plain old fashioned "yard," and had not been translated into a campus.

When Mr. Dwight accepted the office of president, he made the very wise stipulation that he should not be expected to take any chair of instruction in the College, nor be charged with the maintenance of its discipline. To the graduate of today the wisdom of these propositions seems self-evident. But it is related that two members of the Corporation—and to the credit of Connecticut Congregationalism be it said that these two were *alumni* representatives—exclaimed in horror, "Not teach? Not enforce discipline? What *does* he propose to do?" It is to this last question that I shall try to furnish the answer.

The work of the president of Yale, or of any other large university, is a good deal like that of the president of a business corporation. There are a number of parts which need to be kept in harmony; a number of questions of policy to be decided in which no head of any one department has before him the whole series of data necessary for the decision. Whatever may be left to the departments is left to the departments—and very gladly. Each faculty has its dean or director; and this dean or director does three-quarters of the things which the president did fifty years ago. He it is that presides over the faculty meetings. He it is that supervises the arrangement of studies. He it is that tries to temper justice with mercy in the dealings of the faculty with the students, and explains the

situation as well as he can to students or parents who are dissatisfied
with the proportion in which the two are mixed.

The modern president has no longer a study, but an office. In the
place of book-shelves we find letter-files. Instead of tables covered
with laborious and beautifully written manuscript, we find type-
writing machines and efficient stenographers to operate them. The
position of honor is no longer occupied by a Greek dictionary, but
by a telephone of the most modern description; while a private
switchboard puts the president into communication with his treasurer
or his deans by a system of special wires of his own.

The books which he has nearest beside him are no longer the
masterpieces of literature, whether old or new, but current works
on education, catalogues of the leading universities of the country,
presidents' and treasurers' reports from those institutions which
are most similar to his own—not to speak of the financial papers
or railway guides. He does little or no teaching himself; it is his
business to utilize and direct the teaching power of others.

If the president is a wise man, he reaches his office early, in order
to handle his correspondence before the flood of visitors arrives.
The letters come from all quarters of the globe, and their subjects
are as varied as the range of human interests. I received not so very
long since a communication from two corporals on the fighting line
of one of the remotest of the Philippine Islands, who had made a
bet with each other as to the year in which the twentieth century
actually began, and agreed to let the word of the president of Yale
University decide it.

Many of the letters are of course simply handed over to the
university secretary or treasurer. Others contain a more personal
note. Says one correspondent:

"Dear Sir. I have offered you a fair challenge for a public debate with me concerning the method adopted in the creation of the
universe. I hold that it is the duty of the President of Yale University to discuss a topic like this with everyone who is willing to
do so; and unless you name a time and place I shall proclaim you
recreant to your duty."

Another and younger man, who is more interested in the present
than in the past, begins:

"Dear Sir. I write to inquire whether your college is composed
of a baseball nine."

A third correspondent says:

"I feel that I have a call to preach the gospel, and therefore if arrangements can be made for my support I should like to take a course of study in the Sheffield Scientific School."

The appeal for financial aid is one which recurs very frequently, not only from those who are coming to college, but from those whose interests lie outside. Perhaps the most curious letter in my experience ran substantially as follows:

"Dear Sir. I have seen your picture in the papers, and recognize the lineaments as those of a person of generous disposition. Sir, my case is a hard one. My husband is a very arbitrary man. He does not wish to be divorced, and he avoids doing anything which will allow me to get a divorce in New York State, where I am now residing, or indeed in any state this side of Dakota. The fare to Dakota is $67.50. He knows this as well as I do, and not wishing me to be able to go to Dakota, though he sends me money frequently, he never sends as much as this at any one time. Now, Sir, if you will kindly mail me a check for the amount named, you will enable me to be rid of an incubus on my life, and will earn my eternal gratitude."

Before the correspondence is finished the callers begin to come. Their concerns are as varied as those of the letter-writers. There are agents for goods and services of every description, most of whom the private secretary strives to keep away from the limits of the inner office, but with scant success. There are many with ideas intended to be of incalculable benefit to the universe, lacking only the capital to carry them out, and assuming that anything which interests them must interest the head of an institution of learning.

The secretary of the university comes in with two or three letters selected from his enormous mail, which he feels that he cannot answer without consultation with his chief, because they contain points involving an indication of future policy—although it is astonishing how few among his many letters a really efficient secretary finds it necessary to refer to headquarters for advice.

The treasurer comes in with reports of perplexing matters in the work with which he is charged. A legal complication has arisen in Chicago which he must discuss with the president before seeking advice of the solicitor. An unexpected difference of opinion has developed between an architect in New York and the contractor on a certain college building. A bill has been presented from Boston, the payment of which, when entered on the ledger, will involve a new principle concerning the accounts between the different departments of the university. All these matters, and manifold others involving the expenditure and use of money, claim a large part of the president's time.

The president must see that the sums spent upon the different parts of the educational and administrative work are so proportioned that they will further at once the needs of efficient instruction of the students and of scientific progress in the world.

When it comes to obtaining funds as opposed to spending them, the duty of the president, while a most important one, is performed on rather different lines from that which is commonly supposed. President Eliot told me when I first took office that it was generally a mistake for the president of a large university to ask for money directly, except in a case where there had been a previous intimation that such a request would be welcome. He said that the duty of the president should be to have his plans in such clear shape that they would appeal to a man who was interested; and that the president's appeal was far stronger when made in form of a plan than when made in the form of a request. I have become more and more convinced of the soundness of that advice.

After or before the secretary and the treasurer come the student callers,—always welcome if the president is a fit man for his place, —some of them wishing advice as to the arrangement of their studies and their plans for professional life; others seeking cooperation in the many organizations, social, athletic or literary, which form a large part of modern college life; still others, who are brought into trouble by the application of the laws of the college and of the community, who come, either alone or with their parents, to see if some exception cannot be made in their favor.

In this latter case, the students and their parents come to the president today as to a disinterested party to whom they can appeal, rather than as a representative of the faculty, although the president always consults with the faculty officials concerned. When a student inquires regarding the operation of a rule of discipline which appears to have worked hardship in his case, my first question usually has to be, "How does the rule read?" The very fact that I have to ask this question is an advantage. The faculty representatives, in their discussion with the students, are too apt to take their own rules for granted as something inevitable and immutable. A president, meeting the student man to man and examining both the reasons for the law and the reasons for the exception, works out the case in a manner which makes his conclusions seem more impartial even if they really are not so. Sometimes he can suggest a method by which the just demands of the student can be satisfied in a manner which did not occur to the faculty; sometimes he can show the student what are the real reasons which actuated the faculty and make him acquiesce in those reasons, by the simple process of telling him things which he never thought of, but which many faculty members—and especially the younger ones—suppose that every man knows by intuition.

But it should not be thought that any large proportion of the talks between the president and the students deal with questions of discipline. Most of them deal with matters of constructive policy— enterprises of social organization, of literary or scientific activity, of reform in college customs, or a dozen other similar things which the student body has at heart. The editors of the college periodicals, the managers and captains of the various athletic organizations, and the representatives of all kinds of student societies, are frequent visitors at the president's office.

There was a time in the history of European universities, five or six hundred years ago, when the president was the head of the organization of students and graduates that was charged with actually running the institution; while the faculties, under the presidency of their various deans, dealt with the courses of study and the conditions for degrees. I do not believe that we shall ever get back to that state, but I am glad to say that we are a great deal nearer it than we were thirty years ago; for there are many things which must be done by the students or graduates or else not done at all, and the number of those things is likely to increase rather than diminish as the university grows in size.

It is a great pleasure to promote every possible movement in this direction; whether by attending Yale News dinners or Good Government Club smokers, or by cooperating to keep up the old College customs. I attend morning chapel regularly—partly because I like to begin the day in that way, but partly also because it is a student ceremony. The faculty, with the exception of a few members who loyally serve as chaplains, has ceased to go to prayers. The institution is kept up by student sentiment, which rather shrinks from a change that a large part of the faculty would be quite ready to make.

Less frequent than the student calls, but of longer duration, are those of the professors. One man desires to extend the scope of his department, and wishes to know what assistants can be placed at his command. A second desires to apply to the Corporation for leave of absence during the year which is to follow. A third is consulted by the president concerning the merits of various candidates for a vacant position in a line analogous to his own. A fourth has a plan for a scientific publication in which he thinks that the institution can advantageously take an interest.

Outside of the office, I attend as many of the meetings as possible of each of the faculties of the university, especially those where questions of policy and of nominations for teaching positions are decided. The president is by the laws of the Corporation *ex officio* a member of every faculty; and he ought to know enough of their action, and share enough of their sentiments, to be a valued member. He does not, as a rule, preside. He attends in order to know what is going on in each department, and to give the members of that department a knowledge of what is going on elsewhere—to stimulate as far as possible the development of policies that will work for the benefit of the university as a whole. In this work the organization of the University Council, where representatives of different faculties meet for discussion, is a very great help; and the special committees of the Corporation for conference with the different departments are also of much service. But no meeting or series of meetings will accomplish the result required. People whose views are opposed must meet privately and talk things over man to man. The arrangement of such meetings and such negotiations for the purpose of keeping the peace, and, if possible, securing harmony between conflicting purposes, forms the largest single element in the president's work today.

The most effective control which the president has over the hands of the different faculties is exercised through the purse strings. The Corporation is the body which can say whether an expenditure shall or shall not be made. That body cannot, of course, discuss all the details of expenditure; it can only act when a large question of policy is involved. But its executive committee, still bearing the quaint name of "Prudential Committee," does act on these things; and the president, as chairman of that committee, can generally decide which direction of development a faculty can pursue by encouraging the expenditure in one line and discouraging it in another. Technically the president has the right to veto any action of any faculty in the university; and that veto is absolute unless the Corporation should reverse it on appeal. But anyone who is familiar with the working of an absolute veto knows it is a right which it is better to keep in reserve than to obtrude into the foreground. To exercise sufficient authority to guide the many departments of the university in a common purpose, and yet at the same time to leave the individuals so free that they will favor new plans as their own, instead of being antagonized by what they regard as plans imposed by someone else —this is an all important problem in university administration.

Less important, but hardly less exacting in matter of time, are the external duties which have grown up in connection with the president's office. I do not refer to the various receptions, public and private, which have gradually become established customs of the place, nor to the alumni meetings which it is the president's duty and pleasure to attend. The alumni are essentially a part of the university, just as much as the students are; and though the great number of the associations and the distance of some of them from New Haven make this an "external" duty in the sense of calling a man far away from home, they do not make it so in spirit. I refer to the dealings of the university with other corporations, public and private, educational and political. The president must keep in touch with the New Haven city government and its various departments. The mayor must be his friend, and so must the chief of police. His dealings with the state are hardly less close and important than his dealings with the city; and he must be on the watch for every chance which the university may have, by public lectures, by free use of its halls and museums, and by encouragement of the teachers in the schools of the state, to emphasize the fact that Yale earns its right of exemption from taxation by the recognition of public duties.

These tasks, together with the lighter but no less exacting duties of hospitality to students, professors and visiting lecturers, make up the daily life of the college president at home, broken by occasions of ceremony, like the graduating exercises of the several departments or the entertainment of distinguished visitors.

But there is a very large fraction of the president's life which is not spent at home. Here again I do not refer to what might first come to mind, the vacations, short or long, with which the college year is interrupted. These vacations, which are periods of rest for nearly all the students, and for a large number of the professors, are almost as full of business for the president as any other times in the year. For although the routine work of instruction stops, buildings go on, and law suits go on; and the very fact that so many of the subordinates are away renders it all the more necessary for the chief to be on call. What I have in mind are those journeys which the president undertakes in the necessary course of his duties, and which make the sleeping-car a resting place in which he feels quite as much at home as in any other.

Several times every year he will be called to attend important ceremonials at other colleges—either a centennial or other anniversary, or the inauguration of a new president. These ceremonies have recently acquired great dignity and importance. The interest of the program itself, the brilliancy of the academic costume, and above all, the enthusiastic participation of students and graduates, make them scenes never to be forgotten; and although some may smile at them as a kind of pageantry, unworthy of the seriousness of a school of learning, they yet have a most important influence in binding together the world of higher education in a common spirit and common purpose.

There are also meetings of different universities to discuss questions of common interest. For fifty successive years an association of New England colleges has met for such discussions and within the last half-dozen years a similar organization has been formed by a few of the leading universities all over the country. There are institutions like the Carnegie Foundation for retiring allowances to professors. There are schemes, some visionary and some practical, for mutual recognition between educational institutions on different sides of the Atlantic.

It is hard to meet all these inside and outside calls as fast as they come; it would be absolutely impossible, except for the presence, as secretary of Yale, of a man perfectly competent to serve either as prime minister, general intelligence officer, or *alter ego* to the president. I often wonder how *any* university keeps running without Mr. Anson Phelps Stokes.

But those things which most frequently call the president of any of our older institutions away from home are the meetings of the associations of the alumni which are scattered throughout the country. The graduates of each university who live in any one neighborhood almost always form themselves into a society of this kind, keeping one another informed of their movements and refreshing their memories of their college days, from which they are now so far separated. Once a year each of these associations has a dinner, at which every effort is made to secure the presence of the president or one of the older members of the faculty. It is perhaps the greatest pleasure and privilege of the president's office thus to be able to renew his acquaintance with his old friends, and to establish more firmly the communication between the university and its graduates throughout the land.

For in a real and living sense these graduates constitute the university. A college which enlists the work and support of its members during their days of study, and loses their allegiance as soon as they go away from it, does but a small fraction of its possible service.

It is a full compensation for all the fatigues of routine work at home and of long journeys by rail, as I set foot in a distant city, to feel myself surrounded by friends, and to feel that the spirit of the university and of what it represents is not confined to any one place or any one age, but that wherever I travel I find a body of men who remember their college with undiminished loyalty, and carry its spirit into the larger life of the nation as a whole.

The preceding pages give, in Hadley's own words, a description of some of the things that went to make up his life as president. He had no occasion to describe a host of other incidents that composed his day as a whole. That was not his topic, and in any event he was writing for contemporaries and could take for granted their knowledge of the happenings of everyday life. Daily routine varies from place to place and from generation to generation, and I shall try to supply here some of the background which he properly omitted in his own account.

At 6:45 A.M. two resounding blasts from a factory whistle on the water front reached as far as the college world, where they served notice that it was time to get up. I think that most of those who for years rose at that summons associate it particularly with the blackness of winter nights before the dawn, when you rose in an ice-cold room and groped your way to the matchbox and from there to the gas jet on the wall.

Breakfast in the Hadley household was at quarter past seven, and by nineteenth-century standards it was somewhat light. Arthur Hadley took an orange, a bowl of oatmeal with ample sugar and cream, then coffee, bacon and eggs, and toast with plenty of butter.

About quarter of eight he left home and walked to the college, a scant ten minutes' walk at his rapid pace. He had to arrive in time to put on the academic gown which he wore while presiding at morning chapel. Chapel was compulsory for all students in the college: a ten-minute service on six days of the week.

It closed with a peculiar Yale custom which went back to colonial times—the senior bow. The president descending from the rostrum walked down the center aisle of the church. On each side the seniors in their pews stood, faced toward the aisle, and each row bowed stiffly from the waist in unison as the president passed. The moment the president reached the end of the aisle decorum ceased, and the students rushing to get away to classes or to breakfast poured out so fast that visitors wondered how the president escaped being trampled underfoot in the crush.

From chapel Hadley would go directly to his office. In the first years of his administration this was located in a building on the campus, but in 1901 Woodbridge Hall was erected to house the officers of the university. The president's office occupied half of the second floor, and as originally planned consisted of a small anteroom for visitors, another small room for the president's private secretary, and an enormous room for the president himself. Hadley's secretary, Miss Hotchkiss, had been with him for years; she was excellent, indispensable, and knew her own mind. She was positive that the only place in the three rooms where the light came at the proper angle for typing was in the big room—though even there it was hardly what a good typist had a right to expect from an architect. So for twenty years Miss Hotchkiss presided efficiently at her desk in the big room and the president worked contentedly in what was intended for the secretary's room. It was actually an improvement over the original plan, for the big room was also used as the waiting room, while that occupied by Hadley and succeeding presidents made a charming, if somewhat small, office. The original anteroom was vacant for years, and later became the private office of the provost, after that position was created.

In his office as in his home, Hadley had a tendency to arrange his books by color rather than by subject. He would come into a room, look abstractedly at some dark corner of the bookshelves, and remark: "That corner needs a little lightening." Then he would remove whatever drab volumes were there and substitute more brightly colored volumes, some of his favorites for this purpose being the brilliant red volumes of the *Statesman's Year Book*. As he always remembered where he had put the displaced volumes, this was no hardship for him, though sometimes confusing to other users. At home he largely had his way, but in the office he had a more persistent opponent in Miss Hotchkiss. Every few years, when Hadley was away on a summer vacation, Miss Hotchkiss would have all the books off the shelves for cleaning and replace them strictly by subject.

At lunch Hadley might have a committee meeting, but more often he was able to walk home and lunch there. Luncheon was at one: cold meat, hot vegetables, beer, and some substantial dessert, such as pudding or a pie. Vegetables, to Hadley, were principally potatoes, though he would take a few string beans or other green vegetable out of a sense of duty and to set a good example to the children.

After luncheon he would sometimes have to hurry off to a college meeting, but frequently he had time for a pipe before walking back to his office. He had smoked very little until around the age of forty; then his doctor insisted on his smoking a pipe after luncheon and another after dinner, as a deterrent to plunging into work right after meals. His evening pipe was a complacent and restful affair, smoked as he sat in one of those now vanished rocking chairs built with rockers attached by springs to a heavy base. After formal dinners there were cigars—very good ones—for his guests and himself, but when alone he stuck to his pipe. He never smoked while working, but on vacations his pipe was a familiar companion.

The afternoon was as full of work as the morning, sometimes in the office and sometimes at faculty or other meetings. He usually returned home just in time to dress for dinner, which came at 6:30. This was the principal meal of the day, taken in a leisurely atmosphere: soup, meat and vegetables, dessert. With the meal he took wine, usually California wine when the family were alone but imported when there were guests or on special occasions.

Until the dark days of prohibition there were cocktails only when there were guests. During prohibition cocktails of necessity took the place of wine, but Hadley, for the first two years of prohibition, while he was still president, served no illegal beverages of any sort, either for himself or others, as he did not think it fair to violate the law while he was in an official position. After he retired in 1921 he no longer felt under this restraint. Even after retirement, his wife deprecated his having any dealings with bootleggers, but fortunately her scruples did not extend to her sons' procuring liquor and supplying their father, which they did with much pleasure.

Formal dinners, as they were served at the close of the nineteenth century, perhaps call for a passing word if only to show what was required of those living in those days. Helen Hadley kept a record in her engagement calendar of what she served on each occasion and who the guests were. Here, for example, is a dinner given by the wife of a young professor in 1891:

> Oysters
> Soup
> Fish, mayonnaise, potatoes, rolls
> Chops and peas, jelly and preserves
> Chicken, celery and lettuce salad, bread
> Peach Ice, kisses, cake
> Fruit, candies
> Coffee.

A few ladies, coming in to meet an old friend, were given the following luncheon by Mrs. Hadley in 1892:

Grapefruit au rum
Fish, cucumber sandwiches
Patties of sweetbread and mushrooms
Game and salad
Mince rolls
Fruit
Coffee and candy.

When a college president went to dinner in New York, he had to work his way through menus of far more impressive proportions. But it was on the trips to visit alumni, to which Hadley referred in his own account of his work, that the meals became truly lengthy. Here is the menu for the Sixteenth Annual Banquet of the Yale Alumni Association of the Northwest, held in St. Paul on January 5, 1900. On the original card the menu is preceded by the appropriate comment: "None but the Brave deserve the Fare."

Blue Point oysters
Almonds, olives
Green turtle soup, à la Francaise
Filet of sole, à la Joinville
    Windsor potato, cucumbers, celery
Quail, French peas
Oyster patty à la creme
Punch
Philadelphia capon
    Asparagus tips on toast, cranberries
Redhead duck, stuffed and roasted
    Currant jelly, fried hominy, sweet
    potatoes glacé
Fresh lobster salad Bellevue
Nesselrode pudding
Assorted cakes
Assorted cheese, toasted crackers
Coffee and cigars.

The whole was followed by eight after-dinner speakers, none of whom was brief.

At the other extreme from evenings with banquets and after-dinner speeches were the evenings which Hadley could pass quietly at home. Occasionally after dinner he would have to go to evening meetings or to introduce some visiting lecturer. With luck he could stay by his own fireside and smoke and read in comfort. The gas chandelier cast an inadequate light for reading, so the family would pull their chairs around the table on which stood the kerosene reading lamp.

Hadley would generally read biographies. If too tired for reading, he would get out the chessboard and some treatise on chess, and study over old matches. When even more in need of relaxation, he would take down the *Reichskurzbuch* giving the current railroad timetables for all Europe, and plan trips to out-of-the-way spots, checking his connections and working out his routes.

Soon after ten the family retired, after perhaps a bit more to eat. Turning off the gas was simple, but the kerosene reading lamp called for skill. Unless highly qualified, you first turned the wick as low as possible and then blew smartly across the top of the glass chimney. The lamp went out, but with considerable smoke. The alternative method was to blow it out without first turning it down. This avoided smoke and was ideal when it worked, but occasionally the attempt would be followed by a startling rush of flame and smoke up the lamp chimney and into the room. Needless to say, Helen Hadley preferred the more conservative method, while Arthur Hadley was the leading practitioner of the more spectacular school, closely followed by his son Hamilton, who operated under the advantage of enjoying the explosive consequences when they followed.

The daily routine held until Saturday luncheon. After lunch, in the spring and fall, Hadley would take the trolley car out to Yale Field to watch football or baseball or track. Walter Camp was the Yale football coach, and he and Hadley were old friends since college days. Their friendship not only gave Hadley many interesting contacts with college athletics but was of assistance when Hadley and other college presidents were trying to keep intercollegiate athletics within reasonable bounds.

Sundays started with an extra half hour of sleep, and with

a breakfast built around fish balls, fried salt pork, corn bread and maple syrup. After a quiet morning at home the family all went together to the Sunday service in Battell Chapel at 10:30.

The college service was taken in turn by different university preachers, a distinguished group of leading ministers, who came to New Haven to preach. Most of them were well acquainted with the characteristics of an undergraduate congregation assembled under compulsion for divine worship. To newcomers Hadley used to repeat the old warning as to length of sermons: "No souls saved after the first twenty minutes."

The family sat together in their pew, while Arthur Hadley sat on the raised dais beside the visiting minister. From here he gave out the church notices for the week, and once a month pronounced the invitation to the Communion: "All those who, by whatever name, have professed or would profess themselves followers of our Lord Jesus Christ, are earnestly invited to remain and partake of the Communion with us."

College towns are places of fixed customs, and for seventy-five years the Whitneys and the Hadleys foregathered after church before their Sunday dinners. William Dwight Whitney had been Professor of Sanskrit when James Hadley had been Professor of Greek. James Hadley was slightly the senior, and during his life and that of his widow the Whitneys always came to the Hadleys' house after church. After the death of Mrs. James Hadley the Hadleys always went to Mrs. Whitney's. Other parents and children would drop in, and there would be a pleasant half hour of visit and talk by the elders, while the children listened, or read old volumes of *St. Nicholas* in a corner of the big room. Arthur Hadley would be a little delayed in arriving, as he usually stopped off at his office for a few minutes, to look over the mail that had come late on Saturday.

At Sunday dinner there were always visitors present. One of these would often be the preacher of the morning. Usually there were two or three undergraduates. At the time of football games or promenades there would be visiting girls and their parents.

In the afternoon, after the guests had left, the family would go for a walk. When the weather was fine this might be a matter of several miles, going out into the country by trolley, and then walking over the hills or along the shore. In the winter the walk would be along the cleared sidewalks, between the snowdrifts, out to the house of some friend, for tea and a talk. One such gathering place, for the Hadleys and others, was the home of Edward H. Jenkins, on the outskirts of the city. Here, to the delight of the children, the talk would be of the Civil War, or sometimes there were elders present who had been out to California in the days of '49 and talked casually of Indians and desperadoes and unmapped worlds of sagebrush and mountains. On the way back from the Jenkins' there usually would be another stop, to call on Helen Hadley's mother who lived on Prospect Street. Once again at home, there was still one more distinctive feature of Sunday to come. This was supper, at which in the early days Helen Hadley would have a chafing dish on the table and cook special treats for the family.

The activities of the year fell into patterns no less fixed than those of the days and the weeks. In September Hadley would deliver the matriculation address to the entering freshmen at the first Sunday service of the college year. There would be informal talks at various freshmen gatherings and a reception at the president's home for all freshmen. Then came weeks of routine work until the end of November, when the college world from president to newest freshman was caught up in the excitement of the football games with Princeton and with Harvard. For these events, as for other highlights of the college year, the Hadleys would always have house guests, either the parents of students or returning graduates or perhaps some visiting foreigner and his wife. Throughout the year, from time to time, there were lecturers to be entertained, and other visitors from the outside world. Visitors, expected and unexpected, were so frequent that there is constant reference to them in Hadley's correspondence. To take one example out of many, on May 21, 1907, he wrote a son at school, apologizing for the absence of a letter the day before:

Mother wanted to sit up and write you last night; but as it was already 1 A.M. and she has much to do to-day I persuaded her not to. To begin with, we had our big reception last night to provide for. Then Judge Townsend was not well enough to have Secretary Root (who is giving the Dodge lectures this year) stay at his house, so we asked him to ours. Finally, General Kuroki chose Monday to visit us with his staff, and there were all kinds of things to be done for him.

Thanksgiving was a holiday always spent in a reunion of Helen Hadley's family, either in New Haven or at her sister's in Brooklyn. This was a large gathering, with many cousins. In contradistinction Christmas was a Hadley and not a Morris reunion and brought together hardly more than Arthur's immediate family, the only other relative present being his sole Hadley cousin, Mary. The New Year's family reunion was intermediate in size; this was always spent with the Twinings, Arthur's cousins on his mother's side. The Twining sisters, two spinsters and one widow, lived in a house on Prospect Street.

In the early years of his presidency, the Hadleys gave a Christmas party in their home, with tree and candles and refreshments, for all students who lived so far from home that they had to stay in New Haven at Christmastime. With the growth in size of the university this soon became an impossible task and was given up.

In the winter term the college schedule was broken by the Yale Promenade, nominally an affair of the junior class but actually attended by the three upper classes. For a long week end New Haven was inundated with girls and their chaperones. The Hadleys' house would be full, and there would be dinners for the Promenade Committee and their guests. The burdens of the Promenade fell on the president's wife rather than on the president. She enjoyed it, and would take in all the events from start to finish. She had first gone to a promenade as a girl in 1881, and claimed to have missed only one in the next fifty years. In her later years she would still attend, and would sit talking with the patronesses, and watching the children and grandchildren of her contemporaries. Midway in this half century there is a letter from her husband to one of their children at school which reads: "I came home from the 'prom' at half-past-one like a good boy, but left Mother to stay. When she got home I was fast asleep; but as she got into bed I heard a clock strike, and it said, 'one, two, three, four, five, *six!*' "

In the winter or early spring Hadley, accompanied by his wife, would make a trip to address alumni gatherings in other parts of the country. One year he might go to the Midwest, the next to the South, the next to the Far West, and so in rotation. Greatly though he enjoyed the trips, they were exhausting. After a night in a sleeping car he would arrive in some city and at once start on a round of addresses: perhaps the high school in the morning, then luncheon and another address, sometimes more talks in the afternoon, and always in the evening a banquet and a speech to alumni. Depending on the distance to the next city, there would be either another night in a sleeper or a night with his local hosts followed by an early morning train trip to his next stop.

Commencement, at the end of June, was the time of greatest strain for the president. Hadley calculated that, beginning with the baccalaureate address at the Sunday service, he had to make some fifty speeches in four days. Even this figure did not include brief pronouncements, such as his statements when conferring honorary degrees. The speeches ranged in character from formal addresses on which he might have worked for weeks to impromptu talks to reunion classes.

These brief speeches to returning classes, as they came in reunion costume to the president's house after the Commencement baseball game, are well described in Mary Raymond Shipman Andrews' *The Courage of the Commonplace,** and though the particular incident is fiction, the picture is drawn by one familiar with the scene and with the speaker:

It has come to be an institution that after the game the old graduates should go, class by class, to the house of the president of Yale, to renew allegiance. It has come to be an institution that he, standing on the steps of his house, should make a short speech to each class.

* Pp. 64 f. (Charles Scribner's Sons, 1911.)

The rainbow of men, sweeping gloriously down the city streets with their bands, dissolves into a whirlwind at the sight of that well-known, slight, dignified figure on the doorstep of the modest house—this is a thing which one who has seen it does not forget; the three-minute speeches, each apt to its audience, each pointed with a dart straight to the heart of class pride and sentiment, these are a marvel. Few men living could come out of such a test creditably; only this master of men and boys could do it as he does it. For each class goes away confident that the president at least shares its conviction that it is the best class ever graduated. Life might well be worth living, it would seem, to a man who should hear every year hundreds of men's voices thundering his name as these men behind the class banners. . . . [The class] were cheering the president, on the point of bursting themselves into fragments to do it, it seemed. There were two hundred men behind the class banner, and each one was converting what was convertible of his being into noise. Johnny McLean turned to with a will and thundered into the volume of tone which sounded over and over the two short syllables of a name which to a Yale man's idea fits a cheer better than most.

In one afternoon and evening there would be a dozen or more such speeches. Each class took it for granted that Hadley should know its own members but wondered how he was so well acquainted with other classes much earlier or later at Yale. Actually, as Hadley once explained, he had firsthand contacts with fifty years of Yale classes, and had good friends in enough more classes to bring the total well over seventy-five. He reached this larger figure by including his father's students, whom he had first known when he was a child, and with whom he had worked on Yale matters when he was a young president and they were old and leading alumni. But even without these additions, when he entered college the class of 1873 were seniors, and when he closed his term as president the class of 1924 were freshmen. In all the years between there was no class that had not been in college when he was either a student or a teacher or the president. In some instances he might have been away during part of the undergraduate life of the class, but never for all. He had the closest personal friendships with the men in the classes he

93 WHITNEY AVENUE

ARTHUR HADLEY, 1921
AT HIS LAST COMMENCEMENT AS PRESIDENT

had taught, but even as president he had always continued to see much of the undergraduates.

Such was the routine of a president's life. As the years went by there were some changes. Thus in his later years his doctor made him go a little slower and he seldom attended early morning chapel, though he never missed the Sunday service and was still as early as ever at his office on weekdays.

One facet of college life has not so far been described, either in Hadley's own account or in this picture of daily details. This is the matter of faculty politics, which bulks so large in the minds of some. It is recorded that a distinguished member of the Yale faculty, running for an elective office after his retirement from Yale, was twitted by his opponent for having no experience in politics, and replied: "No experience in politics! After being on the faculty for forty years!!"

One reason for this absence of emphasis here is that politics is far less of a factor than many individuals think. A further reason is that Hadley was singularly immune to its influence. He was so thoroughly wrapped up in Yale, and eager only for the good of Yale, that he was impartial in his approach to problems.

Problems, of course, there were. After his retirement, when Hadley was looking back on his work, he was inclined to think that the most exhausting task of a university president was that of helping his faculty members to pull together instead of separately. He even outlined for me, half in earnest, the characteristics of various faculties in their internecine strife, based on the experience of college presidents he had known over the length and breadth of the United States during a half century of teaching and administration.

Subject to the exceptions that accompany any general rule of human relations, it appeared that members of English faculties and of language faculties generally were frequently at odds, and heatedly so. In their case it might take up much of the president's time but was not a serious problem. It was all part of their way of life, and the following year there would be new alignments in the disputes and the old grudges would be forgotten.

Faculty differences were less frequent but more serious in history, or economics, or law; but in those faculties a tactful president could usually work out an accord, because it was a matter of professional pride with any scholar in such a field to be able to see the other man's point of view, however different from his own it might be. In the Divinity School, or in the faculties of mathematics or physics, disputes came seldom, but when they did you had to reconcile yourself to losing one contender or the other, because those professors were used to dealing with absolute truth, and each knew that truth was on his side and on his side alone. Whatever the faculty involved, Hadley always found much with which to sympathize on either side, although the lengths to which selfrighteous enthusiasts would go made him frequently quote the proverb of Halévy: "Virtue is more dangerous than vice, because its excesses are not subject to the restraints of conscience."

CHAPTER X

UNIVERSITY DEVELOPMENT

1901–1914

ARTHUR HADLEY had accepted the presidency because he saw so clearly what Yale might accomplish. Yale was not lacking in fundamental qualities. The traditions were sound. The spirit was excellent, whether among students, faculty, or alumni. The subjects taught were in the main well taught. Everything was there on which to build, but the work of building a Yale which should be in touch with the times called for clear vision, careful plans, and persistence in carrying the plans through.

The plans of the new president were outlined by him to meetings of alumni in different parts of the country at the start of his administration.

He wanted Yale to be a true university, and at the moment it was a conglomeration of schools, of varying excellence and often working at cross-purposes. Students enrolled in one department were normally barred from taking courses offered by another, and there frequently was an equal barrier to the interchange of ideas between the professors in different departments.

He wanted each student to get an education and not a hodge-podge of courses. For the undergraduates this called for something with more central unity than the extreme elective system. For the graduate students it called for a strengthening of the existing professional schools.

He wanted Yale to be a national university, playing a leading part in the nation's school system. Instead, it lacked proper contact with the public schools of the country. If the situation could be set right, Yale would not only be able to influence the development of the educational system of the nation but would itself benefit by getting as students the best men from all ranks and from all over the country.

To achieve his aims, Hadley needed the support of faculty, students, and alumni. To a great degree he could accomplish this by a clear statement of his purposes and by inspiring his hearers to work for the same ends. Over and above this, as a practical matter of administration, he needed increased university funds; that is, funds whose disposal was in the control of the central administration and not of one or another of the competing parts that went to make up the university. These funds he obtained early in his administration and used effectively.

Yale University at the start of Hadley's administration numbered just over 2,500 students. An increase in size was no part of his aims, and although the number rose to something over 3,200 by 1906, it held at approximately that figure for the remaining fifteen years of his term. The practice of different schools in the university varied, particularly in the early years when some of the schools were virtually independent, but the general tendency was to take advantage of increased applications by making more careful selection instead of by increasing in size.

Of the initial 2,500 students, rather more than two thirds were undergraduates, and the balance, in round figures, was made up of 250 in the Graduate School, 200 in the Law School, 150 in the Medical School, 75 in the Divinity School, and 50 each in the Music School and in the Art School.

Physically, the central core of the university was the Old Campus (bounded by Chapel, College, Elm, and High Streets) on and about which the "Academical Department," or Yale College, had its buildings. The term "its buildings" is used literally; the buildings were college and not university buildings. Even the Library was regarded as college rather than university property. The students in the college made up nearly half of the total university enrollment in 1899: 1,224 out of 2,517.

Across Elm Street from the campus were the buildings of the Divinity School. Then came a gap of two city blocks, which was to be filled with Yale buildings during Hadley's administration but which in 1899 was still occupied by private houses. After this gap, north of Grove Street, came the buildings of the Sheffield Scientific School, in which the balance of the undergraduates were enrolled.

The rest of the university was inadequately housed or houseless. In even earlier days, before the Divinity School had received its buildings adjacent to the Old Campus, the location of the scattered and scanty quarters of three of the graduate schools used to be accurately described by saying that the Law School was on the road leading to the jail, the Medical School on the road leading to the cemetery, and the Divinity School on the road leading to the poorhouse.

One feature of the Yale picture as it existed at the start of Hadley's administration calls for special treatment, both because of its peculiarity and because it furnishes a good example of his handling of an administrative problem. This was the existence at Yale of two independent undergraduate departments: Yale College and the Sheffield Scientific School.

Any university might reasonably have had an academic department and a scientific department, one stressing the classics and the other science. At Yale, however, the independence went so far as to produce two separate and self-sufficient institutions.

The academic department was Yale College, but the college did not think of itself as a department. It was the original Yale unit, founded in 1701, and it regarded itself as Yale and all else as accessory. To become a member of Yale College a student had to present four years' school work in Latin and three in Greek; once in, he had to complete a four-year course before attaining his Yale degree as Bachelor of Arts.

The scientific department was the Sheffield Scientific School, with an independent income controlled by a separate board of trustees. Candidates for this part of Yale had to present only two years in Latin and no Greek; their undergraduate course was only three years, leading up to the Yale degree of Bachelor of Philosophy.

Neither department limited itself in what it taught, but each developed faculties to cover, as well as might be, the whole field of knowledge. A student in Yale College could specialize in science, a student in the Sheffield Scientific School could specialize in literature. Let Hadley describe the situation in his own words, in his annual Report for 1907:

The Sheffield Scientific School is not primarily a school for engineers or technologists, with certain collegiate features added. It is primarily a college. It has grown up under such circumstances that there is a larger proportion of engineers and technologists than usual among its students; but the literary side of education has always been emphasized in the requirements for admission, the course of study, and the choice of members of the Governing Board. A man has to study as much literature to get into the Scientific School as he does to get into Harvard College—not the Lawrence Scientific School, but Harvard College itself. After he is in the Scientific School he has to pursue more additional literary studies to get any kind of a degree—even a degree in engineering—than he has to do to get the Harvard A.B. The names of [Daniel Coit] Gilman and [William Dwight] Whitney and [Thomas R.] Lounsbury, leading members of the Governing Board of the Scientific School and dominant advisers in its policy, represent a succession of literary influences which most colleges, even among those that are ostensibly devoted to the pursuit of the humanities rather than of science, would find it hard to match.

Nor can the Academic Department be regarded as a place where a boy is deprived of the opportunity of indulging his scientific tastes to the fullest extent. . . . It is said that today, under the provisions of the curriculum, an Academic student who wishes to devote himself to the study of pure science, as distinct from its technical applications, can find more time and opportunity to do so in the Academic Department than he can in the Sheffield Scientific School.

By the time of this report Hadley had already accomplished much in getting the two departments to make their facilities available to each other, instead of denying them, as they had in the past. This laid the foundation for an even more difficult task. The university secured funds for building university laboratories, a project which had long been a dream of Hadley's.

The agreement and cooperation of the College and the Sheffield Scientific School on these laboratories had to be worked out in long conferences between committees of the two. Hadley's jubilation when the task was brought to a successful conclusion is revealed in a talk on the subject to the annual alumni meeting at the Yale Commencement in 1910. His remarks were informal, and are given here as they were taken down in shorthand, but what they lack in workmanship they more than make up for in spontaneous frankness:

The initiation of this policy of university laboratories has been attained,—thanks to the wisdom of different persons involved, thanks to the wise influence of graduates,—by a full understanding between the Academical and Scientific departments of Yale, between the College and the Sheffield Scientific School, such as we have never in any previous years approximated. We are working in full and pleasant understanding. There is an immense feeling of happiness about the relations between the College and Scientific School of Yale University.

The Scientific School was established as a department of Yale University more than half a century ago, at a time when even these gentlemen [the older graduates present] find it hard to look back upon fully; established as a department of the university, just like any other department. The gifts of Mr. Sheffield caused it to be named by the Corporation "The Sheffield Scientific School." Now, by-and-by there came into office a man who might possibly have diverted money from the study of Science to the study of Greek or Metaphysics. I don't think he ever would have done it, for Noah Porter [president from 1871 to 1886] with all his devotion to Metaphysics never would have attempted to destroy a department of the university such as we had which was of such promise. But those of us who were in his classrooms remember that his phraseology was at times hard to understand, and a certain indifference on the part of the President made it seem desirable to Mr. Sheffield that part of the property be not in the hands of the Corporation, but put into the hands of a separate Board of Trustees, which has managed that property "wisely and for the promotion of the study of Mathematical and Physical Sciences in the Sheffield Scientific School"—so read the terms of the trust.

Well, what people saw was that there were two boards,—a Corporation and a Board of Trustees; and what inside people saw who watched was that there was a certain amount of rivalry between two colleges. They rushed to the conclusion that they were independent. They were not. They were parts of a whole on such terms that the whole benefited by the prosperity of the parts. . . .

The only thing that was necessary was to have the representatives of the Corporation and the representatives of the Board of Trustees of the Sheffield Scientific School talk over their plans with one an-other beforehand, instead of saying after a thing was done: "Why did you do it so stupidly when we were doing another thing?" This policy of free interchange of ideas has been adopted during the last year.

Hadley had, by the middle of his administration, attained with the College and the Sheffield Scientific School the goal which he had set in his inaugural address of 1899. He had then said that Yale's form of organization had advantages and disadvantages, and that his aim was "to reduce the latter, while retaining the former." In the later years of his administration the distinction between the two departments was further broken down, and by the next administration the old Sheffield Scientific School, as a full-scale college, had disappeared. Hadley had no desire to push matters so far. He saw real advantages in the traditions and achievements of the Sheffield Scientific School, and was more than content to have the College and "Sheff" pursue their independent existence side by side, once they were working in cooperation.

One advantage of the Sheffield Scientific School, to take a concrete example, was that its three-year course of study had developed naturally. The whole organization of the school—educational, athletic, social—had grown up on a three-year basis. Hadley himself was a strong advocate of the four-year course and fought successfully for its retention in Yale College. He appreciated, however, that the supporters of a three-year course had much to their side of the argument. If there was going to be a three-year course, he vastly preferred to have one that had evolved successfully over the years rather than one produced overnight by lopping off a year from a four-year course and re-arranging the fragments.

The popularity of a three-year course as against a four-year one was so great in the early years of the century that the Sheffield Scientific School grew much more rapidly than the College. By 1914 the individual classes in Sheff were as large as those in the College, though the total College enrollment remained larger since there were four College classes in residence at any given time as against three in Sheff. There was strong pressure on the College to reduce its own course to three years, and for a time it looked as though the pressure might prove too great to be resisted. President Eliot at Harvard was advocating a three-year course, and other colleges were considering the matter. Columbia went even further in its proposals, which drew from Hadley the following comment in a letter to his old roommate Worcester (October 8, 1902):

I wrote to Butler, expressing my great interest in his report, but at the same time suggesting the possibility, if not the probability, that some enterprising institution would be found to give the degree of A.B. in one year.

Looking at the matter from the Yale standpoint, I am glad that Columbia has done what she has. If the universities of the country, under the lead of Harvard, made a stand for a three years' course, it would be impossible for Yale to resist the tendency; but if the Harvard reduction is made to be the first step in a race for brevity, the college which keeps out of it has great advantages.

Even though it is an entire digression, I cannot resist quoting the balance of the foregoing letter, together with a portion of another letter written three days later:

I am going to be at N.Y. at midnight of next Tuesday—to put the matter accurately, from 11:00 P.M. Tuesday to 3:15 A.M. Wednesday. Can you join me for a midnight supper at the Century about 11:15?

[Three days later:] Your question about the 3:15 A.M. departure is a natural one. It is due to the fact that I have to make a speech at New Haven at eight o'clock Tuesday evening, and another at

Kansas City at six o'clock Thursday evening; and the 3:15 A.M. New York Central train furnishes the only means of reconciling the two.

The Yale Corporation was the final authority in all Yale matters. Hadley took its authority for granted and never attempted to go against it or circumvent it. His recognition of the complete authority of trustees is set out in a letter he wrote a close friend who was a trustee of an educational institution where relations between board and president were not at the moment harmonious. For obvious reasons the name of this correspondent and the date are omitted.

If there is a difference of opinion between the leading members of the corporation and the president, it appears desirable to present to him clearly and presently the necessities of the situation as the trustees understand them, in order that there may be either entire harmony of financial management or a withdrawal at a time when so many honorable avenues of work are open to able men.

No need for a statement of relative rights and duties arose as between Hadley and the members of the Yale Corporation. He never questioned their authority, and the more attention he could get them to give to university matters the better he liked it. He recognized that the initial formulation of policies lay with him and he would urge his point of view forcefully, but he looked to the Corporation not only for the final decision as a matter of legal responsibility but for advice and guidance in working out the wisest possible final decision.

His feeling toward the Corporation is revealed in one paragraph of a long letter which he wrote, shortly after his retirement, to his old friend Alfred Ripley, who had served on the Yale Corporation and on its Prudential Committee throughout his administration:

It has meant everything to me that you and I were working together during all these twenty-two years. I am the opposite of Mr. Woodrow Wilson in a good many respects; and unlike him, I have to work with others and through others, for my personal satisfaction and enjoyment no less than for the sake of getting things done right. I shall never forget what I owe to you and Henry Sargent and Otto [Bannard], and the other men of the group who have worked together on the Corporation for so many years and seen so many of their ideas carried into effect.

The Corporation and the president were in agreement that the funds needed by Yale were to be used for strengthening the institution and not for growth in numbers. As the slogan of an endowment campaign after the close of his administration went, it was "For a better, not a bigger, Yale." And this principle was carried out in practice, for the university kept substantially the same enrollment from 1907 through 1921, though the endowment, the faculty, the salaries, and the plant all increased. Even with increased resources in hand and more coming in, Hadley appreciated that it was all too easy to spread yourself too thin. In an address to the Yale alumni in Hartford on February 3, 1909, he said:

To the public, the word "university" means a place where all kinds of sciences can be taught and taught well—a place not devoted to the study of letters alone, and not devoted to the study of science alone, but one which prepares men for theology and medicine, law and engineering.

But there is another and truer conception of the word "university," which bases the right of an institution to call itself by that name, not upon the universal range of knowledge that it teaches but upon the universal recognition of the value of its degrees. A university in this sense is not a place which undertakes to teach everything; it is a place which undertakes to have its standards respected everywhere. Practically the universal recognition of the degree has been and is a matter of far more importance than the attempt to teach universal knowledge. No European university has had a prouder history than Oxford; yet the range of subjects taught at Oxford has often been relatively small. No American university has stood higher than Johns Hopkins; but of all important American universities Johns Hopkins undertakes the fewest different kinds of work. . . .

This fact has made it possible for us to live. If the greatest university were the one that was in a position to teach the greatest

number of things Yale's future would be discouraging indeed. . . .
It is in the nature of things impossible that we should do as many
kinds of work as other universities do. It is not in the nature of things
impossible that we should do the work which is actually before us
as well or better than they.

The first increase in endowment had come in connection with
the Bicentennial celebration, but this had been almost entirely
absorbed in new buildings. The value of the productive investments of the university in 1899 was approximately $4,500,000
and by 1904 it had not yet reached $5,000,000. Only a small
fraction of this could be used as the administration might see fit;
the rest was earmarked for one school or another. To this
$5,000,000 might be added the value of the dormitories, per-
haps $1,000,000, and the funds in the hands of the Sheffield
trustees, amounting to another million, but by no possible
method of calculation could the income-producing capital of
Yale be reckoned at as much as $7,000,000.

The financial position was made worse by the fact that over
$1,000,000 of nominal endowment existed only on paper. The
president, in his Report for 1910, explained that in 1905 there
were still included in the balance sheet "Advances to Income,
$235,095" and "Advances for Land, Buildings & Permanent
Equipment, $797,715." The first item represented an actual de-
ficiency in the past of receipts as compared with expenses; capital
had been used to meet current deficits, and the money was gone.
The last item represented capital which should have been in
productive securities but had been used instead to complete
buildings when contributions for that purpose had proved inadequate, or to repair old buildings. Nor was this all; a further
$300,000 was tied up in unproductive real estate, a substantial
part of which came through bequests to the university of mort-
gage notes which had been accepted at their face value, only to
have the notes and the real estate behind them ultimately prove
unproductive.

In his Report the president set out the steps taken to remedy
the situation. In the five years from 1905 to 1910 almost
$5,000,000 of new money was added to endowment, approxi-
mately doubling the actual productive funds. Part of the in-

crease was used to replace past impairments of capital, so that
by 1907 the balance sheet was free of fictitious items. Unproductive real estate was sold. With funds restored to their proper
amounts the rest of the new money which had been raised could
be used to take certain much needed steps. The first was an increase in salaries; the next was improvement in the Library.
After these came the purchase of land necessary for the system-
atic development of the university; the thirty acres of the Hill-
house property were purchased through a gift of $650,000 from
Mrs. Russell Sage for the purpose. Here, on Prospect Street,
the new university laboratories were built.

Hadley saw no reason why the balance sheets of colleges
should be less honestly kept than those of railroads or industrial
corporations. The successive treasurers of Yale during his administration developed a form of financial report which the *Educational Review* (December, 1915) declared might well serve
as a model:

The annual reports of the President of the Carnegie Foundation
have frequently called attention to the inadequacy of the financial
reporting of the universities and colleges of the country, and the impossibility of obtaining from many printed reports the actual facts
. . . Reports like the present report of the Yale Treasurer and its
immediate predecessors should amply satisfy the requirements of
the trustees, alumni, friends and patrons, philanthropists who have
made or who contemplate educational gifts, and individuals and
agencies engaged in educational studies, to whom, according to the
Carnegie Foundation, such reports should make their special appeal.

The professional schools required strengthening even more
than the undergraduate schools. With the undergraduate instruction it had largely been a problem of resolving conflicts
and obtaining adequate funds. In certain of the professional
schools fundamental change in the type of school was required.
The work was pushed forward by Hadley all along the line, so
that changes were taking place simultaneously in different
schools. It will be clearer, however, to trace them here one
school at a time.

The Medical School underwent the most drastic reorganization. Founded in 1813, it had a distinguished history. Reviewing the situation toward the end of the school's first century, the report of the Carnegie Foundation on Medical Education in the United States commended the work done by the school and stated that Yale was one of the two medical colleges in New England that had a claim for continued existence and public support. But this was a claim only, and a claim that had to be speedily made good if the school was not to be left hopelessly behind. While other medical schools were offering their students adequate clinical opportunities and thorough instruction, the Yale Medical School was still operating with a part-time faculty, lax entrance requirements, large classes, and inadequate facilities. That its graduates stood so high in spite of all these handicaps was a tribute to their hard work and to the devotion of the faculty.

In 1907, the last year before the carefully planned reorganization, the Medical School had an attendance of 150. Its total annual budget for all purposes was just under $30,000, principally derived from the tuition paid by the students. Most of the students had only a high school training, some were not even high school graduates. Less than one man in six was a college graduate. With full recognition of what it would mean in decreased enrollment and increased costs, advanced standards were imposed for entrance and better facilities provided for work after entrance. By 1913 the enrollment had dropped to 42, a low point from which it gradually built up until, by the close of Hadley's administration, the school had 119 students, selected from a numerous body of applicants.

The deficits occasioned by the loss in tuition and the increase in expenses were met during the transition period out of general university income; but as soon as the new school had proved itself, an adequate endowment was sought and obtained. By 1914 this endowment was in hand or pledged, with gifts of approximately $2,000,000 secured. Once more the successful raising of the money was due in large part to the efforts of Mr. Stokes.

Anything more than this general account of the reorganization of the Medical School would be out of place here. The detailed carrying out of the plan was not the work of Hadley but of the new dean, Dr. George Blumer, who was the head of the school from 1910 to 1920, when he was succeeded by Dr. M. C. Winternitz. Hadley's decisive part was the insistence, before the reorganization took place, that Yale must have a first-rate medical school or none at all. After the reorganization had been undertaken, his part was to support the new dean and to see that the necessary endowment was raised. On this latter point he made his position clear in his report as president for 1914:

The proper policy of the endowed university regarding its professional schools appears to be this: it should give them what they need to maintain the highest standards, but it should be understood that the aid is of a temporary character. The university ought to have its free income available for making experiments, for developing the departments whose utility has not yet been sufficiently proved to justify an appeal to the public for special endowment. We have been willing, for instance, to carry the Medical School at a considerable deficit for a series of years, to show the public that we can give it a first-rate medical school in New Haven; but the University could not attempt to do this indefinitely without crippling the other schools or preventing the professors in other departments from getting the salaries that they ought to have and deserve to have. In the long run the plan of separate and adequate endowment for the several schools is the only proper one. If after a certain length of time the work of any professional school does not appeal to the public, it seems inadmissible to make it a permanent burden upon other departments.

In the case of the Law School, the Yale Corporation voted in 1906 that beginning with the academic year 1909–10 two years of a college course or its equivalent would be required for admission. The enrollment of the Law School had been 195 in 1899, 294 in 1906, and in the last year before the change it reached 438, of whom 183 were in the first-year class. By 1914 the enrollment had fallen to a low of 133, with a first-year class of 38. From here the numbers built up gradually, a process that continued even though the admission requirement was later raised to a college degree. Here again, the actual details of the program were in the hands of the new dean, Henry Wade Rogers, and of his successor after 1916, Thomas W. Swan.

The requirement of a college degree as a prerequisite for admission to a professional school was opposed by Hadley. This was one point in his educational theory where he was unsuccessful in having his ideas carried into effect. The growing insistence on the requirement, among first-class institutions, carried Yale along with it. In fact, even at Yale, the president was in a minority in his views.

Hadley was heartily in favor of adequate standards; what he objected to was the theory that the absence of a bachelor's degree proved that proper standards had not been met. He welcomed any test of the intellectual ability of the student, or of his educational background, but did not think that education was to be obtained exclusively in colleges. In the course of his losing fight he stated his position many times. It would seem only fair to give as much prominence to causes in which he was unsuccessful as to those in which he was successful, and so his statement in the president's Report for 1902 will be given here at some length; it may be readily skipped by those not interested in lost causes.

Hadley started by summarizing the arguments in favor of requiring a college degree as a prerequisite for admission to professional schools:

1. That some of the very best medical schools and law schools in the country have made the change or are on the point of making it, and that if Yale wishes to be in company with those universities which enjoy the highest consideration at home and abroad she must follow their example in this respect.

2. That those universities which require an academic degree enable the instructors to do a higher grade of teaching and attract a better class of students to their lecture halls.

3. That the professions of law and medicine require for their proper pursuit a high degree of maturity and a broad basis of general culture, both of which are best secured by the requirement of a preliminary period of college training prior to entrance upon the actual study of the profession itself.

I admit the truth and force of all these considerations. I acknowledge the brilliant success of the Johns Hopkins Medical School and

the Harvard Law School in the pursuit of this policy. . . . I see
why each university, seeking its own immediate interest, is under
a pressure to make this change. I see also why so many university
men honestly believe that their public duty coincides with their private interest in this matter. And yet, after all this has been said, I believe the proposed change to be a mistake. . . .

Let us first consider the probable effect of the general adoption of
this principle upon the professions of law and medicine. The requirement that every man who begins professional study in either
of these lines should have had a long course of secondary study is
good so far as it secures maturity of mind. It is bad so far as it makes
him late in entering upon his career of active service to the world.
Whether the evil outweighs the good will depend upon the individual. To the man who has plenty of money for his support during
the early stages of his education, who can afford to wait without
hardship for the professional success which is likely to come in the
long run, and can marry during the early years of his professional
life without fearing that some unavoidable accident to himself may
result in sending his family to the poor-house, the advantage of increased maturity probably outweighs the disadvantage of enforced
delay. For the poor man, unless he be possessed of extraordinary
physical vigor—and sometimes even then—the balance is likely to
turn in the other direction. . . . We have our choice concerning
the question whether we shall increase this difficulty by requiring a
long course of secondary education prior to the beginning of professional study, or shall try to minimize it by putting the opportunity
for such study within reach of the graduates of our high schools as
soon as they are qualified to enter thereon. . . .

We are face to face with a broad question of principle, which
our universities must decide. Shall we require every candidate for
the so-called learned professions to spend a certain length of time in
his secondary education and let him study what he pleases during
that time? or shall we let him spend in secondary education such
time as his pecuniary circumstances and personal interests allow,
and have his course of study adapted thereto—believing that for efficient professional study, as well as for other lines of intellectual effort, the habit of hard work is of more value than the question of
seniority? . . . If we choose the [latter] alternative, we shall say
to the secondary schools, "For those who wish to treat the course
in high school or academy as part of their secondary education, we

will indicate what studies form a proper basis for three or four years of subsequent non-professional work in a college; but for those who wish to treat the course in high school or academy as the whole of their secondary education, we will throw open the doors of our professional schools to all who have the necessary basis of knowledge, no matter where they have acquired it."

And what, it will be asked, is this necessary basis of knowledge?

Without entering at too great length into the discussion of a matter of detail like this, I should be disposed to say that the necessary basis was somewhat higher than is exacted by most professional schools at present, but no higher than the best high schools profess themselves able to give. Every candidate should have a good knowledge of English. I wish the requirement in this respect might be much stricter than the possession of a degree of Bachelor of Arts or Bachelor of Philosophy now indicates. He should have a reading knowledge of ordinary Latin prose; and I should like, if possible, to add a similar requirement for both German and French. He should be familiar with those more concrete forms of mathematics like algebra, geometry or trigonometry, which do not require an exceptional type of intellect to master them. Such a candidate will probably be familiar with a certain amount of natural or physical science—though I should question the importance of making this a prominent condition of entrance into the law school. . . .

It is an interesting though little known fact, and one which seems to me to have an important bearing on the whole problem, that it was worked out in Germany some centuries ago, and was decided in favor of the direct connection between the professional school and the high school, as against the mediate connection by way of a course in arts. . . . The really successful institutions were those which elevated the course in arts to a higher and more independent rank, and helped the secondary schools by accepting their graduates for degrees in law or medicine just as freely and as rapidly as circumstances would admit. . . .

In the case of the Graduate School, Hadley had direct knowledge of the problems, for he had taught there for years and had served as dean from 1892 to 1895, when he was succeeded by Andrew W. Phillips. The individual courses were excellent, but there was duplication in some fields, entire absence of courses in others, and the whole organization, or lack of organization, was such as to hamper growth and development. Under these circumstances the school was not immune from what Hadley termed "a besetting sin of American graduate schools, to lay too much stress on investigation and too little on scholarship; . . . they have encouraged men to discover things that were not worth discovering."

A history of the Graduate School since its founding in 1846 is given in the president's Report for 1913. The picture of the condition of the school about 1900 is drawn from a heartfelt memory of what Hadley had suffered as dean, and indicates clearly the points at which he felt changes were necessary. These changes he was able to secure, and once more the deficit carried by the university during the transition period was ultimately covered by increased endowment secured for the school. The 1913 Report said in part:

Our graduate school has been regarded by many outsiders and by some members of its Faculty as being an attempt on the part of two distinct college faculties, Academic and Scientific, to cooperate in giving what graduate instruction they could. This view of the matter has caused difficulties both in administration and finance.

As long as the Graduate School was regarded as a cooperative enterprise, it was impossible for the Dean and administrative committee of the department to arrange the courses of instruction systematically and economically, or to perfect plans for their most efficient development. Each professor was at liberty to announce such graduate courses as he pleased, subject only to the control or advice of his colleagues in the undergraduate faculty of which he was a member. If two courses were offered which covered the same or practically the same ground there was no means of preventing such duplication. If there was an important gap left which neither professor volunteered to occupy, there was no means of filling it. These evils were to some extent avoided by conferences between officers engaged in the same line of teaching in the two undergraduate departments. But such conferences were purely unofficial, and it was an optional matter with the individual professor whether he should be guided by their results or not. Under such circumstances it reflects great credit on the members of the Yale Faculty that no greater evil resulted from this confusion.

The same sort of difficulty was felt in other matters beside the arrangement of courses of study. In dealing with any and all questions of policy, the organization of the Graduate Department placed it at a distinct disadvantage. Other departments had their governing boards, each composed of men imbued with the spirit of the department and charged with the duty of promoting its interests. The Graduate School had no such governing board. Most of its professors were members of other faculties. The total number of such professors was enormously large. This made the Graduate Faculty unwieldy. The proportion of members that attended its meetings was small; the proportion that took an interest in the subjects discussed at these meetings, except as they might affect the relation between the Graduate School and some other department, was still smaller. To avoid these evils the actual conduct of the affairs of the department was left in the hands of a comparatively small administrative committee. But whenever this committee had to deal with important matters its action required the assent of the Faculty, and this assent by no means followed as a matter of course. The Dean of every other department had at his hand a strong body of men responsible directly to the Corporation, to assist him in formulating his ideas and carrying them out. The Dean of the Graduate School had no such assistance.

The financial difficulties were even greater than the administrative ones. When the graduate instruction of the professors of the Academic Department and the Scientific School was given to the Graduate School as a voluntary contribution, instead of being counted and credited as a contribution from one department to another at the regular scale of interdepartmental allowances, there was a tendency on the part of each Faculty to overrate the importance of the contribution of its own members and to underrate the importance of the contributions of others. As long as the contribution was not reduced to figures but described in merely rhetorical terms, each department thought that it was contributing a great deal to the general work of the University and receiving very little in return. It is easy to see how much such misunderstandings would interfere with effective cooperation.

A still more serious effect of this method of keeping—or not keeping—accounts was the impression which it made outside. Any man who read the Treasurer's Report got a wholly inadequate idea of the work of the Graduate School. Although we were giving graduate instruction which cost us in round numbers seventy-five thousand dollars a year, only a small fraction of this appeared in the Treasurer's Report as an expense of the Graduate School, because the rest had been voluntarily assumed by the Academic Department and the Sheffield Scientific School. Many a man who wished to give money for research hesitated to put it into the hands of Yale University because he thought that we were not spending any more money for graduate instruction than appeared in the Treasurer's Report; nor was it an easy task to convince him of his error.

In the other schools of the university the smaller enrollment did not make the task of reorganization and integration any less difficult. Each had its particular problems, but by sympathy, patience, and persistence they were gradually straightened out. As in the case of the larger schools, the deans were outstanding men, though with varying ability as administrators. It was to their own interest, no less than to that of the university, to have existing deficiencies rectified. In the Divinity School the dean was Frank K. Sanders, later succeeded by Charles R. Brown. In the School of Fine Arts John F. Weir was dean, followed by William Sergeant Kendall. The dean of the Music school was Samuel S. Sanford, followed by Horatio Parker. One new school, founded in 1900, was organized from the start on the desired basis, and rapidly established a leading position for itself. This was the Forest School, with Henry S. Graves as director.

An interesting experiment with a Summer School was started in 1905, with a six weeks' course designed for school teachers and principals and superintendents of schools, although other qualified students were also admitted. Those attending lived in Yale dormitories, and instruction for the most part was by members of the Yale faculty. The quality of the work done at the school was good, and several hundred attended, but after trying the plan for three years it was decided that the drain on the budget of the university and on the energies of the faculty was out of proportion to the good accomplished. In the president's Report for 1908 announcing discontinuance of the school Hadley left the possibility open of its resumption at some future date, but added his belief that such a school should be an incident in the development of a department of education, which Yale did not yet have, rather than an independent arrangement by itself.

Common to all parts of the university was the problem of an adequate salary scale for the faculty. A partial improvement was effected in 1905. Further improvement took place in 1910, and a new salary scale was introduced, which at least put Yale in the front rank, though salaries still remained lower than the president would have wished. In particular, he regretted that the university was not permitted to pay larger salaries to the really outstanding professors. His annual Report for 1910 goes into the reasons for this restriction with great frankness, and he points out that the principal reason was that the various faculties at Yale had broad powers of decision in such matters, and that the professors desired "to avoid anything which should look like a habit on the part of the Corporation of differentiating between individual professors." As Hadley went on to point out:

"The theory that the salaries of all professors must be equal tends to tie the best men down to the level of the weakest; because no university is in a position to pay the weak a great deal more than they are worth without forfeiting its right to ask for added endowment."

The salary scale as put into effect achieved some improvement at this point, for the Corporation insisted on its right to increase any given professor's salary without being thereby obliged to raise the salary of others. While the principle was established, and was to prove valuable in later years, in these early years the actual amount of any differential had to be kept small.

At another point, however, the scale gave full effect to one of Hadley's theories; it was designed to force a decision on reappointment early in a teacher's career, so that the man who did not show full promise would have to leave, instead of being kept on indefinitely in his existing grade. The description of this feature, and of the general working of the salary scale, is given in the president's Report for 1915, after the new scale had been in effect for five years:

Instructors begin at one thousand dollars a year and are gradually advanced to sixteen hundred; assistant professors of the first grade receive two thousand, assistant professors of the second grade twenty-five hundred, and assistant professors of the third grade three thousand; professors receive four thousand, forty-five hundred, or five thousand.

The system has proved a good one. The considerations in its favor which were urged in the Report for 1911 have shown themselves sound ones in practice. The rapid increase in instructors' salaries from one thousand to sixteen hundred dollars enables us to keep men here when they are proving useful. The comparatively small margin between the highest instructor's salary and the lowest assistant professor's salary prevents heads of departments from retarding the promotion of the better men for economy's sake, and prevents men who do not quite deserve promotion from complaining of pecuniary hardship if it is withheld. The shortening of the term of an assistant professor's appointment has proved one of the best features in the system. In the old days assistant professors were kept for five years on the lowest scale of salary. Now the question of their promotion comes up at the end of three years instead of five. In the majority of instances three years is enough to show whether a man is likely to deserve promotion or not. In the former case it is fair to advance him; in the latter case it is desirable to tell him so as soon as possible. There are always a few men with whom the three year term is rather short for deciding whether they are qualified for promotion or not. In these cases we can reappoint them for a year at a time at the old rate. Such a reappointment serves as a notice that they have done reasonably well but must do better if they expect to rise in their profession.

The same considerations apply to assistant professors of the second grade. In the great majority of cases three years are sufficient to determine whether we can promote them to professorships here or recommend them to professorships elsewhere, and if so in what sort of institutions. One of the greatest evils of our old system was that this decision was made too late. It is far easier for a man to change his location when he has served only six years as an assistant professor than when he has served ten years. Under the old system we were often urged, and perhaps sometimes led, to keep people here permanently because we had already kept them here so long that it seemed unfair to compel them to go. Under the new system we decide at an early period whether we want to keep an assistant professor for an indefinite term or not. The effect of this is to reduce the number of cases to a minimum. We have a few assistant professors of the third grade, and they are among the most useful men in the faculty; but as a rule it is not wise, either for the man or the institution, for him to stay here unless he has a combination of qualities which warrant us in promoting him to a full professorship.

But while the terms of appointment and the relative salaries are pretty well arranged, the absolute level of salaries ought to be higher. This is not true of Yale alone; it is true of every good school and college in the land.

Each faculty selected its own members and decided which should be promoted to any vacancy. In the early days of Hadley's administration all that the Corporation possessed was the veto power. The actual appointment was by the Corporation on the recommendation of the faculty in question, and the Corporation had the theoretical right to refuse to appoint. The Corporation did not even have the power to transfer a professor with his own consent to the place where he might be most needed. One department might be overstaffed and another understaffed, but the understaffed department could insist on taking on new teachers instead of accepting some qualified teacher from the overstaffed department.

By the end of Hadley's administration a reasonably satisfactory solution of this situation had been reached. In the matter of appointments and promotions the faculties retained their right to nominate the men to fill their vacancies. On the other hand, with the income from new endowment the Corporation established certain faculty positions for which it retained sole power of appointment, acting on such advice as it might see fit to take. In the matter of assigning men where they might be most needed, the president was finally able to announce in his 1920 annual Report:

Professors of all grades will hereafter be elected to chairs in Yale University and assigned by the Corporation to the School and Department that it may judge most appropriate. Instructors will be appointed instructors in Yale University and be annually assigned to the School or Schools which the Corporation may determine. Recommendations for increase of the salary of an officer of instruction will be presented to the Corporation through the Dean of the School to which he is assigned.

Securing the best possible men for the faculty was Hadley's constant preoccupation. The fact that the right to nominate was not his but in the hands of a group of professors merely meant that more time had to be taken in working with the group in question to secure the best possible choice. He knew the faculty individually and took pride in each outstanding member, whether that member was popular with the public or a genius like Willard Gibbs whom few could understand. If the man selected was not at Yale, there was the further task of persuading him to accept. Hadley's correspondence files reflect the successes and the disappointments of the task. He was always in favor of trying for the ideal man, even though the odds were against his accepting, which naturally increased the number of occasions when the offer was declined and the task had to be begun all over again. This never discouraged Hadley; and near the close of his administration, in writing to ask suggestions for a new appointment, he said:

"Don't refuse to suggest a man's name because he probably won't take it. The best men that I have got were men who probably wouldn't take the places they hold."

When he was successful in getting the desired man he was as jubilant as a schoolboy. If he was writing the news to a friend he would boast of the success with no inhibitions. Thus when Yale secured Ernest W. Brown, the English mathematician, Hadley wrote to Anson Stokes (April 18, 1906):

"He is regarded as the leading mathematical astronomer of his generation. He declined an invitation to Princeton, and refused to consider similar suggestions from Harvard and Columbia. Sir George Darwin was very influential in getting him to come. He told him that in his opinion Yale was the most attractive place in this country for a university man."

Ernest Brown evidently agreed, for he made New Haven his home for the rest of his life, and taught at Yale for twenty-five years.

Reference has already been made to the Library. The importance of this vital part of the university, as well as the needs of the Peabody Museum and of the Art Gallery, will be found stressed repeatedly in the president's Reports and elsewhere. All three were facing the necessity of change if they were to live up to their opportunities. All three found in the president a helpful friend in working out the changes and in seeking funds. A picture of the contrast between old and new in the case of the Library is given in an address which Hadley delivered before the Connecticut Library Association on February 3, 1909:

The character of the library and the library administration has a powerful influence on the kind of students that resort to a university. The work of those students after they get there is determined in large measure by the sort of facilities which the library offers. . . .

Down to about 1885 the real research work of a university, so far as it concerned itself with books, was chiefly done in the libraries of the professors themselves or in the special libraries—sometimes deposited in the general library building of the university and sometimes not—which enthusiasts had collected for particular purposes. There was a separation between the researches which were being conducted at a university, whether by its professors or its students, and the general administration of the library, which it is hard to understand. One of the professors of the old school—and, I might add, one of the more enlightened professors of the old school—said to me only a few years ago, "I conceive that the chief educational use of a university library is to lend an occasional book to a professor who does not happen to have that book in his own library." He regarded the university library as a sort of museum; the actual laboratories where the work was done were the special libraries of the professors.

The last twenty years have witnessed a radical change in this respect. The great multiplication of books and periodicals in many departments of science has made it impossible for any but the wealthiest professors to have private libraries which would meet the needs of research. The increasing number and variety of the researches undertaken by the students has rendered the old-fashioned departmental library inadequate as a place for such research. The university library has to meet these needs, and to meet them on a large scale.

Two affiliated organizations were regarded by Hadley as outstanding additions to Yale. One was the new *Yale Review*, which was started in 1911 by Wilbur L. Cross with Hadley's encouragement and aid. Hadley had been one of the editors of the old *Yale Review*, founded in 1892. Wilbur Cross, in his *Connecticut Yankee, an Autobiography*, has told charmingly of the inception of the project for the new *Yale Review* as he and Hadley walked across the Yale Campus sharing an umbrella on a rainy day.

The Yale University Press was a second affiliated organization which found in the president one of its strongest friends and supporters. This was founded by George Parmly Day in 1908, and after Day came to Yale as treasurer in 1910 the ties between the Press and the university became even closer.

The physical plant needed by the developing university grew prodigiously. Funds were secured, and dormitories built, to house the entire undergraduate body. Classrooms and laboratories were provided. Near the close of Hadley's administration the will of his old friend John Sterling left Yale the funds for the great building program which was carried to completion under his successor, and of which the greatest monument is the Sterling Library.

Many of the dormitories built during the early years of the century have themselves been removed to make way for the present residential colleges. A good example, however, is still standing in Wright Hall. The buildings of this type were planned to secure the largest possible results for the money available. Thanks to careful work by excellent architects they were extremely livable, though built under restrictions as to expenditure that were fortunately not present when the residential colleges were built in later years. In dormitories of this later period the Memorial Quadrangle, with the great Harkness Tower, marks the closing years of Hadley's administration. This quadrangle now houses Branford College and Saybrook College, but the tower still bears the Harkness name.

Numerous examples survive of other types of buildings erected during Hadley's administration. If on the one hand we omit Woolsey Hall and the Dining Hall, which had been planned before he took office, and on the other hand omit the latest buildings such as the Memorial Quadrangle, we find that all the rest have much in common, however diverse the purposes for which they were built. They were designed to conform to a careful architectural plan, but the buildings were worked out first from the standpoint of utility, not of architectural effect. Local stone was used wherever possible. As is bound to be the case, some were less successful than others, but the good ones are excellent, and in the planning of each and every one Hadley took the most intense personal interest, working with the architects at all stages of the plans.

In the entire process of university development Hadley relied on the graduates not only for support but for an active role in the process. He kept them thoroughly informed. This was done in part by trips to meet with alumni associations all over the country. There were some thirty cities, scattered from the Atlantic to the Pacific, that might fairly be said to have been on his circuit. In some of them he spoke frequently; others he visited only at longer intervals. There were many others where he visited and spoke only once or twice during his administration. Besides reaching his immediate audience, his talks were given wider circulation through the columns of the local newspapers and in the *Yale Alumni Weekly*.

The annual reports of the president summarized for the graduates the work done during the year. The formal report was read by many, and in addition the material in it was presented by Hadley, in more popular form, to the reunion classes attending each Commencement. Each class returned for reunion every five years, so this furnished a periodic opportunity for posting graduates who had not kept in touch from year to year. Beginning in 1914 the Commencement gatherings were supplemented by meetings on Alumni University Day, in the middle of the college year, when graduates could return and see the university in actual operation.

Alumni participation had been growing before Hadley's administration, but if one wants a picture of the completely different attitude of the authorities in earlier years, one can find it in the diary kept by Arthur's father, James Hadley, during the 1850's. Under date of September 18, 1852, he records a conversation at a Yale faculty meeting: "Mr. Olmsted having said something about the attempts of Alumni in Amherst and Williams to dictate in regard to college matters, Mr. Woolsey [the President] said, 'Mark my prediction—if our Alumni meet together year after year, with nothing to do but talk, and time enough for that, they will be trying to govern us. You must shut their mouths with long Addresses.' "

The graduates of any university constitute a body of tremendous potentialities for that university. They far outnumber undergraduates or faculty. Their loyalty is extraordinary. They have the advantage over both the professors and the administrative officers through being in touch with all aspects of the nation's life. They accredit the university in the eyes of the outside world, and at the same time their interests have a vital influence on the interests of the undergraduates.

Organization is needed if the possibilities inherent in the graduates are to be realized and made effective. Here the genius of the secretary, Anson Phelps Stokes, came into play. Before his day the alumni associations in different localities, the secretaries of different classes in the various schools, the agents of the Alumni Fund all acted separately. Anson Stokes worked out an organization of graduate effort which became a distinguishing feature of Yale. It centered in the Secretary's Office, and it provided the indispensable mechanism for harnessing to useful purposes the enthusiasm that Hadley and the alumni inspired in each other.

The units of this graduate organization were dual. One was the class. Each class had its secretary who handled its meetings and records and kept the members in touch with each other. Each class also had its Alumni Fund agent, who solicited annual contributions from each member of the class. The records for all these, and the machinery for handling them, were centralized in the Secretary's Office at New Haven, or in some office operating under its supervision.

The other unit was the locality, with its alumni association holding meetings at intervals, either alone or with neighboring associations. Sometimes an alumni association maintained a clubhouse or other permanent quarters. Here again the Secretary's Office had lists of members and information as to the meeting dates, so that speakers could be sent out from New Haven—perhaps the president, if not, some officer, or some member of the faculty, the selection in any case being made with due regard for the likes and dislikes of the alumni in that particular locality.

The president's Report for 1904 explains the new organization and discusses the whole problem of alumni representation, with a history of developments at Yale and a comparison with the system developed at Harvard. Under the new Yale system representatives elected by the alumni in each locality met together at intervals in an Alumni Advisory Board. Hadley gave great weight to the opinions of this board and found the organization most helpful. For his views on the subject of alumni participation generally, stated more frankly than in the formal picture given in his official report, there is an illuminating letter which he wrote to the secretary of a sister institution, in answer to a request for comments on a new plan of graduate organization in contemplation there:

. . . You are clearly right in thinking that the reorganization ought to provide means for doing business easily and effectively, and to secure interest among a large number of people, particularly those who have just graduated. I am not sure that you are right in trying to pursue both aims simultaneously. I think that primary stress should be laid on promoting efficiency. If you accomplish this, interest almost always follows. If you fail to accomplish this, no form of organization will secure the interest you desire.

The way to promote efficiency—the only one ever invented—is to select committees with the utmost care, and then be guided by their advice.

A good many people are afraid of this way of doing business; but I am convinced that their fears are exaggerated, and in the majority of instances groundless. One source of apprehension is expressed in your footnote. You are afraid that committee work will be dominated by the leisure class. I think I can reassure you on this point. The people who actually attend the meetings of committees are from the busy class. The members of the leisure class habitually stay away from the committee meetings, and then assume all the privileges in public discussion that would be rightfully theirs if they had attended them regularly.

There is also some apprehension that if the reports of the committees are accepted with but brief debate, there will be a lack of general interest in the proceedings. I do not believe that that will be the case if the committees are wisely chosen. Indeed, I think that promiscuous discussion does more to kill interest in associations of this kind than any other one cause. A sensible committee report, based on knowledge of facts as they actually are, attracts members to an association. Debate on the subject, so long as it is confined to reasonable requests for information, does not repel them. But when, as so often happens, the member who is possessed of the least information makes the most confident proposals, the effect on those whom you want to interest is very bad indeed. Many people like to flap their own wings, but few enjoy seeing others do it.

. . . The report of a committee will carry weight with the board of your institution primarily on account of the care with which the members of the committee have investigated the facts; and secondarily because the committee has been selected by your graduate association as a body of competent investigators. Whether a group of representatives of the graduates approves the result of this investigation after it has been presented to them, is a matter of relatively less consequence.

Under these circumstances I should not expect much good to come from a discussion of the proposals of an Advisory Council in a large senate like the one which you suggest. In a body of that size it is a practical necessity to accept the results of committee work in all matters requiring careful study and deliberate interchange of views. The hurried discussion that comes in a large two hour meeting or four hour meeting is worse than useless; and parliamentary bodies the world over are successful in their work to the extent to which they recognize this fact.

At Yale the alumni received an annual appeal for contributions, this appeal coming through an organization entirely run by graduates and known as the Alumni Fund. A part of the sums collected would then be turned over to the university authorities to be spent currently; the balance would be added to the principal of the Alumni Fund, the income from this principal in turn being available in succeeding years.

The Alumni Fund had been started in 1891, when just over $11,000 was contributed. Annual contributions averaged a little below this through 1899; then, with the new administration, they started to climb, under a succession of devoted Alumni Fund chairmen and class agents. In 1905 they passed the $50,000 mark, never to fall below that figure again. After 1910 they usually exceeded $100,000. They continued to grow, and during the first World War, when the university was threatened with a heavy deficit, the graduates responded nobly. The fund passed the $400,000 mark in 1917, and had risen to over $500,000 annually by the end of Hadley's administration.

As the gifts increased, the amount voted to the university for expenditure each year grew. To Hadley the Alumni Fund meant freedom. It was a source of income that could be used for each new step in university development. He was careful to preserve this freedom by refusing to use the income to meet recurring deficits. In one way or another he kept it free to be used to meet new situations as need arose.

The Alumni Fund represented freedom to Hadley in a further sense, because it came in small amounts from a great body of donors in whom he had confidence and who had confidence in him. He undertook to persuade the graduates of the merits of the projects he had in mind, and was not in the position of one receiving a large gift from an individual donor, whose wishes might well have to prevail if the gift were to be received at all.

Hadley's trust in the graduates was real. He testified to it many times but never in more sweeping terms than in one letter which he wrote to the Yale Alumni Association of the Southwest: "Cardinal Newman has said that a university is not a school or a group of schools, but an atmosphere; and the Yale Alumni make the Yale atmosphere."

The undergraduates knew little and cared less about all the problems of university reorganization or alumni relations. Their interest was quite naturally in what directly affected them.

Entrance examinations and the required studies leading up to them were realities that no student could overlook. Here, as the years went on, Hadley was successful in realizing his aim of tying Yale in with the schools throughout the nation. The Sheffield Scientific School was always more liberal than the College, but even the College gradually brought its requirements into line with what a good student from a good high school was in a position to offer. It retained one set of entrance requirements adapted to the curriculum of the conservative eastern preparatory schools, but developed another to test the capabilities of men educated in the public schools.

The increasing liberality in the entrance requirements made it possible for men from a wider variety of schools to come to Yale. On the other hand the changes in the curriculum at Yale reduced the variety of courses which a student could elect. A wide range was still offered, and new departments were even set up, such as the Department of Anthropology; but the student was held to some degree of logic in making his choices.

In the president's Report for 1908 Hadley said:

The Scientific School offers a choice between various courses of study, each arranged for a definite purpose. The Academic Department offers a choice between individual studies, so arranged as to help the student in experimenting to see what he is good for. . . .

In the Academic Department we already see the results of this understanding in a reduction of the number of elective courses. There was a time when these were multiplied almost indiscriminately, at great expense and with some loss of efficiency. There was a sort of feeling that a college course ought to provide everything which any student might want to study—a feeling that it was a school in which the student ought to be able to learn the theoretical elements of anything that he intended to study or thought of intending to study afterward. This had been the policy of Harvard; and the great and well deserved success of Harvard in many other lines where she was right led our American colleges to follow her blindly in this one where she appears to have been wrong.

After the extreme elective system had been modified, each student was required to concentrate in one given field, which constituted his "major." He was also required to take a smaller number of hours in some related "minor" field. Certain courses were prerequisites, and as a result the total choice in freshman year was particularly limited. Throughout Hadley's administration it remained necessary to have some knowledge of Latin in order to graduate from the College, although it was dropped as a compulsory entrance requirement.

Hadley believed in retaining the classics for two reasons. In the first place he valued them for their own sake. In the second place, as a purely practical matter, he recognized that top rank men were more available for classical faculties than for any others. In fields such as the sciences the best men were continually being tempted away by offers outside the college world on a more lucrative scale than any university could meet. Some men would stay out of love for their work, some would leave. In the classics, however, a position on the faculty of a great university was the highest post open.

To Hadley the quality of the teacher was always more important than the nature of the subject taught. This was true whether he considered the matter from the standpoint of the teacher or of the pupil. Advising teachers, he said: "It does not so much matter what you teach as how you teach it." Advising students on their choice of courses, he urged them to take "courses which are taught in ways that will make it easy to work hard; not hard to work hard."

Though studies came first, Hadley was no less interested in

all aspects of undergraduate life. He felt that in the eastern universities a peculiar condition existed that did not occur in western —particularly in state—universities. The undergraduates of state-supported institutions included some good men, with a large intermixture of mediocre ones; but the students of outstanding character and ability were most apt to be found in the graduate schools. In the older universities of the East the reverse was true; though many brilliant students were found in the graduate school, the outstanding men were more apt to be among the undergraduates. It might be difficult to fire the enthusiasm of these undergraduates and make them realize their potentialities, but the potentialities were there. Hadley was not disturbed by the fact that few of the undergraduates were planning to devote their lives to academic work; he recognized that there would be "ten men who want to learn things worth learning for one who wants to teach things worth teaching."

Hadley's own account of his contacts with undergraduate activities does less than justice to his interest in athletics—perhaps because his fellow members of the Colby Club were so well acquainted with the fact. He not only attended all games but went to practice sessions as well. His letters to his children discuss the abilities of the various players and describe the prospects in detail.

His familiarity with the subject used to stand him in good stead, because those were the days of intense criticism of intercollegiate athletics. There were frequent meetings with presidents of other universities to discuss what should be done to keep athletics within bounds. Hadley was as keen to correct abuses as anyone else, but he had a real appreciation of the value of training in team play. This he was ready to preach at all times. In 1908 he was invited to deliver the address at Harvard when the annual awards of academic distinction were made, and he took the occasion to point out, in passing, to these men who had won prizes by their individual intellectual effort, that they had something to learn from athletics:

Two generations ago the intellectual idol of the graduates and students of most of our colleges was the leading debater. . . .

Whether the debates of that day were much better than the debates of today we need not undertake to decide. Our fathers for the most part think that they were; our grandfathers are unanimously sure they were. On the other hand, the printed specimens of prize debates that have come down to us would indicate that if our fathers and grandfathers were right the speeches have suffered greatly from cold storage. Be this as it may, the leading debater was the man who won the largest meed of admiration so that college authorities were often led to deplore the fact that students neglected the solid rudiments of Greek and Hebrew for the meretricious joys of oral English expression.

In the third quarter of the nineteenth century all this changed very suddenly. . . . I was talking [of the reasons for this change] with General Francis Walker, a man who, first as a student of Amherst College, then as an adjutant general in the civil war, and afterwards as superintendent of the census, professor of political economy, and president of the Institute of Technology, had the opportunity of viewing this question from more sides than most men. He replied: "The answer is simple. When the nation had to go to war for its very existence, and when our college graduates had the opportunity to serve their country in places of prominence at peril of their lives, the debaters stayed at home and left the athletes to go to the front. This is why, ever since, the country has liked athletes better than debaters."

Of course, this is an over-statement. Had General Walker attempted to say this in a book, instead of in casual conversation, he would have rounded its corners with qualifying adverbs and propitiatory adjectives.

Nothing in which students were concerned was foreign to Hadley, but most of all he was interested in the students themselves. Graduates from many classes have told me stories of his personal attention to their problems. With 3,000 students in residence, he obviously could not have a close acquaintance with all or any major part, but his sympathetic interest could include an unbelievably large number.

His letters to Helen Hadley are full of references to men in college, some of whom she knew, and some of whom she did not: athletes, scholars, sons of old Yale families, interesting newcomers, men in trouble, men doing well. In one series of such letters there is an account of a sophomore, whom she did not know, who was critically ill with scarlet fever. The boy's mother had come on and was with her son, but since she was inside the quarantine line Hadley had been unable to see her. He had sent her some flowers "with as nice a note as I could write." A later note had a jubilant reference to the boy being better. But a few days after that:

My poor little Sophomore, with scarlet fever, died after all. For two or three days they had been quite relieved about him, and then he had a relapse. His people are plain and unpretending—foreigners I think—but very nice, and pathetically grateful for sympathy. The boy, whom I had known and liked for a combination of ability, shyness and good manners, turns out to have been even more of a person than I thought. . . . I did all I could, which was very little, in helping . . .

The quality of Hadley's leadership was summed up by William Howard Taft in an impromptu remark at an alumni gathering. Taft and Hadley had known each other since undergraduate days. In more recent years Taft had been on the Yale Corporation, and in 1913, after his term as President, he came to Yale as a member of the faculty. At his first Commencement as a faculty member he said:

"You don't know how kindly and all-embracing the arms of Arthur Hadley are until you sit with him and under him as an associate."

CHAPTER XI

OUTSIDE WORK

1901—1914

IN Arthur Hadley's first years as president of Yale he limited himself to official duties as closely as possible and declined virtually all outside calls. Some existing commitments he had to honor. For example, when elected to the presidency he was already the president of the American Economic Association, and so had to deliver the opening address at the annual meeting of that association. He gave various other addresses during this initial period, the most important of which are reprinted in *The Education of the American Citizen*.

Beginning in 1901 he decided that he could find time to prepare an occasional course of outside lectures without neglecting his Yale duties. He reached this conclusion only after careful consideration, and after discussing the matter with the members of the Corporation. They not only agreed but urged him to undertake such work. In this period he accepted some such outside engagement about every other year.

The first lectures, a course of six on the "History of Academic Freedom," were delivered at the Lowell Institute in Boston in February, 1902. When the course was suggested by A. Lawrence Lowell the year before, the topic was to be trusts or railroads, but for reasons not indicated in the correspondence the subject was changed. A portion of the lectures was printed in the *Atlantic Monthly* for February and March, 1903, under the title "Academic Freedom in Theory and Practice."

The manuscript of these lectures is now in the Yale Library, and all other unpublished material that has survived is similarly available. About two thirds of the manuscript was omitted in publication, as not of sufficiently general interest. The omitted

portion consists of the history of academic freedom in particular
countries, such as France, Spain, Germany, and the United
States, with accounts of individual institutions in those countries.
In addition to the famous universities of Europe and America,
the lectures treated of such matters as the Litchfield Law School,
the Fairfield Medical College, the projects of the Chevalier
Quesnay de Beaurepaire, and the work of Jefferson at the University of Virginia.

In 1903 Hadley gave the lectures on the Dodge Foundation
at Yale. Although given in New Haven, he regarded them as
"outside" work because alike in preparation and in the audience
for which they were intended they were apart from his normal
duties as president. They were published under the title *The Relations between Freedom and Responsibility in the Evolution of
Democratic Government*. The book, like the lectures themselves,
was enthusiastically received. President Theodore Roosevelt,
writing a friend about "Hadley's admirable volume," went on:
"As Hadley has well said, freedom does not mean absence of all
restraint. It merely means the substitution of self-restraint for
external restraint, and therefore it can be used only by people
capable of self-restraint . . ."

The purpose of the book is set out in a brief preface which is
worth quoting in full, not so much because it describes the book
as because it describes one of Hadley's fundamental beliefs:

For the successful conduct of a nation's affairs, we must have a certain degree of conformity between its political institutions and the
moral character of its members. There is one set of virtues which
fits men to be subjects of a monarchy; there is another very different set which is requisite for the citizens of a free commonwealth.

We find a tendency among many people at the present day to
claim the political rights of free citizens without accepting the moral
obligations which go with them. But the attempt to assume the privileges of freedom and disclaim its responsibilities is fatal to the nation
which tolerates it; and theories of law or schemes of social reform
which ignore this ethical basis of democracy are likely to prove
suicidal.

It is the object of this book to show what this ethical basis of democracy is, how it has arisen, and what happens if we try to ignore it.

The Dodge Lectures, like many of Hadley's addresses, reached a large audience in their published form. The widespread interest in the addresses crops up in the most unexpected places. Sometimes it concerns a particular published volume, as in the case of a review of one of his books in a daily paper in India. At other times the reference is harder to account for, as in the case of a full page advertisement of a sale of men's neckwear in a Milwaukee paper in 1908. This begins: "President Arthur T. Hadley of Yale, in his matriculation sermon, said . . ." and proceeds to quote for a paragraph. Then the advertiser continues: "We try to live up to these principles—and have endeavored to imbue our entire buying and selling organization with these very sentiments, but have never been able to express ourselves so wonderfully—so resourcefully."

Sometimes a remark in an informal address, reported in some newspaper, caught the popular fancy and spread from coast to coast. On one of his early alumni tours in 1900 Hadley spent two nights in Denver, and on one of these he spoke before the Candlelight Club. The subject was "What Shall We Do with the Trusts?" and he stressed a point which he often made—the power of public opinion. After considering what could be accomplished by legal means and paying tribute to the superior effectiveness of the courts in England in dealing with such situations, he went on:

The directors of these large enterprises have a very much greater power than was possessed by any of the directors of small enterprises in the olden time; a very much greater power for good if they manage them well; a very much greater power for evil if they manage them ill. This power is so great that it can only be controlled by public opinion—not by statute. But in America, in spite of many disappointments, we still remain firm believers in statutes. . . . In those cases where it does work at all, it is apt to produce indirect effects very different from what its original measure proposed. . . .

It must be understood that where business has been monopolized and is not subject to the control of competition a man has certain responsibilities that he does not have in dealing with his private business. But someone will say, how are you going to make him understand? There are means enough. Don't invite him to dinner with you. Don't let him come to your house. Disqualify him socially. You may say that is not an operative remedy. This is a mistake. Whenever it is understood that certain practices are so clearly against public need and public necessity that the man who perpetrates them is not allowed to associate on even terms with his fellow men, you have in your hands an all-powerful remedy. It reaches down a great deal lower than you think. There are not so many strata in society after all. We are really more democratic than we sometimes think we are. The power of public sentiment, when it can once be created, is very much larger, very much more overwhelming, than the mere superficial observer would think.

The picture of trust magnates being brought to heel by an absence of dinner invitations from the right hosts was too much for the cartoonists, and they made the most of it. Hadley, however, stuck to his guns, and a generation later, lecturing in Oxford in 1922, he said: *

"When it was first suggested in America that certain abuses of the corporate trust which the law was powerless to reach could be dealt with by social ostracism, the idea was pronounced absurd and made the subject of cartoons in every comic paper. But greater consequences were produced in that way than by statutes or dissolution suits."

In 1906 Hadley delivered five lectures in New York on the John S. Kennedy Foundation, which were published the next year under the title *Standards of Public Morality*. The lectures were given at what is now the New York School of Social Work but was then known as the School of Philanthropy Conducted by the Charity Organization Society of the City of New York. His treatment of the subject may be gathered from the titles of the five lectures: "The Formation of Public Opinion"; "The Ethics of Trade"; "The Ethics of Corporate Management"; "The Workings of our Political Machinery"; "The Political Duties of the Citizen." The book is particularly readable, for as Hadley

* *Economic Problems of Democracy*, p. 147.

explains in the preface, the lectures are printed substantially as delivered on the lecture platform. He had illustrated his points as he went along with a wealth of pertinent stories, which he left in the printed text.

In view of the fact that a comment by Theodore Roosevelt was used in appreciation of a previous book, it is perhaps only fair to give a comment on this book from a man who thought that Roosevelt hardly practiced what he preached. Once more stressing the effectiveness of informed public opinion as against uninformed legislative penalties, Hadley had cited as an example the brilliant work of Charles Francis Adams on the Massachusetts Railroad Commission. Adams wrote and thanked him, but pointed out that these were "not at all the lines which commend themselves to our strenuous president, who looks with contempt on any measure of reform which has not a soldier with a bayonet, or a policeman with a club, in its enacting clause."

During this period Hadley commenced a long association with the Carnegie Foundation for the Advancement of Teaching. In 1902 he had aided Andrew Carnegie in working out the plans for the Carnegie Institution in Washington. In 1905, when the Foundation was established, he became one of its original trustees, and served until his retirement from Yale in 1921. The work took him frequently to New York, as he was a member of the executive committee. After 1914 he was vice-chairman of the board, and from 1917 to 1920 he was chairman.

Hadley received a half year's leave of absence from Yale duties to go to the University of Berlin in the fall of 1907 as Theodore Roosevelt Professor of American History and Institutions. His wife and two sons went with him and they spent the whole winter in Berlin. The family lived in rooms on the top floor of the Hotel de Rome, on the corner of Unter den Linden and Charlottenstrasse.

Hadley gave a general course of thirty lectures, in German, on "Industrial History and Industrial Legislation in the United States." He also had a seminar with selected students. One or two individual lectures in the series were published, but the series as a whole was never printed.

In addition to his academic duties, the Theodore Roosevelt Professor was expected to take an active part in the social and cultural activities of Berlin. This Hadley did with great enjoyment. The lectures themselves started with a gala opening attended by the Crown Prince and members of the cabinet, and closed with a formal academic session at which the university faculty were present in full regalia. On this last occasion the economic faculty was led by Adolf Wagner, under whom Hadley had studied thirty years before, and Wagner closed the proceedings with a moving tribute to his former pupil.

The whole life in Berlin bore out what Hadley had written to Edwin Worcester when the appointment was announced:

The thing that does make me feel queer is the going to Berlin to lecture at the university. When I studied there in the seventies, nothing would have seemed more wildly improbable than that I should return as an *Ehrenmitglied* of the Berlin Academy; and there have been no intermediate stages to soften the transition. I suppose I shall find things sadly changed. They tell me that all the people who read the *Jobsiade* are dead, and that another generation of students has arisen who know not *Jobs.**

The extracurricular activities of the professorship included presentation at court, court functions, and innumerable dinners. At one of these latter Hadley achieved a triumph as an expert in wines that has been embroidered in Yale folklore but which is sufficiently remarkable to warrant telling as it actually occurred. He was known to be a connoisseur of wines, and at a dinner given by a cabinet minister his host asked him if he could

---

* Hieronimus Jobs is the hero of the *Jobsiade*, a poem popular with a bygone generation of German undergraduates, which recounts in doggerel verse the mishaps attending its hero as a candidate at the university and elsewhere. The rhymed title page of the first part reads: *Die Jobsiade, ein grotesk-komisches Heldengedicht von D. C.A.K. Leben, Meinungen und Thaten von Hieronimus Jobs dem Kandidaten und wie Er sich weiland viel Ruhm erwarb, auch endlich als Nachtwächter zu Schildburg starb.* Hadley's own much read copy (all three parts in one volume) had belonged to his uncle Henry Hamilton Hadley, and is the fifth edition (Hamm und Crefeld, 1839).

place the wine which was then being poured. From the interest of those near him at the table Hadley perceived that this was some special test and tasted the wine carefully. He recognized the general district and the year without difficulty, but after several sips confessed that he could not name the vineyard, adding that this caused him the more chagrin because he thought he knew all the great wines of that district and this one was certainly great—markedly reminiscent of three well-known vineyards, which he named. The host and guests listened with mounting excitement, and at the close rose to their feet and drank his health. It was Hadley's turn to express his surprise that naming a district and a year should merit such praise.

"Of course not," said the host, "but you do not realize what you have done. You could never have tasted this wine. It is from a small private vineyard that has been in my family for some centuries and the wine never comes on the market. The three vineyards which you named, however, are the three by which my family's vineyard is bounded."

I cannot qualify as a direct witness, because I was too young to go to formal dinners, but I well remember my father's delight at the breakfast table the next morning when my mother was recounting the exploit. My brother and I, with the skepticism of youth, tried to get my father to admit that luck must have played some part. This he stoutly refused to do, explaining the mathematical odds against picking three correct vineyards by accident out of the hundreds in Germany. We were less convinced by his mathematics than by an analogy he drew. He pointed out, and we conceded, that he often met freshmen he had never seen before, and yet was able to place them correctly, not by luck but by their resemblance to other members of their family in earlier college classes.

There are descriptions of less unusual scenes in letters to his eight-year-old daughter, who was spending the winter with an uncle and aunt in the United States.

A good many canal boats go through the river by my office, and some stop to spend the night there. Some are loaded with brick, some with white sand to make mortar of, and a good many carry apples. Besides these boats there is a wonderful set of ducks.

Right opposite my office on the other side of the stream is a little fenced-off grass plot. I think most of the ducks live there when they are not in the water.

Beyond the ducks and the grass plot, but still right opposite my windows, is the Royal Palace where the emperor and his family live. Each member of the family has a certain flagstaff—I only had room to draw two in the picture—and when that person is at home his or her flag goes up.

After his return to the United States in 1908 Hadley found time to prepare, at the request of the United States authorities, a report on the "Facilities for Study and Research in the Offices of the United States Government at Washington." The report was transmitted to the Secretary of the Interior by the Commissioner of Education under date of November 30, 1908, and was published the following year by the Government Printing Office.* In the letter of transmittal the Commissioner said:

The question has been asked repeatedly in the course of the collection of materials for this number, whether it is intended to have some bearing upon the effort to secure the establishment at Washington of a National University. It seems proper accordingly to make the following statement: That this publication is intended merely to convey accurate information concerning a matter of the highest educational interest, and not to serve as an argument, either pro or con, in any special propaganda. Its immediate purpose is to furnish information to advanced students and directors of research.

Two years later Hadley undertook a much more serious task for the government, this time at the request of President Taft. In 1910 the question of railroad securities was in the political spotlight. The Mann-Elkins Act authorized the President of the United States "to appoint a commission to investigate questions pertaining to the issuance of stocks and bonds by railroad corporations, subject to the provisions of the Act to regulate commerce, and the power of Congress to regulate or affect the

* United States Bureau of Education, Bulletin, 1909, No. 1, whole number 398.

same." The President asked Hadley to act as chairman. Hadley stated his position in a letter of July 12:

My dear Mr. President:—

. . . . I had hoped to receive some word from you regarding your conception of the duties and mode of procedure of the Commission, which the Act itself leaves a little indefinite. In the absence of any such statement, I think I shall advance matters most by telling plainly how the situation looks to me.

A special commission can have one of two forms. It can be a committee of gentlemen of influence representing different sections of the community, to take testimony; and on the basis of this testimony to draft a statute which shall represent intelligent public opinion and have the force of intelligent public opinion behind it. Or it can be a committee of experts, selected for their knowledge of the specific matters involved, to advise the Government on the basis of their own technical judgment; indicating what sort of measures will be practicable for the reformation of abuses and the improvement of railroad management.

The language of the Act seems to indicate that a commission of the former type is contemplated. If so, I regret to say that I cannot accept. I have not at my disposal the time necessary for the taking of testimony; and if I had, I am confident that it would be from the public standpoint a mistake for me to do it. A special commission to take testimony and digest its results, in such a way as to harmonize the public opinion of different sections of the country, should consist either of members of Congress, or at any rate of Government officials with recognized position in our legislative and administrative machinery. If a commission does not consist of members of Congress it simply relieves Congress from the responsibility of taking any note of the testimony that comes before the commission. This perhaps ought not to be so, but it is so in fact. The Tariff Commission of 1882 will serve as an instance. Parliaments and Congresses have always been reluctant to follow the advice of any commission which purported to relieve them of their proper function of interpreting public opinion.

If it be not the duty of the Commission to take testimony, but to give expert advice, using the appropriation to obtain information in the same way that an intelligent business house would obtain information, the case is somewhat different. If the Act could be interpreted in this way I should be very glad to do anything I possibly could to help the government. . . .

A committee of experts should represent at least three elements. There should be one or more lawyers to advise as to how the Government may take jurisdiction in this matter, and at a later period of the investigation how an Act may be drafted so as to leave as few loopholes as possible. There should be one or more financiers to advise regarding the methods and effects of existing practices in the stock market and the means of effecting the necessary changes with the least disturbance of capital. There should be a political economist who is familiar with the practice and legislation of different countries and different states in our own country, and knows how different systems of control have worked to protect the public interest. I believe that such a commission could give useful advice; and while I am not sanguine that its advice would be followed, I think that it would have more chance of being followed than that of a commission intended to represent different sections of public opinion. . . .

If the Act allows you to appoint a commission of experts and to give them the necessary time, say one year, for reaching their conclusion, and if you wish to appoint a commission of that kind, my services would be at the disposal of the Government. I should deem it a privilege and a pleasure to serve on such terms; and the sacrifice of duties at Yale which would be involved would be no greater than any man ought to make when he sees a chance to serve his country. . . .

I have stated these matters very plainly, in the belief that in cases of this kind the plainest statement is usually the most helpful and courteous one.

President Taft replied that he wanted a committee of experts, and Hadley was appointed chairman. The other members were William L. Fisher, Frederick N. Judson, Balthasar H. Meyer, and Frederick Strauss, with William E. S. Griswold as secretary. In October, before the hearings started, Hadley went to Europe, "to get at the necessary knowledge regarding conditions on that side of the Atlantic." He studied the written material and talked with leading experts in England and on the Continent. In one letter to a son at school in the United States he described himself as "more busy than I can possibly tell." In another he excuses the haste of writing with the explanation: "I have been busy investigating railroads all day long. I lunched with some financiers, and am to dine with some traffic men." He had one relative holiday during the trip, when he took time out to represent Yale at the one hundredth anniversary celebration of the University of Berlin.

Hearings began in Washington the end of November, 1910. These were followed by a week of hearings in New York and another week in Chicago. Formal sessions were held during the day, and in the evening the commission would invite selected men to dinner for informal discussions that would often continue far into the night. After a study of the material collected, a few additional hearings were held in New York in March.

Hadley always regarded it as a particular triumph that he secured a unanimous report by the commission, and thought that the concessions necessary to secure this were well worth while. His labors to secure unanimity had to be many times repeated. Hadley was always most discreet in avoiding references to any particular individual, the nearest he ever came being to tell me, years later, that as was usual on committees, the member who had been least diligent in attendance took it upon himself to be most diligent in objections. A hurried note to his wife after one of the early sessions on the form of report simply says:

"Sessions of the Commission were squally, but interesting. How we are ever going to agree on a report is more than I can see. I was acting the part of peacemaker to-day, with rather indifferent success. However, we may hope that the people have got some of the bad stuff out of them."

The unanimous report was presented on November 1, 1911, and was received favorably not only by the public generally but by the most diverse elements among the public. It was useful in part as the basis of some later legislation, but was perhaps most important as a clear presentation of the facts in a controversial field. It developed the history and theory of the subject for thirty pages, closing with two pages of "Points to be Emphasized," of which the sixth and last reads:

Upon the whole, your Commission believes that accurate knowledge of the facts concerning the issue of securities and the expenditure of their proceeds is the matter of most importance. It is the one thing on which the federal government can effectively insist today; it is the fundamental thing which must serve as a basis for whatever additional regulation may be desirable in the future.

An appendix carried suggestions for a statute under which railroads would file in advance with the Interstate Commerce Commission a full statement as to securities to be issued, together with complete financial reports and a full disclosure of the interest of any director. The Commission in turn could call for more information and could make public all information. The report, however, pointed out the limitations of such a process:

We are told that if it was possible to standardize food by a pure food law, it ought to be possible to standardize railroad securities by a securities law. It is possible—to the same extent and no more. The pure food law enables a man to know what he is buying. It does not certify that the thing he buys is good for him. That is left to his intelligence. The government cannot protect the investors against the consequences of their unwisdom in buying unprofitable bonds, any more than it can protect the consumers against the consequences of their unwisdom in eating indigestible food.

One recommendation in the report was adopted widely in other fields of financing. This was "shares without par value." Such shares, while not unknown previously, had been little used. Now states commenced to adopt legislation making their issuance a simple matter. In later years Hadley conceded that the Commission might have been less sweeping in its endorsement if it had foreseen the abuses to which no par value stock lent itself; but he continued to believe that the advantages outweighed the disadvantages.

Another unexpected by-product of the work of the Commission, of a personal nature, especially pleased Hadley. The elder Mr. Seligman had listened for a morning to the examination of witnesses by the chairman at a public session. At the close he took Hadley aside and said: "If you ever get tired of your job at

New Haven, there is a partnership for you in Seligman Brothers right off." As Hadley wrote in reporting the incident to his wife: "I realize he knew I would never act on his offer, but all the same I think he really meant it."

Hadley's report as chairman of the Railroad Securities Commission also played a part in an interlude so brief that it hardly existed at all. The report had been favorably received by liberals and conservatives alike. When the Republican nominating convention in 1912 threatened to split the Republican party in a three-way fight between Taft, Roosevelt, and La Follette, one group worked out plans to put Hadley forward as a candidate on whom all could agree. The move was not going to be made so long as there was any hope of rallying the party behind Taft, and if this failed the group counted on the personal support of Taft in securing the votes of most Taft delegates. It was hoped that La Follette would finally acquiesce because of the popularity of the securities report with the Progressives, and that even more support could be obtained from the Roosevelt adherents who were voting from motives of antipathy to Taft quite as much as enthusiasm for Roosevelt. However, Taft secured his majority, and the plan was never tried out.

Two years earlier, as a personal friend of both Taft and Roosevelt, Hadley had taken part in an attempt to bring them together and heal the split in the Republican party. A luncheon was given, under Hadley's auspices, at the home of Mr. Henry C. White in New Haven on September 19, 1910, at which there were present President Taft, Ex-president Roosevelt, Secretary Norton, Lloyd Griscom, and Hadley. The next day Hadley gave out an agreed statement as to the cordiality which marked the meeting, but that was all.

In 1913 Hadley was asked to join the Board of Directors of the New York, New Haven, and Hartford Railroad and accepted, serving for the rest of his life. He recognized that the task would be time-consuming but thought it his duty to undertake it. The New Haven railroad was in difficulties. Its attempt to create a transportation monopoly in southern New

England had collapsed, with consequent loss to its stockholders. Money had gone for expansion that should have been used to keep the property up to date, the morale of the employees had suffered, and there had been a succession of train wrecks with severe loss of life. When Hadley went on the Board in September, 1913, he did not realize how bad the internal situation was, though it was apparent that much was wrong. Once a member, he worked hard and effectively with the new management that was trying to set matters right. Among other duties, he was one of the committee of three that met with Attorney General McReynolds in the attempt to reach a working compromise of a threatened government antitrust suit.

Editorial approval of his election was widespread and unanimous. Financial papers saw in him an expert whose advice could do much to set the tangled affairs of the road in order. Leftwing papers hailed his election with delight as bringing in a man who would get to the bottom of what was wrong and not connive at shady transactions. A theme common to papers of all types was expressed by the *Minneapolis Journal* (September 28, 1913):

Dr. Hadley will be a minority in the Board, perhaps a minority of one in his larger equipment of knowledge and judgment. But the power he will exercise is not measured by votes. His position resembles that of the advisory committee of expert bankers attached to the Federal Reserve Board in the complete banking law. With singular authority he will advise and recommend acts and omissions in the broad public interest, that would have averted the demoralization of the last few years.

In 1914 the Federal Government announced its intention of going ahead with the antitrust suit, and President Woodrow Wilson accompanied the announcement with a personal attack upon the motives of the directors of the road. Even strong Democratic papers protested, and expressed their confidence in Hadley. The Republican *Boston Transcript* went further and brought in by innuendo past difficulties of Woodrow Wilson with his Board of Trustees when he was president of Princeton (July 26, 1914):

When any one, even the President of the United States, accuses the president of Yale University of bad faith, of failure to live up to his agreement, New Englanders are "from Missouri." They remember that no board of trustees of Yale University has ever questioned either the veracity or the good faith of Dr. Hadley, and they are disposed to believe that his service on the reorganization directorate of the New Haven has been inspired by the same high purpose and characterized by the same fidelity to honor and integrity that make him so valuable an asset not only to Yale but to the nation.

Hadley made no attempt to gloss over the past misdeeds of the New Haven. In a public address he stated that "the present condition of the New Haven road was brought about by a combination of some unwise finance with a great deal of unwise operation and unwise politics." Now that the events of the period are past history, a less formal statement in a letter to a classmate may be quoted (to Elmer P. Howe, November 2, 1914):

If ever the whole story of this and some other transactions could be written it would make a very interesting document to the layman and lawyer alike. Our old friend Ed Robbins is by no means squeamish, and Ed, before he got on the other side of the thing, once told me in a burst of frankness that a certain transaction violated the elementary principles of law, ethics and expediency, all at the same time!

Hadley continued his outside work of academic character, in spite of the time required for practical railroad problems. In 1912 he delivered the McNair Lectures at the University of North Carolina, published in 1913 as *Some Influences in Modern Philosophic Thought*. In April of 1914 he gave the Barbour-Page Lectures at the University of Virginia and in May the Ford Lectures at Oxford University, the two series being published together in 1915 under the title *Undercurrents in American Politics*. This volume was very much in line with his earlier lectures which have already been discussed. It falls into two parts, the first entitled "Property and Democracy," the second "Political Methods Old and New," which were respectively the

Oxford lectures and the Virginia lectures. The six-page Table of Contents is an excellent example of a "Brief" in the literal sense defined by Webster as "a formal outline of logically related headings, setting forth the main contentions with supporting statements." The whole, as the title indicates, is a picture of the actual operation of American democracy, as opposed to the way it is supposed in theory to operate.

The Ford Lectures were only a part of Hadley's duties at Oxford. Some years later, when Harvey Cushing was writing his life of William Osler and asked Hadley for possible material, he replied:

While I have known Osler all my life and had him at my house two or three times, my closer acquaintance with him dates from 1912, when we were thrown rather closely together at the two hundred and fiftieth anniversary of the Royal Society. Mrs. Hadley and I had a most delightful two weeks' visit with the Oslers at Oxford in May, 1914, when I was invited to the University with the ostensible object of giving some lectures and the real object of looking to see what was the matter with the Rhodes Scholars.

The description of Osler which Hadley gave appears in Cushing's book.* As for the lectures, whether or not they were the real reason for the trip, they were a success. Writing to a son in America immediately after the last lecture he reported: "My lectures worked out nicely—at any rate I had more students at the last lecture than I did at the first, which is said to be as much of a test at Oxford as it is at Yale."

Some Influences in Modern Philosophic Thought, the 1912 McNair Lectures, is most revealing of all as to the lecturer himself. In a slim volume of some twenty thousand words he gives his views on education, science, politics, and ethics, closing with a chapter on the spiritual basis of recent poetry. The whole constitutes a charmingly presented picture of the changes brought by the nineteenth century.

The volume includes an appendix "On the Meaning of the Term Philosophy" which gives Hadley's views so characteristically that it deserves to be quoted at length:

* II, 326, 406–408.

When these lectures were delivered I was asked by two or three persons what the word philosophy really meant. This is a much easier question to ask than to answer. A study of the definitions and the illustrative passages given in the Oxford Dictionary leads one to the conclusion that the English word philosophy can be used in as many different senses as Mark Twain found for the elusive German word *Zug;* which, as he truthfully remarked, could mean anything from a bank check to a railroad train. Under such circumstances each man may, within certain broad limits, choose his own definition. A philosophy, as I understand it, is a set of working hypotheses which a man adopts in order to harmonize, as far as may be, his prejudices with his experience.

There are certain ideas or prejudices which we accept without proof and take as starting points in our own reasoning. It is in this manner that we assume our own existence, the existence of other people like ourselves, the reality of an external world of some kind, and an underlying orderliness in the events of that world. None of these things is capable of proof, in the ordinary sense of the term. The *Cogito ergo sum* of Descartes does not represent the real reason for believing in a man's own existence. It is simply a means of making a belief which we already possess appear logically plausible. I know of no better name by which to call these assumptions than the old and somewhat abused term innate ideas. They are based on inherited habits of action and thought, which have lasted throughout so many generations that they have become unconscious if not instinctive. They represent prejudices rather than reasoned judgments regarding the universe; and they exemplify in a striking degree that superiority of prejudice over reason which Burke so cogently set forth.

Side by side with these innate ideas or prejudices there gradually come into our lives other ideas which we acquire consciously as the result of teaching and observation. Our own experience of everyday life and the truths of history and science which we learn from others supplement our preconceived notions of the universe, and as we grow older begin to conflict with them. Out of this conflict comes a readjustment of our prejudices. No man, however strong his innate ideas, holds them in quite the same form at thirty that he did at fifteen. But though men modify their preconceptions they never reject them. However much a man may become imbued with the facts of physics, he puts them in a framework of metaphysics of his own. . . .

The attempt to get a system of working hypotheses which shall satisfy our instincts without conflicting with our experience is the most difficult problem which logic presents. For we are not trying to compare the validity of two similar kinds of proof or even the results of two different kinds of evidence. We are adjusting a set of formulas derived from the inherited experience of the race to the limitations set by the acquired experience of the individual. The process of achieving this result is philosophy. The result, when we get it, is *a* philosophy—good or bad, as the case may be.

A few years later, writing to his brother-in-law Robert T. Morris, he said (June 10, 1915):

. . . To the pragmatist—and 1 am a thoroughgoing pragmatist—every phenomenon is a phenomenon of nature, whether it is more easily expressed in physical terms or in psychical terms; and every formula a hypothesis which will probably have to be rejected or modified some day, after it has served its purpose in scientific development, just as we are today rejecting the formula of the conservation of energy.

As for nature versus metaphysics, I should say that discovery of new truth was by the process of hypothesis and verification; that the perpetual tendency of writers and thinkers was to let their hypotheses outrun their verification; that the hypothesis, running in advance of the verification, is metaphysics in Aristotle's sense of the word; and that the use of the name "metaphysics" as a term of reproach is justified only when a man gets his mind so fixed on the making of hypotheses that he overlooks the need of verifying them before he publishes them.

Equally revealing as to Hadley himself is a list of his favorite books. President Eliot of Harvard, shortly after his retirement in 1909, had sponsored a "Five Foot Shelf" of books. As the Hadley family were sitting around an open fire on a rainy day in the country, and other occupation palled, the children badgered their father into telling them the books he would put on such a shelf. He made his position clear that he would never do such a thing commercially but finally yielded in the family circle, and the books were duly listed by one of his sons. Some years later the old list turned up, and Hadley was cross-examined into making a few changes. I give the revised list here, as it stands in schoolboy handwriting in an old notebook, although it may well omit some books that he would have included had he been going into the matter more seriously.

The Psalms, Ecclesiastes, Isaiah, The New Testament—King James version.
Homer: *Odyssey*—Butcher and Lang translation.
Sophocles: *Oedipus at Colonus*—"Any good translation."
Dante: *Inferno*—J. A. Carlyle's translation.
Omar Khayyám: *Rubáiyát*—FitzGerald translation.
Goethe: *Faust, Wilhelm Meister's Lehrjahre*—"Any good translation."
Shakespeare: *Hamlet, Macbeth, Julius Caesar, Merchant of Venice, Henry IV, Henry V, Richard II, As You Like It.*
Milton: *Paradise Lost.*
Bunyan: *Pilgrim's Progress.*
Defoe: *Robinson Crusoe.*
Smollett: *Roderick Random.*
Coleridge: *Ancient Mariner.*
Wordsworth: *Intimations of Immortality.*
Scott: *Ivanhoe, Old Mortality, Guy Mannering.*
Thackeray: *Vanity Fair.*
Dickens: *Bleak House, Tale of Two Cities.*
Arnold: *Tom Brown at Rugby.*
Carroll: *Alice in Wonderland, Through the Looking Glass.*
Browning: *The Ring and the Book.*
Whitman: *O Captain, My Captain.*
Kipling: *Kim, The Recessional.*
Green: *Short History of the English People.*
Adam Smith: *Wealth of Nations* (abridged edition).
A good dictionary.
A good atlas.

On the last two items I know his preferences, because in the interval between the original list and its revision I entered college and he outfitted me with the largest size *Webster's Dictionary* and with an even larger Stieler's *Handatlas*. There is a footnote to the list stating that he would have included the *Hex-ameters* of Horace but felt there was no adequate translation. He reluctantly omitted Euclid on the ground that it was not literary. He omitted Blackstone's *Commentaries* because the volumes would take up an unwarranted fraction of the shelf.

An even more personal note as to Hadley's outlook on life is furnished by the statements on a sheet of paper which I found in going through Helen Hadley's records, tucked in the back of her engagement calendar for 1903, and endorsed in her handwriting, "A.T.H. Feb 24, 1903." It reads as follows:

1. Tell nothing but the truth to any one. If a case arises where it is hard to be both truthful and courteous, put all the thought you can spare upon solving the problem.

2. Tell the whole truth to yourself. If you have made a mistake, face the facts squarely. Do not worry about it, for a mistake is seldom fatal unless it has been repeated. But do not excuse it, for this means that you will surely repeat it until it becomes fatal.

3. Do not think about one piece of business when you ought to be thinking about another; and above all things, do not think about any piece of business when you ought to be sleeping.

4. Believe in people's good intentions, even when you cannot approve their actions or concur in their judgment; but beware of concurring in their judgment or approving their actions merely because you believe in their good intentions.

5. Believe in your friends, in your associates, in your work. Believe in God just as fully as your intellectual constitution will allow —not necessarily as the subject of a creed, but as an unseen ruler of the universe, who is somehow going to bring things out more squarely than our limited vision can comprehend.

CHAPTER XII

WAR AND RECONSTRUCTION

1914–1921

THE first half of the president's Report for 1914–15 is devoted to military training. This was only in part due to the fact that Europe was already at war. Colleges were quick to feel the effects of the war, but even before 1914 Hadley had been actively interested in military training. He was one of a small group of educators who believed in its value both for the nation and the individual, and beginning in 1912 plans had been worked out with the army and the navy for summer training camps for students. When Woodrow Wilson was elected President, and appointed Josephus Daniels as Secretary of the Navy, the naval camps were abandoned; but Secretary of War Lindley M. Garrison went ahead with the army plans.

There was a modest beginning in 1913 with a summer training camp at Gettysburg; in 1914 there was an eastern camp at Burlington, Vermont, and a western camp in California. In 1915 there were camps at the start of the summer on the same undergraduate basis, the camp for the East being at Plattsburg. This was followed by the first of a series of "Plattsburg Camps" for the general public, and summer training camps moved out of the college world into the world at large and onto the front pages of the newspapers.

The earlier type of student camp is of interest from the educational standpoint, even though its development was cut short by the advent of war and the need for more widespread instruction. Hadley took a leading part in developing the system and valued it highly. The following description of the place of such camps in college education is from his 1914–15 Report:

The course of instruction has been carefully planned by General [Leonard] Wood and an able body of younger officers. It demands hard work of the student; but it achieves correspondingly large results. . . .

To those who are interested in the Yale tradition of public service it is a gratifying fact that Yale has had a larger aggregate enrollment in the different United States student camps than any other institution in the country. At the Plattsburg encampment alone there were more than eighty Yale men. Under these circumstances we have had considerable opportunity to watch the educational effect of this system; and I have no hesitation in saying that, wholly aside from their military value in preparing a reserve of partly trained officers for possible service in the event of war, the camps have an educational value that much more than justifies their organization and their maintenance.

In the first place, they fill half of a student's vacation with mental and physical training of an extremely exacting type.

One of the difficulties under which the modern world has suffered is the tendency to make college vacations too long for the good of the students. The professors need more weeks of vacation than the students do. They are older, and their work is more exacting. They need time for research and writing and independent work of many kinds; and the chance of getting that time during the college term is small. An institution that should content itself with two months of actual vacation would find it hard to persuade good men to stay on its instructing staff, or to keep them in good condition if they did stay. Under these circumstances the length of vacation has been adapted to the professor's needs rather than the student's needs. In the old days this did less harm than it now does; partly because the average professor in the old days did less outside work, and partly because the average student did more. A large proportion of the students in some of our older institutions spent a good deal of their vacation in work, which ranged from school teaching during the winter to haying during the summer. There are still a good many who do this, and are compelled to do so as a means of self-support. But the majority of our students have no regular and exacting occupation during the long vacation. Those who are serious try to carry out regular courses of reading—often with somewhat indifferent success, the spirit being willing but the flesh weak. Those who are less serious spend their vacation in a round of visits and sports, commonly innocent enough but not possessing great educational value.

It is clear that if half of the long vacation of such a student can be filled with hard and interesting work of almost any kind, it is a gain from the educational point of view. It is far better on all grounds for him to work while he can work advantageously and take only the rest he actually needs, than to contract habits of idleness by taking twice as much rest as he needs. The English universities have met this difficulty by the establishment of a reading term, which encourages men to come back for independent work before the professors and tutors begin their lectures. We are trying to introduce something of the sort at Yale. But the number of men whose attention can be engrossed by a reading term must for the present be comparatively small. It is a great advantage to have as many of our students as possible spend five weeks in a life which trains them in regularity, order and intelligent use of mind and body for complex ends, and familiarizes them with a line of life and work which, whether we approve of it or not, has nevertheless played and is playing a supremely important part in the world's history.

For the education received at summer camps is not a training in the showy side of military service, as some suppose; nor is it a matter of routine drills, as others think. It is a training in the exercise of the intelligence on problems of interest and importance. And, wholly apart from its physical and intellectual value, it gives a training in the sense of public obligation.

By the time summer camps ceased to be undergraduate affairs, their place at Yale had been taken by another form of military training. In the summer of 1915, with the war in Europe threatening to become world-wide, Hadley asked General Leonard Wood how military interest at Yale could best be directed to serve the immediate needs of the army in the event of war. General Wood answered that one lesson of the war was the need for a great expansion in artillery and that Yale could best serve by training artillery officers.

In those days it was necessary to improvise in order to secure such training. It was arranged that if as many as one hundred undergraduates were willing to enroll, application would be made to the State of Connecticut to form a national guard battery of field artillery. The State of Connecticut could then be supplied by the national government with the guns and other equipment necessary to outfit a battery in the national guard. In addition the army would assign one or more regular army officers as instructors.

Plans were made that summer, and enrollment took place after college opened in the fall. The undergraduate organizers knew that there was much interest among the student body but were somewhat doubtful as to how many men would actually be willing to enroll in the national guard for a program of intensive training. Under Hadley's guidance they did not trust to chance, but spent two weeks in laying the foundations for a popular appeal, working through the columns of the *Yale Daily News* and through every other undergraduate channel available. The result was so sweeping as to be embarrassing. As reported in the *News* of November 13, 1915:

. . . After the matter had been thus explained to the student body, application blanks were placed in Yale Station [for the College] and Byers Hall [for the Sheffield Scientific School]. It was expected that the necessary number of men would hardly be obtained within several days, but the response of the students surpassed all expectations. The blank forms were set out one morning at 9 o'clock, and before noon of the same day more than enough men had already signed. By nightfall more than four hundred had handed in applications, and during the following days this number increased to nine hundred and fifty.

So many applications were received, in fact, that it was necessary to delay the work of organization until it was certain that this large number could be accommodated. . . . The Government, however, soon issued orders authorizing the enlistment of four batteries in the place of one, and the work of organization went ahead. . . . At first only about twenty men a night could be handled by the three medical officers detailed for the work, but as matters were systematized, and undergraduate clerks broken in, the number rose to fifty or over. To date over 400 have enlisted. Some inevitable delay has arisen since so many of the men joining are minors, who must send their enlistment papers home for their parents' signatures before they can be examined and sworn in. . . .

Funds for an armory have been guaranteed by graduates interested in the work. Here the drills will be held, and until its completion much of the work of handling the guns can be done in the baseball cage.

Hadley not only encouraged the plan but worked behind the scenes in ways unknown to the undergraduates. There was, for example, the matter of obtaining gifts for construction of an armory. Securing the best regular army officer possible to command the batteries involved conferences in New Haven and in Washington and a good deal of firm insistence on the qualifications necessary.

The commander obtained proved ideal. He was Robert M. Danford, then a lieutenant in the Fifth United States Field Artillery, who twenty-five years later as Chief of Field Artillery was to prepare the artillery of the United States for the second World War.

In June of 1916 the national guard was called into federal service against Mexico. In addition to the four batteries at Yale, there was a Connecticut battery at Stamford and another at Branford. The six were combined into a regiment under the command of Colonel Danford, which became the Tenth Field Artillery, there being in those days only nine artillery regiments already designated. Two years later the artillery was to expand so many times over that many of the students from the Yale batteries became the commanding officers of batteries or battalions.

The Tenth Field Artillery was so newly organized and scantily trained that it was thought better not to move it to the Mexican border in June. Instead it went to the government training area at Tobyhanna, in Pennsylvania, to go through a course of intensive instruction under its commanding officer that made subsequent army training camps seem restful. By the end of the summer, when the unit was trained, no additional troops were being moved to the border, and the batteries were mustered out of federal service under a general army order affecting all college units. Even though Hadley thought that the return of the unit to state service might mean that the government would employ it in maintaining order in the strikes which were then spreading, he wrote a friend: "While I do not like the prospect of having the militia actively employed in this way, I will own that I feel very much more content to have our boys engaged in maintaining public order at home than in attempting the same task for a body of reluctant foreigners."

The army and the university alike now wished to establish a Reserve Officers' Training Corps at Yale, under legislation enacted during the summer of 1916. The difficulties in the way of achieving this goal, and the roundabout method devised by Hadley and the army for reaching it may serve as an example of the sort of red tape with which Hadley had to deal during the next two years. As explained in his Report for 1917:

No member of the National Guard was eligible for membership in the Reserve Officers' Training Corps; and the Yale undergraduates who were most actively interested in military service were at that time members of a unit of the National Guard, the Tenth Field Artillery. . . . Though discharged from Federal service, they were not discharged from State service, and in the uncertainty regarding our future relations in Mexico the Administration was unwilling to grant such discharge. Our plans for organization were therefore blocked for the time being. Fortunately, the War Department saw the importance of the artillery unit of the Reserve Officers' Training Corps which we proposed to establish, and removed the obstacles which stood in our way by the simple expedient of withdrawing Federal recognition from the four Yale batteries. This gave their members the right to ask discharge from the State of Connecticut and to become members of a Reserve Officers' Training unit at Yale.

By the time this was accomplished it was the beginning of 1917 and Yale was rapidly passing to a war footing. The various steps are set out in the president's Report for 1917. Side by side with the R.O.T.C. Colonel Danford organized a course of practical instruction in artillery work, three hours a day, for men who were not in the regular course but who wanted to get quickly as much experience as they could in drill and in the handling of guns and gun teams. Twelve hundred students enrolled and were taught for the most part by fellow students who were in the regular course and who had Tobyhanna experience.

In March the Yale Naval Aviation Unit, which had been training since the previous summer, was called out for further training and was sent to Palm Beach. A Naval Unit enrolled three hundred men. On the administrative side, an Emergency War Council was set up by the Yale Corporation, consisting of the president and five others, "with power to make rules, issue statements, and decide doubtful cases, subject to the general jurisdiction of the Yale Corporation, in connection with Yale problems growing out of the national situation."

During this initial period of tension and preparation the undergraduates had shown admirable restraint, the most striking instance being on the occasion of an unpopular address by a leading pacifist. In the prevailing war hysteria the incident provoked a flood of protests, but Hadley had no doubts in the matter. In fact, it was he who had counseled the undergraduate leaders to let the speech take place as scheduled and to use their influence to calm the more violent students who wanted to ride the speaker on a rail and throw him out of the city. To quote again from the 1917 Report:

During the two months that elapsed between the breaking off of diplomatic relations and the actual declaration of war Yale stood for free speech. She has been blamed for it within the college walls as well as without. She was gravely criticized for allowing Dr. Jordan to make a peace speech a few days before war was actually declared. But we held that it was irrational to prepare for a war in behalf of freedom by suppressing freedom of speech; and that men's convictions would in the end be firmer as well as wiser if they had heard the arguments on both sides squarely presented. I was proud of our students the night Dr. Jordan spoke. They gave him a fair chance to say what he wanted to; and the very fact that he was not interrupted made the weak points in his case more apparent than anything else could have done. When war actually came the peace men in the college, having had their say at a proper time, did not continue to say the same things at an improper time, as has been done in so many other places. As we had not sat on the safety valve, we had no untimely explosions.

As men went off to war, an academic war raged over the conferring of war degrees. Yale's action was set out in the president's Report for 1918:

Yale's position in this matter is intermediate between two extremes. On the one hand there are men like President Lowell of Harvard, who say that the Bachelor's degree should not be given for military service at all; that it is not a reward or recognition of loyalty, but a certificate that a man has pursued certain studies enumerated in the college catalogue. On the other hand there are those who say that all who go into the army should receive the Bachelor's degree and not be asked to complete the course at all. The amount of criticism that we have received from the advocates of both extremes is about equal.

With those who hold that we should not recognize war service at all I have no sympathy. With those who say that we ought to give a degree to every 1918 man who entered the army, as Columbia did, I have a great deal of sympathy; but I think that they are wrong. A degree is not primarily a reward of loyalty. It is a certificate that a man has done certain things and can do certain things, . . .

The college which defers giving the degree, and gives it only on the basis of specially meritorious service, says: "Our degree is valuable; come back and get it if you can. If you cannot we will accept absent work instead of present work provided the record warrants it."

Under the rule then adopted by Yale no degree could be received unless a student had completed the studies of his junior year. If he had, and had a good service record, he could get a regular degree after the war by returning for one full term's work. If he did not return, but had a good service record or died in service, he received a degree *honoris causa*, which was treated not as an honorary degree but as "a special form of degree in course, given under conditions created by the present war." Students who had not completed the work of junior year could get a degree only by returning to Yale after the war and completing the course.

By the time the university was fully in the war, all resemblance
to its peacetime appearance was gone. Hadley in the fall of 1918
sent a sketch map to one of his sons in service by way of proof
that the father was in fully as military an atmosphere as the son.
On it he had drawn all the well-known university buildings but
had substituted up-to-date names. His own office, Woodbridge
Hall, was labeled Civil Administration. The New Haven Green
appeared as the Parade Ground. The Old Campus housed Field
Artillery, Chemical Warfare, Premedical, and Engineers. As
stated more formally in the president's Report for 1918–19:

During the first half of the year Yale was engaged in two kinds of
military teaching. It served as a camp of instruction to train men who
had already been called into the service of the United States for
scientific work in connection with the Medical Corps and the Signal
Corps; it also served as a military college to train a body of cadets
who had been inducted into the service but not yet called to active
duty. Yale was thus at once an officers' training camp and a military
university.

Our work as an officers' training camp . . . was organized in
three sections, the Army Laboratory School [600 students], the
Chemical Warfare Service Station [50 students], and the Radio
Officers School [500 students] . . .

The courses of military and naval training for students regularly
enrolled in Yale University, which had been established in 1917,
were continued in the autumn of 1918, with this important modifica-
tion, that the students pursuing these courses were no longer civil-
ians, but members of the organized forces of the United States,
temporarily held for duty at Yale but subject to military or naval
discipline. . . . The senior officers of the Army and Navy were not
simply professors of military or naval science at Yale; they were
actually in charge of more than four-fifths of Yale's student
body. . . .

The total enrollment in the Naval Training Unit was about five
hundred. . . . More than nine hundred of our students were enrolled in the Army Training Corps.

The final organization described in the Report was reached
only after many struggles with red tape and administrative con-

fusion. So long as the draft age remained twenty-one, the situation was not impossible. Both the army and the navy encouraged men to take officers' training courses until twenty-one, instead of enlisting earlier in the ranks. This permitted a three-year course, which was described by Hadley in a letter to a son, February 2, 1918:

We have been working out a full three years' artillery course to last during the period of the war. It has six hours of theoretical military work each week, three hours of French (or other modern language if the student already knows French), three hours of science, and three hours of History and Government. The students are, I believe, quite enthusiastic about it, and I think it will enable us to get men here from the preparatory schools.

A day-to-day picture of the situation is given in Hadley's letters during this period. His sons were overseas, and he wrote them frequently. On September 6, 1918, he records:

Just at present we have joys and responsibilities of our own in connection with the new draft law, which reduces the age to eighteen. The war department propose to "induct" all students over eighteen into the service no matter what their physical qualifications or disqualifications may be. It believes that anybody who is strong enough to go to college is strong enough to serve the government in some capacity. Boys so inducted will be virtually enlisted; they will receive the pay of privates and have their college expenses paid by the government. They will take a course of study similar to that already provided for the R.O.T.C., Naval Training Unit, Signal Corps Unit, or Engineers' Reserve. After a brief period, boys who have reached the age of twenty will be divided into four classes, which will be assigned (1) to Officers Training Camps, (2) to further special studies at College, (3) to non-commissioned officers training camps, (4) to the ranks as privates. We hope not to have many class 4 men. The plan in its outline is a first rate one.

After a somewhat longer period the same weeding out process will be applied to the boys of 19; and still later, to the boys of 18. The boy who enters college before he reaches the age of 18 can join the S.A.T.C. [Students Army Training Corps] and wear the uniform, but must pay his own expenses. He has a full year before he can be called into the service; and if he is physically and mentally capable, should have a first rate chance of making Class 1.

Our boys have done splendidly at the Camps just closing.

A few days later, on September 11, he wrote:

"Things are badly confused here trying to carry out the war department plan for militarizing us, but we shall get them straight somehow. I have been so busy for the past three days that if there is any news to tell it has escaped my notice."

And a fortnight later: "Business here is much messed up. The Committee on Education and Special Training is giving us orders which we cannot possibly carry out." As his 1919 Report said:

The situation was further complicated by the fact that the whole work of military instruction in our colleges was placed under the hands of a civilian committee in Washington which was unfamiliar with the special needs of field artillery and the steps that Yale had already taken to meet them. We were also handicapped by the absence of nearly all our older students; for when the military age was reduced to eighteen the War Department recommended practically every member of the Yale R.O.T.C. who had reached that age for a commission in field artillery. This was a most gratifying evidence of the value of the instruction which we had given during the previous year; but it created a shortage of cadet officers which crippled us seriously in dealing with the large number of freshmen whom we wanted to train.

On October 22, 1918, Hadley wrote to a son in France:

Yale is recovering from Spanish influenza and settling into her stride for the term. We have our troubles, but seem to be better off than most other places. . . . The Northeastern department inspector is quite a good man, and his visits help more than they hinder. Your friends of the A.G.O. are quite meek since the day four weeks ago when I asked them for authority from the Judge Advocate General's office for a very absurd thing which they were doing.

We have between 1700 and 1800 regular students this year, besides 950 in the two officers training schools (Army Laboratory School and Radio Engineer Officers School) making about 2700 in our buildings and laboratories. Of our students, about 1500 are in uniform (Field Artillery 500+, Navy 550+, Engineers and Chemists 400). We have therefore only a little over 200 civilian students. People have adjusted themselves to the new conditions much quicker than I thought they would. But they are all very proud to be so closely connected with the service, and pleased with the way things are run.

On the financial side the war meant a staggering deficit in the annual budgets. Hadley and the officers of the Alumni Fund went before the graduates with an account of the needs of Yale, and the response broke all records. Contributions to the fund had been running something over $100,000 a year, with an all-time record of $131,000 in 1911. In the year ending June 30, 1917, the graduates gave $425,000, in the following year over $500,000, and in 1918–19 the amount was nearly $600,000. These extraordinary contributions made it possible for the university to meet its operating deficits.

When the armistice came on November 11, 1918, Hadley found that the changes called for by peace brought as many problems as those posed by war, and there was no longer the wartime spirit on the part of all concerned to aid in meeting them. On November 17, 1918, he wrote a son:

"The S.A.T.C. is getting restless and the Naval Unit still more so. The Government has not yet told us what we are to do about the situation here now that the war is over, but promises to do so very soon."

On November 20 he amplified this:

Demobilization is about as bad for a college as for an army; in one way worse because the college does not know in advance when and where it is going to be ordered to demobilize. The boys who were willing to eat coarse food or study French with a will when they thought they were preparing themselves for army service, now have lost appetite both for the food and the French. It is really pretty inconvenient not to know what is ahead of us. I suppose we shall probably go on pretty much as we are for four weeks longer; that then the army Lab. men, Radio Engineers and other technical details will be taken away, and undergraduates readjusted to their old basis somewhat more slowly.

What made matters particularly difficult was that Yale itself was in the process of readjusting its old peacetime organization. It would have been difficult enough to go back to a known and tried peacetime basis, but many graduates were demanding that the opportunity be taken to set up a new and improved Yale. Within limits this was all to the good. Plans in this direction had been worked out before the war, and progress had already been made. The difficulty lay in the fact that an active group of graduates now pressed for even more sweeping changes in the form of more administrative officers, more faculty, and higher salaries. They showed postwar impatience at any delay regardless of whether or not funds were available to meet the cost of the changes.

If Hadley had been less tired from the strain of the war years and the press of administrative details, he might have been able to please all concerned, though it would have been difficult in the extreme. As it was, when the graduates returned for the annual Alumni Day on February 22, 1919, and he outlined the attitude of the administration toward the plans which were being pressed by the graduates, he for once put his worst foot forward. He had always been an advocate of higher faculty salaries, and he thought that in his speech of February 22 he was again stressing the point and once more explaining the difficulties of paying adequate salaries and the reasons which led men to stay at Yale at half of what they could make in outside industry:

From the standpoint of University administration, the one vital question, which throws all others into the background, is the question of salaries. A university must have strong men in its Faculties. The character of its professors is more important than the system of organization or the scheme of studies. . . .

To get good men, we must pay them a living wage,—not necessarily a wage that they would receive in other lines of industry:—the pleasure of work in a place like Yale and of association with its traditions will make our Faculty content with half the pay they have elsewhere. . . .

Nearly everything that has been proposed this morning has merit —if we had money enough to carry it out. But no reform is worth carrying out if it is going to tie our hands in such a way as to drive good men from Yale to other colleges, or from college service into business and professional life. What, from the standpoint of the administration, should determine which of the many desirable reforms should be put into effect first? The answer is this: Where a reform will enable one man to do the work which was formerly done by two, put it into effect as speedily as possible; where it will require two men to do the work which was formerly done by one, defer it to a more convenient season. . . .

Some would favor an immediate increase of all salaries and an appeal to the graduates for the large additional sum, probably two hundred and fifty thousand a year, which such readjustment would necessitate. I cannot believe that this is wise. For a specific need, like the field artillery training in which Yale took the lead and which enabled her to say "Prepared" when the roll of colleges was called two years ago, we can properly spend money which we have not in hand and rely on the graduates to make good the deficiency. But a recurrent deficit is a different thing. It cannot, and should not, be met in this way. It may be that for a year or two, during the immediate period of reconstruction, we shall have to appeal to the generosity of our graduates on a larger scale than usual; we should not make plans of development which put us under the permanent necessity of resorting to such an appeal.

He was to say the same things later in a form which won acceptance, but on that Alumni Day he had put them with unfortunate bluntness and aroused a storm of protest from graduates. This was a new experience for Hadley, and the very fact that the graduates had always supported him in the past made him take it the more to heart. For weeks he could not sleep at night for worrying as to whether or not he might be wrong, since he had not been able to prove his point to the satisfaction of the graduates. In particular it grieved him that his work of twenty years should seemingly count for nothing in their eyes. Actually this period of extreme despondency did not last long, and it is probable that the objectors were never in the majority. Within a few months his later speeches, made with his old felicity of presentation, had explained his position in its proper light and won acceptance.

During the period of bitterness immediately after the speech the *Yale Alumni Weekly* had headed its opening page "Reconstruction Action Demanded," and went on to say (February 28):

. . . Last Saturday the largest number of graduates who have ever attended Alumni University Day came back primarily because they were interested to know at first hand what the Alumni Committee had proposed to the Corporation and what the University administration was planning to do to meet the public Yale opinion as expressed by that Committee and by graduate and Faculty contributors to these columns. If they were as inspired by the one as they were disappointed by the other, they showed their sentiments. . . . Any attempt to block progress is opposed to the best interests of the University at this juncture. . . .

We confess to an entire inability to understand or to accept the point of view regarding Yale reorganization which the President of the University gave to the graduates on Alumni University Day. We refer to the two matters of Faculty salaries and an indefinite delay in adopting a reorganization plan because of temporary financial conditions.

The storm might never have broken, if Hadley had phrased his February 22 speech as he did a subsequent brief statement on March 7. The latter, though it actually did not commit him beyond his previously expressed position, met with general approval:

". . . Equally important is the recommendation that increased salaries should accompany improved methods of teaching and increased efficiency. I shall advocate immediate efforts to raise the money necessary for this vitally important purpose."

As soon as the program of reconstruction was actually adopted by the Corporation, Hadley pressed loyally for the accomplishment of all its features. Privately he thought it emphasized paper organization at the expense of flexibility, and that at points it stressed reform simply for reform's sake. For this he had no sympathy, and it was at this period, in 1920, that in writing to Harvey Cushing about William Osler he said:

"Even in the quiet halls of Oxford, reform had begun to make its disturbing presence felt; and for advice Oxford instinctively turned to Osler as one who knew the habits of the intruder and was familiar with the measures which were necessary to keep him quiet."

But once the plans were adopted Hadley came out in his annual Report for 1919 as strongly in favor of the provisions he did not like as for the provisions which he had long advocated. In the latter class were such matters as university appointments for the faculty rather than appointments in the separate schools. The recommendations, as listed in the 1919 Report, were as follows:

1. A four years' undergraduate course of study leading to the Bachelor's degree for all students, Scientific as well as Academic.

2. The transfer of the Select Course from the jurisdiction of the Sheffield Faculty to that of the Academic Faculty.

3. A joint freshman year for both Academic and Scientific students.

4. Control of student morale and discipline to be taken out of the hands of Deans of Faculties and put in charge of a Dean of Students.

5. The members of the Faculty to be professors and instructors in Yale University, to serve where their powers were most needed, rather than to be men who owe primary allegiance to the several Schools whose governing boards had nominated them.

6. The University Council, and the Provost who was to act as its Chairman, to deal with the larger problems of University organization, on which the Corporation had hitherto acted under advice from the separate faculties.

Hadley in this Report could not resist pointing out to the reformers that not all their steps were original. Speaking particularly of the recommendations of the Graduate Advisory Committee as adopted by the Corporation's Committee on Educational Policy, he said:

The suggestions of the Committee are not so new as some of the older graduates suppose. Many of the most important ideas in the report were under consideration before the war began. The Governing Board of the Sheffield Scientific School had already taken the first step toward the adoption of a four years course. . . . The war simply gave us opportunity to carry out promptly and as part of a general scheme a number of changes which would have come less systematically and with less public notice in the course of a few years' development.

In his official report he could hardly picture the wartime change in the Sheffield Scientific School as frankly as he did in a letter written March 8 to Anson Phelps Stokes just after the action took place. After explaining why the Corporation had found it advisable to authorize the organization of instruction by departments under the jurisdiction of the Prudential Committee, he went on to relate his experiences at the meeting of the Governing Board of the Sheffield Scientific School:

There was quite an amusing scene at the Governing Board meeting where I presented and explained this action. Never have I seen a more astonished body of gentlemen than the members of the Governing Board of the Scientific School when, in answer to their inquiries, I read them parts of pages 28 and 29 of the by-laws of the Corporation. Finally one of the older men said: "Then the Governing Board's whole power is dependent upon the consent of the Corporation." I said yes. He next said, "What is there to prevent the Corporation from abolishing the Governing Board?" I said, "The practical thing that will always prevent it is the wisdom of the men who are themselves members of the Governing Board. The only theoretical obstacle to its abolition is the necessity of giving five days' notice in advance to the members of the Corporation before it can be done." A sort of awed hush came over the meeting. When we passed to the powers and duties of the Director, however, a majority of the men became suddenly, and in some instances flagrantly, cheerful.

By Commencement of 1920 Hadley was able to report good progress in carrying out reorganization plans. The common freshman year was organized under Dean Angier. Arrangements were complete for adding the fourth year to the Sheffield Scientific School course and for transferring the Select Course to the College. Williston Walker was provost, and Burton Twichell was dean of students. Faculty appointments were henceforth to be in Yale University and not in the separate schools. A new salary scale was in effect, and steps were under way to raise endowment to meet the cost of increased salaries; in the meantime the Alumni Fund was once more filling the gap. Under this new scale instructors started at $1,500 and went to $2,500, or exceptionally $3,000; the range for assistant professors was from $3,000 to $4,000, or exceptionally to $5,000; associate professors received $4,500 or $5,000; professors $5,000 to $8,000, with plans for increasing the maximum to $10,000.

The university was also making good progress so far as the undergraduates were concerned. An unexpectedly large proportion returned to complete their studies after the war, so there was little break in the traditions of the place. From the class of 1918, some of whose members were entitled to receive war degrees on their service records without returning, the number returning to earn their degrees exceeded those receiving war degrees. In the classes of 1919, 1920, and 1921, the total withdrawals to enter service had been 1,118, out of whom 889, or nearly 80 per cent, returned.

Other activities picked up where they had left off, and work which had been suspended during the war was resumed. The Harkness Memorial Quadrangle was carried to completion during 1920, and the dedication ceremonies took place in January, 1921. The first of the Sterling Memorial buildings, the University Chemical Laboratory, was begun the same year. John Sterling, of the class of 1864, died in 1918, leaving his fortune to Yale—a legacy by which the university ultimately benefited to the extent of over $40,000,000. Only a minor portion of this amount was actually received and credited to Yale funds during Hadley's administration; the major part was paid over during the administration of his successor, including the funds for the great Sterling Library building.

During the years immediately following the war certain new developments were selected by Hadley for comment in his Reports as particularly significant. One was "the creation of an active and vigorous Department of Education." Another was the development of the Industrial Science Course in the Sheffield Scientific School. A third was a still further improvement in the matter of entrance examinations, designed to meet even better the needs of boys entering from high schools.

The normal round of university life was soon resumed. In fact, much of it had continued during the war, changed only by the uniforms and the military bands. There had been Commencements during the war, but from the standpoint of the graduates the greatest came in 1919, when most of the classes held reunions, either regular or delayed. For Hadley this meant a record number of speeches to returning classes, but he enjoyed every one of them.

When Hadley became president at the age of forty-three he had said that he was not going to continue beyond sixty-five. This was generally known, and as he approached that age speculation became rife as to his successor. At the same time various friends urged him to continue longer in office. In order that there might be no doubt as to his position, he wrote the Corporation in the spring of 1920, stating the facts and asking to be relieved from active duty on June 30, 1921. He added:

"I am making this request more than a year in advance, because I regard it as important for the continuity of Yale's progress that my successor should be chosen next autumn, and have at least six months at his command in which to consider plans for the future, before assuming the actual duties of his office."

The successor chosen was James Rowland Angell, a graduate of the University of Michigan, for whom Hadley had the greatest admiration. This admiration increased as he watched President Angell discharge the duties of the office. As far as Hadley's personal choice was concerned, however, he had been in favor of selecting a Yale graduate rather than an outsider. This did not prevent him from welcoming President Angell heartily, and alike on official occasions and in the family circle he found Angell a joy and a delight. Hadley was particularly careful not to meddle in college affairs after his retirement, but the new president would drop in of evenings to chat with the old. Some of the pleasantest evenings I have passed have been in the library of the house at 93 Whitney Avenue, while the two presidents relaxed and talked, the ex-president in an old rocking chair and the new president stretched out at length on the sofa.

Hadley's announcement of his intended resignation brought many letters from friends, and his actual retirement brought yet more, together with formal resolutions of appreciation. To repeat the tributes is a temptation, but it is in Hadley's replies that the significant information is to be found. Answering a letter from Barrett Wendell at Harvard he wrote (April 12, 1920):

. . . I do not find my strength giving out, and am hoping actually to do more work in the next five years than I have done in any similar period in the past. But things have reached a point at Yale where the immediate problems of reconstruction after the war are pretty well settled and where plans for the future, involving the use of the Sterling gift and other large gifts, will have to be determined. These ought to be made by the man who is going to carry them out, and the carrying out will be a matter of ten or fifteen years to come.

Under these circumstances 1921 is a natural time to make the break; and I, for my own part, shall be glad to be relieved of the necessity of fixing salaries and adjusting difficulties between faculties in order to take up some of the industrial problems, particularly the railroad problems, of the country. I have kept in touch with my old work sufficiently to do this, and have been offered one or two directorates which ought to give me first rate opportunities.

Although his strength was not giving out, he recognized that the work was telling on him. To Hamilton Holt, who wrote suggesting that retirement should mean more articles for the *Independent*, he replied (May 6, 1920):

One of the greatest difficulties of recent years is that I have been pumped so dry by the daily claims of administrative work that my brain is not filled with partly conceived articles to the degree that it ought to be, and generally was until a few years ago. Under these circumstances I am afraid that some more water will have to run into the reservoir before we can talk about distributing it.

Looking back some years later, Hadley told his daughter he was sure he had been right in retiring at sixty-five:

I knew it was time for me to retire. When new propositions came up I could see both sides, and could see that the bad just about balanced the good. That showed I was too old. When I was younger I could see both sides, but was prepared to put the new propositions through in spite of the bad, trusting to keep the good and discard the bad. That is the only way progress is possible in an administrative job.

CHAPTER XIII

RETROSPECT

ARTHUR HADLEY closed his final Report as president with a review of developments during his administration. This was his considered judgment on the past twenty-two years, and it seems best to give his account in his own words. The preceding chapters have traced his plans and have followed his work in converting those plans into reality. This chapter views the scene in retrospect, with all the advantages and disadvantages involved in hindsight.

In concluding the last of my annual reports to the Alumni, it seems appropriate to look back over the twenty-two years and summarize what has been accomplished in the development of university ideals and methods during that period.

President Dwight had laid the foundation for this development with much wisdom and foresight. He had secured an Act of the Legislature making "Yale University" the corporate name of the institution. He had arranged working agreements between the separate faculties by which they acted in cooperation with one another, instead of pursuing their several courses independently. He had placed the details of administration of each school under the supervision of its dean, and had thus made himself president of the institution as a whole in a different way from any of his predecessors. But in spite of the large work that he had accomplished and the yet larger ideals which he had constantly in mind, Yale had still remained a group of colleges. To make it a university in fact as well as in name it was necessary to establish a centralized control of buildings, of income, and of procedure.

At the beginning of President Dwight's term of office there was not a single permanent building which the Corporation had an unquestioned right to administer according to its own best judgment for the benefit of the university as a whole. The Peabody Museum and the Observatory were under the control of outside trustees or managers. The Library had been constructed to a very considerable extent with College funds, and the College had always been accorded special privileges in connection with its use. The educational buildings and appliances were all held as trusts for the benefit of separate schools, whose faculties had a prescriptive right to advise as to the manner in which they should be used. These schools were very unequally provided with places to live in. Three-quarters of the buildings existing in 1885 belonged to the College; the other quarter was divided between the Theological School, the Art School, the Scientific School, and the Medical School. Neither the Law School nor the Graduate School had any permanent home whatever. Even under President Dwight's administration no very substantial progress was made toward remedying this state of things. Of eighteen additional buildings completed during his term of office, only three—the Chittenden Library, the Gymnasium, and the Infirmary —were University buildings in the true sense of the word. Of the other fifteen, eleven were given to the College or built out of College funds, three belonged to the Scientific School, and one to the Law School. A University building plan seemed as far from realization as ever.

A long step forward was taken in the years from 1899 to 1902 by the erection of the Bicentennial group: a University dining hall, assembly hall, and offices of administration. Ten years later the purchase of the Sachem's Wood estate gave the opportunity for the establishment of University laboratories of pure science: Physics, Zoology, and Botany. These were the first of our educational buildings—using the word in its narrower sense—that were under University control; that could be used by the students of the Graduate School, the College, the Scientific School, the School of Forestry, or the School of Medicine, as need might arise, and were managed by the Corporation under the advice of committees in which members of different faculties sat side by side. The great gift of Mr. John Sterling will enable us to carry this development of laboratories still further; and also to establish a Memorial Library which will be in a fuller sense a University institution than could possibly be the case with one which was situated on the College campus and largely built with College moneys. Among other University buildings of the last twenty years are the Yale Bowl, the Yale Boat House, the Artillery Armories, the Carnegie Swimming Pool, and the University Heating Plant. No account of what we have been able to do in this connection would be complete without a grateful reference to the generosity of an unknown friend who has assisted the Treasurer of the University in acquiring land for this development somewhat in advance of the necessity for its immediate use.

And while the general needs are being thus provided for, we have been able to take better proportionate care of the separate parts. For the first time since Yale became a university the buildings available for the use of the several schools now bear some relation to their respective needs. In the College, the last twenty years have witnessed the virtual completion of the main quadrangle by the construction of the Linsly Memorial and of Wright Hall. The Berkeley Oval has been still more definitely completed by Fayerweather, Lampson, and Haughton Halls. And above all, a new quadrangle, or rather group of quadrangles, has been given by Mrs. Harkness as a memorial which in its various courts and entries epitomizes the whole history of Yale and is at the same time a work of surpassing beauty. The Scientific School has secured a social center in Byers Hall, and has been equipped with classrooms in buildings like Kirtland and Leet Oliver and with laboratories of applied science like Hammond, Mason, or Dunham. It has also been able to provide housing for its students; mainly through the gift of two beautiful buildings by Mr. Vanderbilt, but partly also through the cooperative spirit shown by student societies. The quadrangle of the Divinity School has been completed by the Day Missions Library. The Music School has been housed in Sprague Memorial; while the Dispensary, the Brady Laboratory, and other buildings in immediate connection with the New Haven Hospital, represent the beginnings of an adequate home for the Medical School. The Graduate School has no permanent buildings of its own; but the construction of University laboratories has given its teachers better quarters and facilities than they could have obtained if separately housed. Projects for the Forest School and for an additional Medical School building are well under way. There are still two schools for which no adequate provision is being made, the Law School and the Art School; and we are unable to furnish proper accommodation to the women who are attending our Graduate and professional schools in constantly increasing numbers. But with these exceptions and that of the Peabody Museum the housing problem of the University stands in fairly satisfactory shape.

Besides these changes in the number and the distribution of our buildings, we have also made progress toward a harmonious architectural plan.

Since the days of the Old Brick Row, Yale's buildings have been singularly lacking in unity of style, of material, or of arrangement. From time to time efforts were made to secure some sort of uniformity; but beyond a gradual improvement in the architecture of individual buildings, very little was accomplished until the election of Mr. Farwell to the Corporation and the appointment of Mr. Frank Miles Day as Consulting Architect of the University in 1913. Mr. Day's death, just at the time when his influence was making itself most effectively felt, was a great disappointment to those of us who believed, with Newman, that one of the greatest educational forces in a university is the character and beauty of its buildings. Fortunately we have been able to fill his place by the appointment of Mr. James Gamble Rogers, whose work in the Memorial Quadrangle is the best possible proof of what he can do for Yale and for America in this great educational field.

Of at least equal significance with this building development has been the growth of University funds and University income.

At the beginning of President Dwight's administration the total amount of University funds available for general purposes was less than $350,000. If we added to these, as we properly might, the funds available for the Graduate School, the Library, and the Observatory, the amount still fell short of $500,000. It is obvious that the income derived from a sum like this was entirely inadequate to support the general needs of a university. These had to be met by contributions from the income of separate schools; partly from interest on their endowment, partly from their tuition fees. The greater part of the burden fell upon the College, and the faculty of the College, naturally enough, assumed a good deal of authority in saying how this money should be spent and in making sure that the College got the largest share of the benefits. Considering the difficulties by which he was confronted, President Dwight did a great deal to bring order out of this chaos; but to the very end of his administration he was hampered by lack of University income, and had hard work to secure the consent of separate faculties in order to get money to meet the general needs. In 1899 the funds of the University available for general purposes amounted to less than $850,000—only nineteen per cent of the total endowment. Under conditions like these any consolidation or centralization of authority was impossible.

Immediately after the completion of the Bicentennial buildings a quiet but determined effort was made to increase the general income of the University, as distinct from its departmental income. Little success was achieved during the first three or four years; but in 1905 a group of important gifts, including one of a million dollars from John D. Rockefeller, enabled us, for the first time in Yale's history, to bring the general funds of the University into proper relation to the special funds of the several schools and departments.

A single illustration will suffice to show how this change increased the power of the Corporation to secure needed reforms. As early as 1847 an attempt had been made to organize a graduate school of Philosophy and the Arts, and much excellent work of graduate instruction was done in the latter half of the last century. But the cost of graduate instruction can never be met by the tuition fees of the students, and there were hardly any separate endowments to support the School as a school. The work, therefore, had to be maintained by professors in the College or the Scientific School who gave part of their time to graduate work—their salaries being paid out of the income of their respective undergraduate schools. Under these circumstances anything like an independent development of the Graduate School as an organization was impossible. It consisted of two separate bodies of teachers and students, who sometimes worked harmoniously and sometimes inharmoniously. Not until the University was in a position to compensate these schools out of University income for the time spent by their professors in teaching graduate students was it possible to organize a graduate faculty that would work as a unit. This change in the status of the School took place about 1907; and it was followed not only by superior efficiency in instruction, but by superior facility in getting endowment and buildings.

The movement thus begun has continued to the present day. Donors have seen the advantage of centralized administration, and have learned that the old habit of tying up gifts for specific purposes may result in making them less useful instead of more so. The total amount of funds now available for the general use of the University, as distinct from its separate schools and departments, is over $13,700,000; representing fifty-three per cent of our total endowment in 1921 as against nineteen per cent in 1899.

Detailed figures of the endowment of the University and its separate schools at the close of each of the last three administrations read as follows:

	1886	1899	1921
University	$344,655.66	$841,904.06	$13,730,735.56
Library	55,677.65	308,256.22	998,582.03
Observatory	10,000.00	322,415.51	524,609.32
Graduate School	79,350.00	164,400.00	2,103,905.57
Academic	941,246.53	1,568,278.07	2,410,061.83
Scientific	152,223.01	405,907.53	837,836.50
Freshman Year	. . . .	. . . .	150,492.63
Divinity	413,585.49	646,810.16	1,356,256.06
Medical	27,651.57	105,794.13	2,056,283.58
Law	11,600.00	82,813.77	501,904.39
Fine Arts	75,200.00	103,250.00	168,924.48
Music	. . . .	5,000.00	88,467.05
Forestry	. . . .	. . . .	748,951.70
	$2,111,189.91	$4,554,829.45	$25,677,010.70

The effective endowment of the College and the Scientific School is from fifty to seventy-five per cent larger than these figures would indicate, because the College dormitories, and the productive property (dormitories and investments) in the hands of the Sheffield Trustees, represent regular sources of income to the schools in question. But even if the table were so revised as to make full allowance for this fact, its significance would be unchanged, as the general University funds would still be about fifty per cent of the total.

The financial and educational position of the University has been greatly strengthened by the growth of the Alumni Fund.

When this fund was established in the last years of President Dwight's administration the aims and hopes of its projectors were very modest. They desired to afford men of moderate means who could not contribute largely to University endowments the chance to make small gifts to current income year after year; and they hoped that the aggregate amount of such gifts on which the University could depend might reach $10,000 annually.

But as the utility of the Fund has become more and more evident and the organization for collecting it has improved, the total amount of gifts has exceeded this expectation thirty and forty times over;

increasing by nearly fifty per cent the amount of University income available for general purposes, enabling us to improve our instruction in Law or Medicine before we had secured the special endowment necessary for the purpose, and allowing us to begin our preparations for war service in 1915 instead of waiting till 1917. It was the Alumni Fund which enabled us in each successive year to meet as they came the expenses and losses entailed by the war, and begin the next year without a deficit.

The indirect effects of the Fund have been as striking as the direct ones. For an Alumni Fund means more than can be represented by dollars and cents. It means intellectual liberty for the institution, in the largest and best sense of the term. A college that is dependent on the state can seldom be kept wholly free from politics. A college which is supported by a church is liable under the best of conditions to the evil of denominational control. A college which owes its prosperity to a few individuals finds it hard to be wholly independent of their individual wishes. But the college or university which successfully appeals for support to its graduates as a body is by that very fact free from the control of a class or a party and able to meet the emergencies which arise as a free and self-determining institution.

The effect of these changes is shown in the annual reports of the Treasurer and in the successive editions of the Laws of the Corporation which are printed by the Secretary's Office.

Until 1900 the different schools of the University were dealt with in the Treasurer's Report as though they were in fact separate institutions administered by a single office. The College, the Scientific School, and the various professional schools, each had its own funds and its own account of income and expense. To know the financial position of Yale as a whole the reader had to add different accounts together, and eliminate or balance cross entries as well as he might. On Mr. Tyler's accession to the office of Treasurer he made two important changes. He began his Report with a consolidated balance sheet and a consolidated income and expense account, from which the cross entries had already been eliminated; and he listed the funds of the different departments one after another, and the income accounts of the different departments one after another, so as to show that they were parts of a united whole. Mr. McClung in 1906 and 1907 went one step farther. He utilized the large increase of University funds to liquidate a complex mass of interdepartmental advances and claims, and a less complex but more indefensible set of advances to income which had been accumulating on our books for nearly half a century. As a result, our published accounts for the first time in many years showed present facts as they actually stood. Finally, Mr. Day in 1910 consolidated the investment account of the University, so that the Corporation no longer held different securities for the benefit of separate funds (except when this was specifically directed in the deed of gift), but carried the funds on the books as general liabilities of the Corporation, balanced and secured by the collective body of productively invested assets.

The old statutes of the University were, like the old Treasurer's Reports, groups of separate records affecting separate institutions. No two faculties stood in the same relation to the Corporation; no two institutions connected with the University were administered by the same, or by approximately the same, methods. At the close of the nineteenth century the laws of the Corporation were still based upon what had been written by President Thomas Clap one hundred and fifty years earlier. Much had been omitted, and many things added; but the additions had not been digested, nor the old laws recast to meet modern changes. The edition of the By-Laws printed in 1907 was the first attempt to define the procedure of the Corporation, the rights and duties of its officers, the authority of the faculties, their relations to one another and to the Corporation, in terms that indicated that Yale was in fact a university. A second edition of the Laws was printed in 1915; a third, embodying the results of our recent reconstruction, in 1920.

The effect of publications like these upon the actual conduct of the faculties and their members is far greater than might appear at first sight. They prevent conflicts and misunderstandings. They lead professors to realize the relation of their own work and their own faculty to the University as a whole. Equally important has been the influence of these Laws upon the Corporation itself. The members of that body, for the first time in many years, have gained a full sense of their own powers and responsibilities. There were decades in the history of the institution when the Corporation made very little inquiry into the business of the Medical School, of the Law School, or even of the Sheffield Scientific School. So long as the financial responsibility for the conduct of these schools was largely outside of the Corporation, this aloofness was natural and justifiable. But when Yale became a university in fact as well as in

name, it was of the utmost importance to treat all departments alike
and give equal measure of interest to the affairs of all.

This meant giving more time to the work. The statutes in force
twenty-two years ago contemplated but two regular meetings a year.
This number was soon increased to five, and now reaches ten. Under
the special exigencies of the year 1920–21 there have been fourteen
Corporation meetings—besides a much greater number of meetings of the Prudential Committee, which is invested with nearly all
the Corporation's powers.

Another effect has been the voluntary abandonment of what was
known as the "ministerial tradition" among the Successors of the
Original Trustees. In the charter of 1701 it was provided that the
Fellows of the Collegiate School should be ministers of the Gospel
in the Colony of Connecticut. This restriction was not repeated in
the charter of Yale College in 1745; but the usage continued unchanged, and none but Connecticut Congregational ministers were
chosen as Fellows until the twentieth century. It was thought that
the provision made in 1872 for six representatives of the graduate
body would give sufficient opportunity for outside viewpoints to be
presented. But the growth of new problems, educational, financial,
and administrative, made the continuance of a large clerical majority
an anomaly; and the publication of a book of University statutes
threw this anomaly into greater relief. To the credit of the ministers
be it said that they recognized this fact and abandoned the old usage,
not as a reluctant concession to public opinion, but as a result of their
own personal judgment as to what was right.

No account of the changes in Yale's organization as a university
would be complete without some reference to the increased opportunities which have been given to graduates for participation in the
discussion and conduct of University affairs. Down to the year 1900
this participation was largely confined to athletic matters. There was
a sort of division of labor, by which the graduates attended to the
body and the faculties and Corporation to the mind. The graduate
control of athletics has been continued and extended in connection
with the building of the Yale Bowl, the Yale Boat House, and other
things requiring large expenditure of money; but side by side with
this there has gradually grown up a system of intellectual control
through the Alumni Advisory Board. This body differs from the
Harvard Board of Overseers from the fact that its work is what
its name implies—an advisory one. But the Corporation has profited

by that advice in a remarkable degree; sometimes in matters which the Corporation has referred to the Board, like the retention of Connecticut Hall or the development of the loan fund system, and sometimes in matters which graduates took up on their own initiative. To this latter class belongs the work of the Committee on Plan of University Development, which was one of the two or three most important single influences—in some respects the most important of all—that led to the adoption of the University reorganization of two years ago.

Side by side with these changes in control we have witnessed equally important changes in the course of study. These have been discussed in detail in successive reports, and I shall content myself with summarizing the general results.

The terms of admission for undergraduates have been readjusted to meet the needs of the country as a whole. Twenty years ago the College required candidates for admission to present the results of four years' school work in Latin and three years in Greek; and even the Scientific School required two years of Latin. A great many good schools, particularly in the West, were unable to give their boys this preparation; and it became necessary for Yale to choose between its character as a national institution and its position as an upholder of the old classical traditions. It chose the former; and it chose wisely. I am myself one of those who think that the value of classical study is underrated, and that of some forms of science overrated, by the American public to-day. But in determining the subjects on which to base its requirements for admission and to lay emphasis in its college curriculum, a university must meet the public demand. It will render greater service by insisting on good methods of study in things that the nation wants to know than by teaching things that the nation does not want and refusing to teach others.

As a result of this change, the old line of demarcation between the College and the Scientific School is breaking down. We now have a joint Freshman Year, with a faculty of its own. We are doing away with the Select Course in the Scientific School. This course was originally designed to meet the requirements of two groups of students: men who, without intending to become scientific experts, wanted to know enough science to employ experts intelligently in their business; and men who had no immediate professional interest in scientific study, but simply wanted a modern college course instead of a classical one. Under the present arrangement the members of the former class will go to the Scientific School, taking courses in Administrative Engineering or Industrial Science; the latter will go to the College, and make experiments for themselves under the elective system to find out what line they are fitted for, deferring their professional study till after graduation.

In the professional schools themselves we have increased the strictness of our requirements for admission, and have greatly increased the efficiency of our teaching. We have not attempted to make the same entrance requirements for them all, as some misguided friends of standardization would have us do. A student who wishes to achieve the greatest development in painting or music must begin technical studies earlier than the one whose powers lie in the direction of law or theology. To defer the professional study of painting until a man had the general culture and maturity of mind which is requisite in a first class lawyer would mean deferring the training of hand and eye until too late. But in the lines that require maturity of judgment for their successful pursuit we have insisted upon a good college education as a preliminary.

We have in the last twenty years learned to offer both teachers and pupils greater opportunity for independent work. We have increased our laboratory equipment fivefold. We are giving our instructors more time for research than they ever had before— though in many cases somewhat less than could be desired. We are affording the student better facilities for study of his own, by the use of the laboratory in physical and natural science, by the introduction of the case system in law, and by the development of modern methods of teaching in history and in literature.

The fear has been expressed by many of the graduates that we may carry this movement too far, and fill our professorial chairs with men who can perhaps show a few of the best students how to investigate, but will fail to teach the great body of students principles that they need to know. There is some force in this objection, particularly as concerns the younger students; and one of the great advantages in organizing the Freshman Year, with its separate faculty, is that we can provide places of honor and influence for men whose tastes and abilities lie in teaching rather than in research and can get the student started with the right kind of inspiration. But for the older students the capacity to show the way is even more important in good teaching than the capacity to transmit knowledge. The thing that differentiates a college from a school is that the boys are old enough to guide themselves, to make their own mistakes, and to learn to distinguish right and wrong by actual experience.

Whatever may be said by admirers of times gone by, there seems to be no doubt that Yale students in recent years have taken advantage of their opportunities and that the kind of teaching given has been justified by the results. The matter was brought to an acute test four years ago at the beginning of the war. In answering their country's call our Yale boys showed not only loyalty but intelligence. In departments of the service like field artillery, which demanded mental training and the power to grapple with technical problems, the modern Yale education stood the test. In the critical days of June and July, 1918, much of the artillery of the regular divisions was officered by students and recent graduates of Yale. Part of this result was due to the exceptional character and ability of our first commanding officer, Robert Melville Danford. Part may fairly be credited to Yale traditions and the Yale system of instruction; for the same experience was repeated in other branches of the service. Looked at as a test of our education, the war gave us ground for pride and satisfaction. We had taught our boys to meet intellectual emergencies.

But the training which a university gives its students in the classroom or outside of it represents but a small part of its influence. It should not only teach its students how to do things; it should show the public what things have been done and what things ought to be done. Its work should be a source of inspiration to the community in which it dwells. Its teaching and its administration should be a help to the schools of the state and of the country. Its investigators should be in active contact with the country's business, both private and public. Its creative work in science and letters should be published to the whole world.

In looking back over the last twenty years it is a great pleasure to see how much has been accomplished on all these lines. The contact between the American colleges and the public life of the community during the latter half of the nineteenth century was quite inadequate. This was specifically true of Yale, where many of our best scholars and men of science—Willard Gibbs was a striking example—were allowed to remain practically unknown until their reputation among European specialists became so great that their fame ultimately reached their own country. Those were days when twenty times as much was said of what our colleges were doing in

athletics as of what they were doing in science or letters; and when
the community's interest in their achievements was of a good deal
the same character as its interest in a professional baseball nine.

To-day we have established other lines of contact and other forms
of public interest. Our collections have been thrown open to the
people of New Haven as they never were before; and the response
has been overwhelming. Thousands of visitors of all ages from New
Haven and the surrounding towns have spent their Sunday afternoons in the Peabody Museum or the Art School. Equal success,
though of a somewhat different kind, has attended our opening of
the Observatory to visitors, and the various exhibitions which we
have organized in the mechanical laboratories. Particular commen-
dation is due to Mr. Keogh for his activity in making Library material accessible to public view on every important anniversary.

Among the many lines in which this public work of the University
has developed, the most striking results have been obtained in the
Music School. This has been made a center of musical education
and musical culture for the city and for the state. Woolsey Hall
is now available for concerts by the people no less than by our own
Symphony Orchestra or by professional visitors. In the public exercises of the School which have been held at the end of each academic year there has been a combination of three things which gave
the utmost satisfaction: the high character of the work done by the
pupils in the way of composition and performance; the large variety
of races and antecedents which were represented on the platform;
and the enthusiastic way in which New Haven and the surrounding
country thronged to hear first-class music created and interpreted
by its own people. This is the sort of thing that means most to a university.

One source of Yale's isolation in the latter part of the nineteenth
century lay in its policy toward the public schools. The attitude of the
faculty was not exactly one of indifference, but it often looked like
it. Yale College had been organized on the old classical lines, and
most of the members of the faculty were slow to change. They
wanted boys prepared in Latin, Greek, and mathematics. They
overvalued training in those subjects, and undervalued the powers
of able boys who had studied other things. Members of the faculty
tended to say to school teachers and superintendents, "We are
arranging the best course that we can. If you do not prepare boys
for that course your pupils can go somewhere else for their final

preparation." The evil effects of this policy were heightened by the fact that we had made no adequate provision for the training of teachers in secondary schools. Our Graduate School devoted its chief attention to the development of doctors of philosophy, who generally laid more stress on research than on teaching and hoped to become college professors on the basis of such research.

This attitude on the part of the faculty has slowly but radically changed; and I regard this as one of the most important achievements of the last twenty years. The alterations in the entrance requirements and in the courses of study are less important than the change of spirit in which those requirements are administered or these courses of study arranged. We are recognizing for the first time that we are part of a larger whole, and must arrange our work, not with an exclusive view to our own efficiency and convenience, but to do the most we can for the training of the country. In my opinion the chief prospective value of our new Department of Education will come from promoting this spirit of cooperation. Yale will probably never be a place for a very large teachers' college. Its situation in a city of moderate size, while it is good for much of its regular work, puts it at some disadvantage in this respect. But it can and should be a place to which the teachers of the country will look for the same kind of leadership that we have already assumed in law and in medicine, in music and in forestry.

For this habit of leadership is the all-important thing for us to develop. A university is distinguished from a college, not so much by the universal range of subjects taught, as by the universal recognition which its achievements command, whether they be in few lines or in many. It was in this particular that American universities fell farthest behind those of Europe. They did not get into the game. Practical men in business and in politics did not look to them as places for getting advice as to how the affairs of life could be most successfully conducted. America had allowed the teaching of theory and the study of practical problems to get too much separated. In this respect the contrast with France or Germany showed itself very strongly. If a practical problem in France or Germany needed solution, men looked to the universities for help in solving it. This caused technical problems of every kind to be studied more thoroughly, gave greater vitality to university teaching, and made the career of a college professor an attractive one for the most ambitious men.

When the war came, and we had to do our technical work with no help from Germany and comparatively little from France, people awoke to the necessity of asking advice from colleges on a good many lines where they had not previously done so. This gave our professors an opportunity to show what they could do—first in war, and afterward in peace. By our promptness in organizing an artillery school, by our development as a place of training for army laboratory men, and by our readiness to let our professors go into every line of Government work, from the preparation of depth bombs to the study of the races of Eastern Europe, we rendered direct and conspicuous public service in a way that had not been possible in previous times. We have made it our effort to retain the advantage thus gained. We are giving advanced courses of technical instruction to officers of the United States Army. We are building laboratories where we can do pioneer work in industrial science both for the Government and for private corporations. We are encouraging all agencies, whether public or private, to look to us for the same kind of help that the universities of France and Germany have accustomed themselves to render. Our whole system, both of instruction and laboratory organization, in the Medical School and the Graduate School, is based upon this modern conception of public service.

And besides encouraging our men to secure practical results, we have been making Yale a place where results could be published to the world. Foundations like the Silliman Lectureship have attracted discoverers with new ideas. The *Yale Review*, under the able editorship of Professor Cross, has become a medium of public discussion second to none in the country. The Yale University Press, in the hands of Mr. Day and his associates, has not only encouraged Yale men to write things that were of permanent value to science and letters, but has caused men of science and letters all over the world to look to Yale as a source of intellectual light.

The student body has responded to these influences. Its extra-curriculum activity is no longer confined to sports. The Elizabethan Club is not simply a center of literary interest among its members; it is a recognized element in Yale life. The Dramatic Association, which appeals to a still larger number of students, is no mere place of organized amusement; it is a place where good plays are seriously studied, and produced in a way which reflects credit on Yale as a whole. The development of these institutions has been accompanied by an increase of serious writing on the part of the undergraduates.

They are beginning to do things in both poetry and prose that are worth while, and that are read by the general public, not because the writers are promising, but because the writing is good.

It has been well said by Cardinal Newman that a university is not a school but an atmosphere. The English university student has lived in surroundings that gave an atmosphere of loyalty and reverence, and appreciation of what was best in life. The German university student breathed a different air; he lived in an atmosphere of energy and technical efficiency. Neither received a complete education which met the needs of the whole man. America has tried to combine the two systems of training, building its colleges on English lines and its professional schools on German ones. But something more is needed than the joining of two systems; we must have a place where all students can feel simultaneously the two kinds of university influence—the spiritual and the intellectual. For the Yale of to-day, the one is exemplified in the Memorial Quadrangle, the other in the University Press.

I cannot close without a word of grateful acknowledgment to the many friends to whose cooperation Yale's progress is due. To mention even a small part of them by name would be impossible. I did not believe that any man who conducted an enterprise about whose needs and policies there was such difference of opinion could expect so much loyal support and so little unfriendliness or coldness as has fallen to my lot in the last twenty-two years. To the Corporation and its officers, to deans and faculties, to the alumni of every part of the country and to the students of every class, I owe more than I can ever hope to recount or to repay; and the very best wish that I can offer for my successor is that he may fall heir to the same friendship and support which I have received in such full measure from my fellow-workers.

CHAPTER XIV

ACTIVE RETIREMENT

1921–1930

IN June, 1921, Hadley presided for the last time as president at the events of Commencement Week. At the close, on Commencement Day, came the inauguration of his successor, James Rowland Angell, into whose hands the outgoing president transferred the university in a simple but impressive ceremony. That day was centered on the new administration and plans for the future. Hadley's last important address as president was his baccalaureate, preached at the start of Commencement Week: "The Race That Is Set Before Us." For the last time he delivered his charge to the seniors, saying:

Gentlemen of the graduating class: We have spent these last years together in a place where for more than two centuries men have consecrated their lives to the service of others; where teachers have worked hard for small worldly reward; where they have been more concerned to follow out the truths of science and philosophy than to gain ease and comfort by so doing; above all, where men of distinguished talents and eminence among their fellows have been making an honest effort to follow the teaching of our Lord Jesus Christ according to the measure of their understanding. Out of their self-sacrifice has grown a spirit of self-sacrifice. By their example even more than by anything that they taught in the classroom, men have been prepared to render public service in church and civil state.

The first two weeks of the summer were spent in answering letters of good wishes on his retirement, and in going through office files to make everything ready for his successor. This last was a slow process, and on July 8 Hadley wrote President Angell:

I hoped to get everything cleaned out of my office before leaving for the country today; but the sorting of twenty-two years' accumulation was a larger task than I expected. I am therefore availing myself of your kind permission to leave a few things in the office until August. . . . My telephone address is Newtown, Conn.; but in any minor matters I would much rather that you and Miss Chatfield should misappropiate my property than telephone me about it in vacation!

Once at Newtown, Hadley settled down for a real rest and the most complete vacation he had enjoyed for years. Best of all, when the autumn days came and college opened, he and his wife stayed on in the country until the middle of October. During the three months' holiday he spent the time sitting in a hammock under the trees smoking a pipe, or tramping about the countryside, or reading whatever came to hand. Between times, in his new-found leisure, he wrote delightful letters to his children, of which a portion of one will serve as an example. It describes what appears to have been the one exciting event of the entire summer.

On Sunday [July 31, 1921] Zoar got up an excitement of its own which compares favorably with anything you can get. At ten o'clock on the fateful morning in question, John Beach and I were returning from a half-hour's walk in our woods. As we reached the hill garden the clouds to the north looked as though a river storm was brewing, and I went up onto John Kean's road to see what the day was going to be like. I had hardly got out into the open, when I saw low black clouds forming rapidly about two miles due west of us, and hurried down to bring things in. I remembered that both kerosene lamps had been left in the corner under the telephone fuses, and I moved them to the other corner of the room.

I had just left the telephone room and passed into the sitting room—my hand was still on the latch—when the lightning struck. Sound first, then flash. This was nothing new to me; but the novelty, and an unpleasant one, was to see the whole front yard, as far as the road, full of fire, like a heavy snow storm of burning iron filings blown out of a Bessemer converter, or the stars of fifty rockets bursting in a high wind. I rushed out to the porch to see what was really happening. In the second that it took me to get there the storm of stars had cleared up; but the rubber of the telephone wire under the eaves was burning brightly, and I set myself to put that out before the shingles could catch, as they might easily have done since the rain was only just beginning to fall.

Just as I got this fire under control John Beach appeared round the corner of the house, and I asked him if he saw where the lightning struck. He said "right in the middle of the front yard." I asked him if he saw a shower of fire and he said "no." Without inquiring into the divergence of human testimony, I asked him to see if there was any fire on the outside of the house besides what I had just put out, while I went inside to investigate. Beyond wrecking the fuse box, the bolt had done no damage in the telephone room. As I returned to the sitting room, your Mother entered from the dining room, and said "That lightning struck just *back* of the house. I was standing at the window and saw it come down by the garage, raising a tremendous cloud of smoke. You had better go up and see that the garage is not taking fire." More divergence of human testimony!

Meantime the lightning was striking over and over again within half a mile or so, but the rain had begun to fall very heavily, and all real danger was over. It was quite clear that the garage was not on fire, and when I went up the lane a few minutes later to check on the water tank on the hill, the tank appeared to be all right.

But the following things had happened, and apparently all at once.

(1) The telephone wire from the porch to the further side of the road, over one hundred feet long, had *disappeared*. The copper had exploded, volatilizing the surrounding rubber and leaving only torn fragments, mostly an inch or two in length, of the fabric which had held the rubber together.

(2) A tall oak tree on the opposite side of the house, on the edge of the woods just beyond the gate to the lane, had also been struck by lightning. The tree itself was not much damaged; but the lightning had dug a curious channel for itself, like a gigantic ant-run, through which it had moved toward the garage, throwing a length of snake fence into the air, hitting the wire fence above the gate, charring four posts of that fence and splitting two others. When it reached the open gate, it dug itself another channel across the lane from one post to another, and then went on its gay way toward the ram-pit. There were other minor indications of a pretty ubiquitous tension, but these were the things chiefly in evidence.

This might seem to have been enough; but more transpired the next morning. I found our tank empty and no water coming in. I was much worried as to the many possible places (most of them hidden and hard of access) at which the lightning might have torn the pipes. Fortunately the trouble was at the ram-pit itself, where the electric current, preferring iron to lead, had torn out a section of lead pipe to signify its disapproval. The water connection is all right now, and the summer has been wet enough to let us pump plenty of water into the tank to make good the loss.

The telephone wire has also been replaced. The Company's expert was much interested in finding that the wire had gone up in a shower of sparks. Though our fuse box was so wrecked that they put in an entirely new one, the telephone instrument was not damaged— indeed some say it works better than it did before. Thus endeth all happily.

On their return to the New Haven house in the fall, Hadley established himself in the room on the third floor which he had used as a study thirty years before, in the days when he was working at home instead of in a college office. Here he collected his books and started intensive reading to make up for lost time and to prepare himself for the book on industrial economy which he hoped to write. He had tried to keep in touch with current economic literature during the twenty-two years of his presidency, and in a sense he had succeeded; but it was one thing to keep in touch with a subject and another to have the exhaustive knowledge of source material that was needed for the task before him.

Hadley had no illusions about the length of the work ahead. He told me that he had his choice of two alternatives. He could, in the years remaining at his disposal, complete a book that would be sound, receive good reviews, be put on the shelves of all libraries, and add nothing to the sum of economic knowledge. The alternative was to attempt a really great work, in the full knowledge that the odds were all against him. He was always fond of computing odds, and reckoned—all too correctly, as events were to prove—that he had only one chance in ten of living to write the book, that if he did write it there was one chance in ten that it would be great, and that if it should be great there was one chance in ten that it would be really great. He added that a man at thirty with a family to consider was not entitled to take one-in-a-thousand chances, but that a man approaching seventy should have that privilege.

While the work was under way Hadley's life settled into an enjoyable routine. On most days he worked in his study. As in his earlier years, particular pieces of research would lead to occasional articles in magazines or serve as a basis for addresses. Each Tuesday he would go to New York for meetings of the executive committees of the New York, New Haven, and Hartford Railroad and of the Atchison, Topeka, and Santa Fe Railway. At less frequent intervals he would also go to New York to attend some dinner. In particular, since 1902 he had been a member of the Round Table, a dining club in New York which met monthly, and he now had more time at his disposal for going to these dinners.

The events of the college year were no longer insistent tasks but pleasant occasions for seeing friends who were returning to New Haven. The house at 93 Whitney Avenue was still full to overflowing for the week end of each big game in the football season, as well as for the Promenade and for Commencement. At Yale gatherings Hadley would usually be called upon for a word or two, but his remarks could now be merely light and informal, free from worry as to announcements of policy or decisions on courses of action.

These brief talks were enthusiastically received. In part this was due to the freshness and vigor of their subject matter, in part to the pleasure of the hearers in listening to the man who had been professor or president in their youth. On one occasion, when Yale in 1927 was engaged in an endowment campaign, there was an hour's broadcast of speeches over a nation-wide radio network, while Yale graduates at dinners in many cities listened to the speakers. Hadley went on the air in Chicago, and Yale men everywhere cheered delightedly as the familiar accents were heard. Whether on the radio or in person, he was always sure of a friendly reception.

Various organizations of which he was a member claimed some

of his time, though he kept himself as free from such demands as possible. Among these were the general societies of the American learned hierarchy: The American Philosophical Society, founded in colonial days, the slightly younger American Academy of Arts and Sciences, and the more recent National Institute of Arts and Letters. He was president of the latter in 1925. Youngest of all was the American Academy of Arts and Letters; he had been one of the original fifty members at its founding in 1904. Other groups were of a more specialized nature, such as the College of Electors to the Hall of Fame at New York University, of which he was a member for thirty years. In the case of most foreign societies his connection was nominal and involved no expenditure of time, as with the British Academy, of which he was a corresponding fellow. In his later years the same was true of the British Association for the Advancement of Science, though at the start of his membership, in 1890, he had given considerable time to its affairs.

Societies in his own field claimed somewhat more of his time. At the close of the century he had been president of the American Economic Association; he continued to keep in touch with its activities, and one of the last addresses he delivered was presented at its annual meeting in December, 1927, on "The Meaning of Valuation." He also kept up his interest in the International Institute of Statistics, of which he had been a charter member since its organization in 1886. His activities here covered half a century and ranged from correspondence on its problems to attending international meetings as a delegate, the last of these which he attended being in Brussels in the autumn of 1923. Getting at facts and presenting them accurately always appealed to him, and he gave substantial time after his retirement to a group of institutions organized for this purpose. The first of these was the Institute for Government Research and the next the Institute of Economics; he was a trustee of each, as well as of the Brookings Institution of Washington, with which both later merged.

A list of the other societies to which he belonged would only parallel that which could be made out for the president of any leading university, and would not reflect Hadley's special interests. This is not to say that he was indifferent to the activities of the other societies; he often took the keenest interest, because any activity or any problem could interest him.

Now that Hadley was no longer burdened with administrative work he felt years younger, and turned to writing with his old zest though not at the pace that had marked his earlier years. One of his first magazine articles after retirement, "What Is Education?" was published in *Harper's Monthly* for December, 1922, and is included in *Education and Government*. Part of it, dealing with limits to the proper field of schools and colleges, was couched in franker terms than Hadley had felt free to use when still president:

In every institution above the primary grade, the budget problem is a serious one. In many of them it looks like a hopeless one. It *is* hopeless, so long as we stick to present methods. We cannot teach the existing number of high-school and college students in the way their parents want them taught without spending more money than the community is willing to pay—and perhaps more than it *ought* to pay. For there is a point beyond which further taxes cripple the life of the community more than further opportunities for education help it; and in some districts it looks as though we had pretty nearly reached that point. . . .

We must approach the problem from the standpoint of the community, considering what it most requires in the way of education, how far this must be provided in the schools themselves, and how far it can be left to other agencies. When we have thus learned to separate the essential from the non-essential, and the things the teacher ought to undertake from the things which he ought not to undertake, we shall find the way to give better education than we now do at less cost; utilizing a moderate staff of well-paid instructors to the best advantage, instead of paying lower salaries to a larger variety of teachers than the actual necessities of the case require. . . .

But, someone will say, "where will people get their knowledge if not in the schools?" They will get it in the same way that they now get nine tenths of it; through observing what they see, listening to what they hear, and reading what they require in books and periodicals. The thing for the schools to do is to teach them to observe and listen, and above all else to read. . . . If parents and teachers can once recognize that it is the business of the student to get the information and of the teacher to show him how, we shall have laid the foundation for a twentieth-century school system which shall combine the merits of both of those which have preceded it.

If the pupil is expected to read things for himself, we can cut from our high schools and colleges nearly all those courses whose primary object is to give information, and concentrate the teacher's power in helping his pupils to do their own reading and thinking to the best advantage. We cannot well remove all information courses from our primary schools or the grammar schools; partly because the children in the lower grades have not yet learned to read well enough or easily enough to be expected to get all their information from the printed page, and partly because information courses, in the hands of a good teacher, may be made an effective means in helping to form habits of order and of imagination which are quite as important for the very young pupils as habits of thinking. But if we can reduce them to a minimum in the high schools and take them wholly out of the curriculum in the colleges, we shall cut down the cost of education at a point where it is now very large, both in the aggregate and per capita. We cannot put everybody through a single course of study as our grandfathers tried to do; for there are three or four different types of mind that have to be reached by different methods and developed in different ways. But we can do away with the idea that each student must have a chance to learn the particular subject he is going to use in after life, and substitute the better and more economical plan of training him in *methods* that he is going to use by subjects which he probably will not use. We can train him for the *kind* of profession for which he is fitted instead of attempting to forestall the professional school or the office in teaching him the details of its practice.

But what of the boy who, when he reaches high-school or college age, is too lazy or too uninterested to do his own part in his education, and get the necessary information by reading? To this question there is but one answer. Take him out of school and set him to work.

I am afraid that this suggestion will provoke a good deal of adverse criticism. There is a general feeling that education is so good a thing, and indoor work in shops so undesirable for growing boys and girls, that we ought to try to keep everybody in school, as far as we can, till the age of sixteen or seventeen. If going to school means education in the full and proper sense of the word, as distinct from merely sitting at a desk and picking up information, this is probably true. But if the student is going to evade doing his part in his own education, then I say that it is better for him to work . . . than to make use of the public-school system as an asylum for the wilfully uninterested. Higher education at public expense should be regarded as a privilege to be earned, not as a right to be abused.

Three years later, in November, 1925, Hadley made the most of being able to write freely as an individual, instead of under restrictions as the head of an educational institution. He entered the lists against the Prohibition Act with an article in *Harper's Monthly* on "Law Making and Law Enforcement." The approach is ingenious; while the article is an attack on prohibition, it makes no reference to liquor or to the Volstead Act beyond a footnote stating: "I have purposely confined my illustrations to matters of past history, where the evidence is all in, and the public has given its verdict. It would confuse rather than clear the issues to discuss the effect of laws like the Volstead Act, where the evidence is not yet all in, and the public is far from having reached the judicial frame of mind necessary for a verdict."

The particular illustration which he was discussing at the moment was the "simple though somewhat perilous remedy" known as nullification. His comment on the example he had just given reads: "The Fugitive Slave Law was thus nullified by the people of the North; the Reconstruction Acts were thus nullified by the people of the South. . . . The attempt to enforce the Fugitive Slave Law converted the misunderstandings between North and South into public menaces. The attempt to enforce the Reconstruction Acts not only resulted in abject failure but left a legacy of bitterness behind it which lasted for many years."

Such an article in such a controversial field did not go unchallenged. The counterattack was led by Senator Borah, the newspapers joined in, and when the storm was at its height one facetious Yale graduate wrote offering to use his influence to get

Hadley sent to the federal prison at Atlanta rather than Leavenworth because the climate was so much pleasanter.

In 1921 Lord Bryce gave in London the inaugural lecture on the Watson Foundation, which was administered by the Anglo-American Society. Hadley the next year went to England to deliver the first full course of Watson Lectures, at London, Birmingham, Manchester, Sheffield, Cambridge, and Oxford. Besides the lectures there were numerous banquets and entertainments, which Arthur Hadley found fatiguing but which Helen Hadley enjoyed to the full. When the course was ended the Hadleys went on to France, and ultimately returned to the United States from Marseilles on a leisurely steamer.

The Watson Lectures were published in 1923 under the title *Economic Problems of Democracy,* and a German translation came out in 1926.

Hadley's approach to the subject was from the angle of his current studies on his projected book dealing with industrial economy. In his opening paragraph he explained:

"Instead of making the constitutional systems the primary object of our inquiry, and the work of national housekeeping—which is simply the English for Political Economy—an incidental one, we shall take the housekeeping problems first in order, and the methods of dealing with them second."

The Watson Lectures followed by forty years his early work on railroad transportation, but time had not made him any less critical in his examination of the facts or less outspoken in the course which he advocated. Summing up, near the conclusion of the lectures, he said (p. 135):

For three generations we have been teaching a philosophy of business that was, fundamentally, an appeal to self-interest. We have been resting comfortably in the belief that if each man was encouraged to pursue his own ends in a clear-headed way, competition would secure efficiency in production and just distribution of rewards. Now this was never wholly true—selfish people were never quite clear-headed enough to make the theory work out as it should, and were continually doing inefficient or unjust things from stupidity or shortsightedness; but with the amount of competition which prevailed in the first half of the nineteenth century, it came tolerably near being true. With the progress of industrial consolidation in the latter half of the nineteenth century it has ceased to be true, even in this rough way, . . . success today is quite as apt to depend on advantages in collective bargaining as on success in competition. . . . Success in competition is usually won by public service—increased production at minimum cost. Success in collective bargaining is usually won at public expense—limited production at maximum cost. A degree of selfishness in business transactions which under nineteenth century conditions was safe and generally advantageous for the community has become under twentieth century conditions unsafe and generally disastrous. . . .

We have a double task before us—to frame a new system of ethics which shall keep nations sound and strong after competition has been abandoned, or limited, and to educate the public to accept this new system and the obligations which it imposes.

To build up a new system we generally have to begin by clearing out some of the deadwood of the old system; and the case in hand is no exception. We have two large pieces of ethical deadwood to remove; the belief on the part of the capitalists that property right is something sacred and the belief on the part of the working man that labor creates value.

A trip to Europe in 1923, to attend the Brussels meeting of the International Institute of Statistics, did not result in any book but proved a delightful holiday. He and his wife went on after the meeting to the south of France, and returned by way of Italy and the Adriatic.

In the spring of 1924 Hadley delivered a course of lectures at Leland Stanford University. These were published the next year as *The Conflict Between Liberty and Equality*. The lectures trace developments from the early days when liberty and equality went hand in hand down to the present day when we face "the issue between liberty and equality; the relative importance from the standpoint of the nation of allowing our individual citizens to develop their own powers in their own way—the claim of liberty—or of having all citizens given opportunities as nearly equal as possible for the pursuit of happiness—the claim of social justice." He rejected Blackstone's definition of liberty as "the right to do anything which the laws permit," since this might amount to no more than civil equality, and instead defined liberty as "the power to use intelligence as a determining factor in our conduct."

Before leaving for California Hadley had lectured in Pittsburgh, and after his return he delivered the Memorial Day Address at Yale. Then he and Helen Hadley sailed for England where they spent six weeks, partly going through a round of functions connected with the 1924 London World Power Conference and partly visiting old friends: Parmoor, Acworth, Stamp, and others. During this same trip they celebrated the birth—on the other side of the Atlantic—of their first grandchild, who was named Arthur Twining Hadley, II, in defiance of the principle of not repeating Christian names that had governed the naming of Arthur Hadley himself and of his own children. The departure from principle not only provoked no adverse comment on Arthur Hadley's part, but the namesake was hailed with delight.

At the World Power Conference Hadley presented a paper entitled "State *versus* Private Management of Power Plants," which is reprinted in *Education and Government*. As was to be expected, private management came out ahead, at least for the time being:

Such are the economic reasons which underlie and explain the fact that government management has been fairly successful in standardized industries, and habitually unsuccessful in progressive ones. As the electric industries constitute a field where there is exceptional room for progress in the immediate future, both on the operating and on the commercial side, it seems most undesirable that electric power generation should become a government monopoly at the present juncture. If a particular group of municipalities believes that it can get its light and power cheaper by organizing a cooperative agency, let it do so; or if the government thinks that it can develop some of the nation's water power to better advantage than private companies, let it do so. But let it go into the competition on equal terms with the private companies as to taxation and regulation. In this way and in this way only can it prove whether it is really cheaper and better for the community.

This paper was representative of one line of work in which Hadley was engaged after his retirement. His connection with railroad management had strengthened his long-time interest in the railroad rate structure, and his interest extended to electric public utilities as well. In addition to theoretical studies of the problem, he acquired firsthand experience as a director of the Engineers Public Service Company.

Some of his papers in this field are reprinted in *Education and Government:* "Factors in the Railroad Situation" (1923), "Principles and Methods of Rate Regulation" (1927), "The Meaning of Valuation" (1928). This last paper which he read at the annual meeting of the American Economic Association in December, 1927, was his final contribution in his chosen field.

During these years Hadley continued to serve on the executive committee of the Atchison, Topeka, and Santa Fe Railway, as well as on that of the New York, New Haven, and Hartford Railroad. He was faithful in his attendance, including all inspection trips. As he explained in a letter to the president of the Santa Fe early in his service (April 20, 1920):

". . . It seems to me that there is no way in which a director can do better service to a company than by getting personally acquainted with division superintendents, their problems and their points of view; and a pleasanter way of doing one's duty than by making a trip over the Santa Fe is very hard to imagine."

The friends he met on the trips stood him in good stead on other occasions, and when he was traveling on other business he was continually running across such friends and enjoying their company. In the summer of 1926 he went to San Francisco as an expert witness for the Pacific Gas & Electric Company, and his letters to his wife are full of accounts of his railroad friends. A postcard dated at Mojave on August 21, 1926, reads:

Needles was hot enough to suit anybody. The natives said "not so *very* hot; only 108." But when you unthinkingly draw water out of the faucet marked "cold" and find it 108 when you put your hands in to wash, it gives you quite a shock. . . . The chief engineer of our Gulf Lines (G.C. & S.F.) has a private car on the train, and I am having lots of fun meeting the operating men who come on to see him.

A year later he appeared as an expert for the Northern Pacific. In April of that year he and his wife had landed at Seattle on their way back from a trip to the Far East, and having a few days on his hands Hadley quickly found himself involved in the work. He wrote one of his sons (April 15, 1927):

I have been meaning to write you every day since we have landed, but the time has been surprisingly crowded. As soon as it appeared that they [Yale] wanted me to speak in Chicago instead of New York on the 20th, I took up some work here on certain Northern Pacific matters which Howard Elliott had wished me to look into. They proved very interesting indeed, and I hope that I can be of some help to the Company in certain rather difficult questions which come up early in June regarding tax valuations. Meantime the hospitality of Seattle is unbounded. . . . Perhaps it is fortunate that we leave tonight so that your mother will have a chance for a good rest in Vice-President Williamson's very comfortable business car on the Northern Pacific. Williamson is a '98 man whom I knew quite well when he was in college.

In June Hadley returned to the Pacific Coast to testify. He was working so busily on the case that his correspondence with his wife was for once mostly by postcard and telegraph. The card announcing his safe arrival will serve as an account of the trip, and at the same time indicate the fineness of his handwriting, as all that follows is on the back of one postcard:

Olympian Hotel, Olympia
Monday, 7:30 A.M.

"It is hard to find time to write, when conferences and redrafting are claiming all your time and strength, and when during the intervals scenery is so attractive and trains so jerky. We had a most interesting party across the continent—Williamson, Lyons the General Counsel of the N.P., and White of the White Motors, who joined the party for the fun of it. I had got hold of some new facts in St. Paul; and Dudley of the Milwaukee was on the train with a

lot more, and views of his own too. Not that I was devoid of amusement:—the weather was good and the scenery at places quite overwhelming. I rode on the electric engine across the main divide of
the Rockies, in the course of which I ran the train ten miles without
disgracing the family. At Spokane we heard that the place for taking
testimony had been changed from Seattle to Olympia, which was
rather inconvenient. But I am very comfortable here, in a clean and
courteous hotel, with lovely views from my window. Next time I
write I hope to be able to tell you all about the testimony, which
should come Wednesday.

The hearings went well and Hadley proved an excellent
witness. In a letter written on the way home he made an incidental comment: "In the cross-examination last Thursday the
Judge said to me in an aside—*You're* enjoying it, aren't you!"

Helen Hadley delighted in an incident of one trip on the
Santa Fe. Shortly after the train started the conductor came
through to get the tickets. Hadley felt in the pocket where he
thought he had his pass and could not find it; tried another pocket
with no more success; rose to his feet and began going through
all his pockets in growing excitement and with his characteristic
nervous, jerky motions which became more extreme as the search
continued in vain. Finally the conductor patted him soothingly
on the shoulder saying: "There, there, old man, take it easy;
you'll never get anywhere in the world or amount to anything
if you hurry like that"—just as Hadley finally produced in
triumph the missing pass as a director and member of the executive committee.

Hadley traveled much during these years, not only back and
forth across the continent on business but overseas to visit parts of
the world he had not seen before. In the late winter and early
spring of 1925 he and his wife went on the *Patria* of the Fabre
Line to the eastern Mediterranean. For the first time they saw
Athens, from there went on to Constantinople, and so by various
ports to Cairo, with brief trips inland to Baalbek and to Jerusa-
lem. Only in 1926 they made no trip abroad; but early in 1927
the two went for the first time to the Far East, taking the *President Cleveland* of the Dollar Line from the West Coast to

Manila and back again. Their brief visits on shore were spent with Yale graduates or with old friends, and strenuous sight-seeing was mixed with dinners and speeches all the way from Honolulu to Manila and back again. In the spring of 1928 they went to the West Indies, and in the spring of 1929 to the Mediterranean.

After Hadley passed seventy his family realized how much his strength was gradually failing; he worked shorter hours, rested more, and took short walks in place of long tramps. It was not so noticeable to others, because he rose to the challenge of any special occasion and seemed his old self. He could still be the life of a dinner party, or score off an adversary in cross-examination. At the time of the hearings in Olympia in 1927 when the judge commented on his enjoying the cross-examination, Hadley was seventy-one. Only a few months before his death he appeared before the New York Public Utility Investigating Commission, preferring to testify rather than submit a written statement "because I talk better than I read." An economist on the Commission suggested that one of his statements was not supported by authority. Hadley adduced in reply a German citation of jaw-breaking complexity. The economist queried the authenticity of the citation. Instead of exhibiting the least annoyance Hadley replied happily that he was grateful for the implied compliment to his German but that he was really incapable of fabricating such idiomatic German on the spur of the moment.

Because of his apparent vigor, Hadley was urged to undertake various enterprises that he had the good judgment to decline. In 1926 the Democratic party in Connecticut urged him to accept the nomination for the United States Senate, but he declined. Again in 1928 he was urged to run, and on this occasion Alfred Smith added his personal plea, but again he refused.

The work on his magnum opus went forward through the years but remained in the stage of reading and research. Not even the one-in-ten chance of completing the book was realized,

much less the one-in-a-thousand of a great work. From his talks
with me, and from the few notes I could find, I know that his
aim was to produce a study in which industrial economy would
be distinguished from political economy, the former being
treated as a field which could properly be considered a science
and developed by exact methods, in contradistinction to the latter which he regarded as an art rather than a science. He hoped
that by accurate work in industrial economy it might be possible
to ascertain what relative wage levels in different occupations
would attract workers in the right proportion to each occupation.
He believed that it should be possible in this way to adjust the
labor devoted to different pursuits so as to have production in
the various fields fit the true needs of the community.

The title of the book was to be "Principles of Industrial Economy and Their Application to Current Political Problems."
In discussing the application of the principles he planned to
deal with at least three problems: internal price regulation
(whether by direct or indirect means), public finance, and international trade. Included in the notes is a much revised draft
of a definition of political economy as the art of so ordering the
affairs of the commonwealth as to promote the health, progress,
and contentment of its members, and their safety from within
and from without; danger from without is from conquest, danger from within may be from treason, internal unrest, or stagna-
tion.

During this same period Hadley was one of the numerous
special editors of *Webster's New International Dictionary*, being in charge of definitions in economics, as he had been in the
previous edition as well. It is interesting to note that he was
scrupulous in keeping his individual theories out of the standard definitions which he was revising or composing. His dictionary definitions are completely orthodox.

In June of 1929 Hadley attended what was to be his last
Commencement. The careful engagement calendar kept by
Helen Hadley records the dinners and the guests, beginning on
the Saturday before Commencement Week and running through

the Yale-Harvard boat race on Friday at New London and the departure of the last guests on Saturday morning. Once more there were impromptu speeches to returning reunion classes after the ball game on Tuesday, a speech at the alumni luncheon on Wednesday, and, last of all his Yale speeches, a final word at his senior society that evening.

The summer was spent at Newtown as usual, with visits from the children and eldest grandchild. The family were urging him to write his reminiscences, and during the summer he worked out the outline for the book. It was his practice in writing of this type to block out the topical arrangement; with this as a guide he would then plan in detail what he was going to say, after which he would dictate the complete draft. He finished the topical outline before leaving for the trip on which he died, but he had reserved the dictation for his return. Where possible I have followed his topical outline in this book, but much of what he planned to write was in his memory only and not to be found in correspondence or other records. His outline follows:

REMINISCENCES OF A POLITICAL ECONOMIST

I. The Background (Down to 1865)
>   Family traditions
>   Old New Haven
>   Civil War Memories

II. Early Education (1865–72)
>   School Life
>   The Hopkins Grammar School
>   Home reading and interests
>   My father's influence

III. College and University (1872–83)
>   Undergraduate life and interests
>   Graduate study in Europe
>   Four years as tutor at Yale
>   The Colby Club

When he talked with me of the book of reminiscences, it was clear that he had in mind just what the title implied, and not a formal autobiography. As one example of the type of reminiscence which he planned to include, he told me that in his description of his Berlin visit of 1910 he was going to give various conversations with German friends who were overly frank on the subject of a possible European war. One such story which stuck in my mind, though unfortunately I have no recollection of the name of the German, was of a staff officer who explained the technical reasons—mainly concerned with the relative progress of artillery programs in the various countries—why 1914 would be the most advantageous date for Germany in a European war. While such stories might have been the most interesting part of the book, I regret even more the loss of his comments on the world of classrooms and research, where he lived so long and observed so wisely.

After leaving Newtown there was a busy month. Hadley appeared before the New York Public Service Investigating Commission, as already described. Helen Hadley was occupied with arrangements for what her engagement calendar notes as "reception and dance for the children." The "children" were now all in their thirties and all married; in fact the party was primarily to welcome the most recent daughter-in-law. There were the usual guests for fall football games, and a Thanksgiving party in New Haven for the whole family.

On December 2, 1929, Arthur and Helen Hadley sailed from New York on the *Empress of Australia* for a world cruise. In the Mediterranean they were on familiar ground, but they saw the sights so vigorously that by Cairo Arthur Hadley was ill and had to take things easier. By Bombay he had recovered; as this was new country to him he once more undertook more than he well could do, and after visiting Delhi and Agra was laid up for a few days. Nonetheless, at Sumatra the process was repeated; the party rose at five, breakfasted at five-thirty and indulged in a day's sight-seeing somewhat too strenuous for a man of seventy-three. In spite of such interruptions he enjoyed the trip and was able to take most of the succeeding shore excursions, including five days in Peking with a trip to the Great Wall.

After leaving Peking Arthur Hadley was once more very tired, and as the ship approached Japan he was again taken ill, this time developing pneumonia. Within forty-eight hours he died, in his cabin at 1:00 A.M. on March 6, 1930, as the ship lay at anchor in Kobe harbor.

Friends in Japan did all they could for Helen Hadley, and as the ship was returning directly to the United States she remained on it with the body. At Honolulu she was met by her son Hamilton and his wife, and on March 30 they arrived in San Francisco. Here, in spite of the sadness of the occasion, Helen Hadley was as much amused as her hosts were horrified by an incident that has lived in Yale legend. A delegation from the Yale Club of San Francisco arrived at the pier with condolences and a band; the latter had not been fully apprised of the circumstances and, as Helen Hadley approached, burst into that stirring Yale football tune, "Boola, Boola."

Railroad friends extended every courtesy as they crossed the continent. The party arrived in New Haven on April 4, but the university was in the middle of spring vacation, and the funeral was not held until it was once more in session on April 11. The service was in the Battell Chapel that Arthur Hadley had hailed in his undergraduate doggerel verse and where he had officiated as president for so many years. It was conducted by Anson Phelps Stokes, and the choir once more sang his favorite anthem, Chadwick's "Ecce Jam Noctis."

Arthur Hadley is buried in the family plot in the old Grove Street Cemetery. The cemetery is flanked on two sides by the buildings of the university, and the plot itself lies in the section where the faculty in his father's day had chosen their lots. Near by are the graves of his father's colleagues and of his own: Woolsey, Porter, Thacher, Dwight, Whitney, Gibbs, Dana, and many others—neighbors and friends.

BIBLIOGRAPHY

THE following bibliography lists first the books written by Arthur Twining Hadley, and then the articles and addresses which appeared in periodicals or in separate reprints. The articles and addresses are not complete, as Hadley kept no list of his writings and many of his articles appeared in college papers or other periodicals not covered in any index of current periodical literature. No attempt has been made to include newspaper reports of speeches to Yale alumni associations in various cities. It is believed, however, that all important items have been included, as well as all those listed in the *Report to the President of Yale University for 1929–30*. Unpublished material in the possession of the author is being deposited in the Yale University Library.

BOOKS

RAILROAD TRANSPORTATION, ITS HISTORY AND ITS LAWS. New York, Putnam, 1885.

> A Russian translation by Kiev was published in 1886. A French translation by Arthur Raffalovich and L. Guérin was published in Paris, 1887, by Guillaumin, under the title Le Transport par les Chemins de Fer, Histoire, Législation. This contains certain additional material, pp. 191–193.

ECONOMICS: AN ACCOUNT OF THE RELATIONS BETWEEN PRIVATE PROPERTY AND PUBLIC WELFARE. New York, Putnam, 1896.

THE EDUCATION OF THE AMERICAN CITIZEN. New York, Scribner, 1901.

THE RELATIONS BETWEEN FREEDOM AND RESPONSIBILITY IN THE EVOLUTION OF DEMOCRATIC GOVERNMENT. New York, Scribner, 1903.

> Republished in 1911, New Haven, Yale University Press; London, Henry Frowde, Oxford University Press. "Dodge Lectures on the Responsibilities of Citizenship."

BACCALAUREATE ADDRESSES AND OTHER TALKS ON KINDRED SUBJECTS. New York, Scribner, 1907.

STANDARDS OF PUBLIC MORALITY. New York, Macmillan, 1907.

Lectures delivered in 1906 on the Kennedy Foundation in New York.

SOME INFLUENCES IN MODERN PHILOSOPHIC THOUGHT. New Haven, Yale University Press, 1913.

McNair Lectures at the University of North Carolina, 1912.

UNDERCURRENTS IN AMERICAN POLITICS. New Haven, Yale University Press, 1915.

Barbour-Page Lectures at the University of Virginia (1914) and Ford Lectures at Oxford University (1914).

THE MORAL BASIS OF DEMOCRACY. New Haven, Yale University Press, 1919.

ECONOMIC PROBLEMS OF DEMOCRACY. New York, Macmillan, 1923.

Watson Lectures, England, 1922. A German translation was published in 1926 under the title Probleme der Demokratie. Stuttgart, W. Kohlhammer.

THE CONFLICT BETWEEN LIBERTY AND EQUALITY. Boston and New York, Houghton Mifflin, 1925.

Leland Stanford University Lectures, 1924.

EDUCATION AND GOVERNMENT. New Haven, Yale University Press, 1934.

Selected articles and addresses.

ARTICLES AND ADDRESSES

1873–76

In *Yale Literary Magazine:* Molière, *39:*139–143; Ulysses, *40:*5–9; The Romantic Element in History, *40:*160–163; The Earl of Warwick, *40:*343–347; The Prodigal Son (on Dubufe's picture of that name), *41:*8–12; Parnassus, *41:*92–96.

Articles written while an undergraduate at Yale.

1884

Overproduction; Post Office; Profits; Reciprocity; Speculation; Subsidies; Transportation; Weights and Measures. In *Cyclopaedia of Political Science,* ed. John J. Lalor. Vol. III. Chicago, Cary, 1883–84.

Competition and Combination, *Andover Review*, 2:455–466 (Nov.).

<small>Substantially reprinted in *Railroad Transportation*, 1885. See note therein, p. 63.</small>

Much of the material included in *Railroad Transportation* originally appeared in 1884 and 1885 in articles, often unsigned, in the *Railroad Gazette*, to which Hadley continued to contribute through 1892, and in the *Independent*, in which much of the writing on economic subjects during these years was by him.

1885

First Annual Report, Second Series, of the Bureau of Labor Statistics of the State of Connecticut. Hartford, Case, Lockwood & Brainard.

1886

Second Annual Report, Second Series, of the Bureau of Labor Statistics of the State of Connecticut. Hartford, Case, Lockwood & Brainard.

Economic Laws and Methods, *Science Economic Discu:__ __ __* Richard T. Ely, New York, The Science Company, pp. 92–97.

Railways, *Encyclopaedia Britannica*, 9th ed., New York, Scribner, 20:223–255.

The Difficulties of Railroad Regulation, *Popular Science Monthly*, 29:1–11 (May).

Yale, *Independent* (July).

Private Monopolies and Public Rights, *Quarterly Journal of Economics*, 1:28–44 (Oct.).

Railroad Abuses, at Home and Abroad, *New Princeton Review*, 2:355–365 (Nov.).

Les Grèves aux États-Unis, *L'Année Économique*, ed. Arthur Raffalovich, 1885–86.

1887

American Railroad Legislation, *Harper's New Monthly*, 75:141–150 (June).

1888

Section on "Le Socialisme" in chapter on États-Unis, *L'Année Économique*, ed. Arthur Raffalovich, 1887–88, pp. 254–261.

Comparative Statistics of Railroad Service, *Bulletin de l'Institut International de Statistique, 3:*25–36.

Reprinted as a pamphlet by Héritiers Botta, 1888.

Steamship Subsidies as a Means of Reducing the Surplus, *The National Revenues,* ed. Albert Shaw, Chicago, McClurg, pp. 126–134.

The Workings of the Interstate Commerce Law, *Quarterly Journal of Economics, 2:*162–187 (Jan.).

Remedies for Railway Troubles, *Forum, 5:*429–435 (June).

The Railway in Its Business Relations, *Scribner's, 4:*473–488 (Oct.).

Reprinted under the same title in *The American Railway,* ed. T. M. Cooley, New York, Scribner, 1889, pp. 344–369.

Some Difficulties of Public Business Management, *Political Science Quarterly, 3:*572–591 (Dec.).

1889

American Railroad Statistics, *Publications of the American Statistical Association,* New Series, No. 1, pp. 241–253 (June).

Read before the Association, Apr. 25, 1889.

Obituary of President Woolsey, *Nation,* No. 1254, pp. 27–28 (July 11).

Railroad Business under the Interstate Commerce Act, *Quarterly Journal of Economics, 3:*170–187 (Jan.).

The Outlook for Industrial Peace, *Forum, 8:*53–60 (Sept.).

Political Science Quarterly: review of *The Consumption of Wealth,* by S. N. Patten, 4:534–536 (Sept.); review of *Éléments d'Économie Politique Pure,* by L. Walras, 4:679–681 (Dec.).

In *Dictionary of Philosophical Terms,* New York, Macmillan. Editorship of the definitions relating to economics.

1890

The Prohibition of Railroad Pools, *Quarterly Journal of Economics, 4:*158–171 (Jan.).

1891

Railroad Problems of the Immediate Future, *Atlantic Monthly, 67:*386–393 (Mar.).

Railway Passenger Rates, *Forum, 11:*215–220 (Apr.).

Recent Railroad Legislation and Its Effect upon the Finances of the Country, *Proceedings of the Convention of the American Bankers' Association,* New York, pp. 37–42.

Address at the convention of the American Bankers' Association held at New Orleans, Nov. 11, 1891.

1892

The first number of the *Yale Review* appeared in May, 1892, Hadley being one of the editors. From 1892 until his election as President of Yale in 1899 he contributed numerous unsigned editorials and many book reviews, in addition to signed articles. The principal articles he contributed are included in this bibliography under their respective dates, but the editorials and book reviews are not included.

The Admission of Women as Graduate Students at Yale, *Educational Review,* 3:486–489 (May).

Legal Theories of Price Regulation, *Yale Review,* 1:56–67 (May).

In *Johnson's Cyclopaedia* (1892–93), editorial work on Political Science.

1893

Ethics as a Political Science, *Yale Review,* 1:301–315, 354–367 (Nov., 1892, and Feb., 1893).

Reprinted in *The Education of the American Citizen,* 1901, pp. 100–134. These articles contain the substance of a course of four lectures delivered at Yale in 1892.

Jay Gould and Socialism, *Forum,* 14:686–693 (Jan.).

The Relation between Interest and Profits, *Hand-Book of the American Economic Association* . . . [Baltimore] American Economic Association, Jan., 1894, pp. 56–62.

Abstract of a paper delivered before the sixth annual meeting of the Association at the University of Chicago, Sept. 11–15, 1893.

Interest and Profits, *Annals of the American Academy of Political and Social Science,* 4:337–347 (Nov.).

Also separately printed as a pamphlet, Philadelphia.

Bank (with John Jay Knox); Commerce; Commercial Crises; Currency; Metayer; Political Economy; Rent; Taxation, *Johnson's Universal Cyclopaedia,* New York, Appleton.

Socialism and Social Reform, *Forum,* 18:184–191 (Oct.).

Reprinted in *The Education of the American Citizen.*

Recent Tendencies in Economic Literature, *Yale Review*, *3*:251–260 (Nov.).

Population and Capital, *Publications of the American Economic Association*, *9*:557–566.

Paper read before the American Economic Association, Dec. 27, 1894.

1895

Yale University, *Four American Universities*, New York, Harper, pp. 47–91.

Misunderstandings about Economic Terms, *Yale Review*, *4*:156–170 (Aug.).

1896

Government Administration of Industrial Enterprise, *Yale Review*, *4*:398–408 (Feb.).

In *Dictionary of Political Economy*, ed. R. H. Inglis-Palgrave. Vol. II *et seq.* London and New York, Macmillan, 1896–99. A number of articles signed A.T.H.

1897

In *Review of Reviews*, *15*:45–46 (Jan.). Article in a symposium entitled "Some Practical Suggestions from Students of Finance."

Economics and Jurisprudence, *Economic Studies*, *2*:36–37 (Feb.).

The Duty of the Government Toward the Investor, *Economic Studies*, Supplement, *2*:117–120; 132–133 (Feb.).

The Good and the Evil of Industrial Combination, *Atlantic Monthly*, *79*:377–385 (Mar.).

The Different Meanings of Cost, *Quarterly Journal of Economics*, *11*:310–311 (Apr.).

Francis A. Walker's Contributions to Economic Theory, *Political Science Quarterly*, *12*:295–308 (June).

Some Fallacies in the Theory of Distribution, *Economic Journal*, *7*:477–486 (Dec.).

1898

The Relation between Economics and Politics, *Yale Law Journal*, *7*:194–206 (Jan.).

Opening address at the annual meeting of the American Economic Association, Dec. 27, 1898.
Reprinted in *The Education of the American Citizen.*

Rate-Making and Taxation, *Hand-Book of the American Economic Association,* *3*:80–88 (Feb.).

Abstract and discussion of paper read before the American Economic Association, Dec. 30, 1897.

Methods of Teaching Economics, *Economic Studies, Supplement, 3*:105–106 (Feb.).

1899

The Elementary Teaching of Political Science, *Seventh Annual Report, Schoolmasters' Association of New York and Vicinity,* 1898–99, pp. 81–92.

In Mill, J. S., "The World's Great Classics," *Principles of Political Economy* . . . , revised ed., New York, Colonial Press, 2 vols. Introduction.

Sociology, Economics and Politics; lecture in Philadelphia, ... 27, printed in *Counsel upon the Reading of Books,* 1902, q.v.

Inaugural Address as President of Yale University, Oct. 18, 1899, *Yale Alumni Weekly, 9*:33–35, 39.

Reprinted in *The Education of the American Citizen,* 1901, under the title "Yale Problems, Past and Present."

The Formation and Control of Trusts, *Scribner's, 26*:604–610 (Nov.).

Reprinted in *The Education of the American Citizen.*

In *Dictionary of Philosophical Terms,* New York, Macmillan, 1899, editor of the department of economics.

Economic Theory and Political Morality, *Publications of the American Economic Association,* Third Series, *1*:45–61.

Opening address at meeting of the American Economic Association, Dec. 27, 1899. Reprinted in *The Education of the American Citizen.*

1900

From 1900 to 1921 Hadley annually presented his *Report of the President of Yale University.* These reports dealt not only with the developments of the current year but also with current university problems of a general nature. They were published annually by the University.

During these years Hadley also delivered the matriculation addresses
to the undergraduates in September and the baccalaureate addresses
in June. These addresses, with a few omissions, were collected by
Hadley and separately printed in the volumes entitled *Baccalaureate
Addresses* and *The Moral Basis of Democracy*. In this bibliography
separate references are not given to either the reports or the addresses,
except for addresses which were not included in the two volumes referred to (reference is then made to the copy of the *Yale Alumni
Weekly* in which the address appeared) and for addresses which were
also reprinted separately and are so listed.

Our Standards of Political Morality, *Independent,* 52:97–101 (Jan. 11).

Reprinted in *The Education of the American Citizen.*

The Policy of Steamship Subsidies, *Review of Reviews,* 21:325–328
(Mar.).

The Real Danger in Trusts, *Century,* May, 1900, pp. 152–153.

The Problems Which Confront Our Colleges at the Opening of the
Twentieth Century. Comments by the Presidents of Dartmouth, Yale,
Western Reserve, Williams, and Oberlin, *Education,* 20:588 (June).

The Greatness of Patience.

Baccalaureate address of June, 1900; separately reprinted with additions under
this title, New York, Crowell, 1901.
Also reprinted in *Baccalaureate Addresses,* 1907.

Political Education, *Atlantic Monthly,* 86:145–151 (Aug.).

Address delivered at Vassar College, Apr. 27, 1900.
Reprinted in *The Education of the American Citizen.*

The Direction of American University Development, *Yale Alumni
Weekly,* 10:47–48 under the title "Political Trusteeship."

Address delivered at Vanderbilt University, Oct. 23, 1900.
Reprinted in *The Education of the American Citizen.*

Fundamental Requirements in School Education, *The Education of the
American Citizen.*

Address delivered at Norfolk, Conn., Nov. 20, 1900.

Conflicting Views regarding Entrance Examinations, *School Review,*
8:583–592 (Dec.).

In *Outlook,* 66:797 (Dec. 1). One of a series of lists in a symposium
entitled "The Greatest Books of the Century."

The Relation between Higher Education and the Welfare of the Country, *Independent*, *52:*2959–2963 (Dec. 13).

Address delivered at the Farmers' Convention at New Haven, Dec. 11, 1900.
Published in *Thirty-Fourth Annual Report of the Secretary of the Connecticut State Board of Agriculture*, Hartford, Case, Lockwood & Brainard, 1901, pp. 29–36.
Reprinted in *The Education of the American Citizen*, under the title "The Relation between Higher Education and the Public Welfare."

The Demands of the Twentieth Century, *Proceedings of The New England Society of New York City*, New York, pp. 34–38.

Address delivered at the Ninety-Fifth Anniversary Celebration of the Society, Dec. 22, 1900.
Reprinted in *The Education of the American Citizen*.

1901

Railroad Economy in the Nineteenth Century, *Evening Post*, Jan. 12, 1901.

Reprinted in *The Nineteenth Century*, pp. 443–453.

Use and Control of Examinations, *Educational Review*, 21:286–300 (Mar.).

Reprinted in *The Education of the American Citizen*.

Government by Public Opinion, *University of California Chronicle*, 4:65–79 (May).

Address delivered at the University of California, Mar. 23, 1901.
Reprinted as a pamphlet, Berkeley.
Also reprinted in *The Education of the American Citizen*.

Alleged Luxury among College Students, *Century*, 62:313–314 (June).
The End in Education, *Outlook*, 68:761–766 (Aug. 3).

Address delivered at Hill School, May 25.

Address of Welcome at the Yale Bicentennial. In *Yale Alumni Weekly*, 11:124 (Jan.), "Issue of Commemoration." Delivered Oct. 21, 1901.

Reprinted in *The Record of the Celebration of the Two Hundredth Anniversary of the Founding of Yale College*, Held at Yale University . . . October the Twentieth to October the Twenty Third, A.D., 1901. New Haven, 1902, pp. 250–253.

Introduction to Adam Smith's *On Colonies*, Congressional Press, Washington, D. C.

1902

Railway Economics and Legislation; Technical Education in the United
States, *Encyclopaedia Britannica,* 10th ed., New York, Scribner.

The Twofold Cause of Betting, *Century, 64:*803–804 (Sept.).

The Purposes of the American University, *Yale Alumni Weekly, 12:*25
(Oct. 22).

Address delivered at the inauguration of Chancellor Strong of the University
of Kansas, Oct. 17, 1902.

Needs of the Country, *Yale Alumni Weekly, 12:*44–45 (Nov. 5).

The Meaning and Purpose of Secondary Education, *School Review,
10:*729–741 (Dec.).

Sociology, Economics and Politics, *Counsel upon the Reading of Books,*
by H. Morse Stephens, Agnes Repplier, Arthur T. Hadley . . .
Houghton Mifflin, 1902.

From lectures in Philadelphia, 1898–99, arranged by the American Society for
the Extension of University Teaching, pp. 139–171.

1903

Academic Freedom in Theory and in Practice, *Atlantic Monthly,
91:*152–160, 334–344 (Feb., Mar.).

Portions of the Lowell Institute Lectures delivered the previous year.

The Task of a College President, *Youth's Companion,* June 4, 1903.

The Place of the Professional School in the Modern American University, *Bulletin of Northwestern University,* Series 2, pp. 17–29
(Nov.).

Education for Citizens of a Free Commonwealth.

Address at Wheeling, W. Va., Nov. 3, 1903.
Printed in *Annual Report 1903–4 of Superintendent of Schools,* Wheeling, pp.
67–72.

Preparation for Politics, *Harper's Weekly, 47:*1778 (Nov. 7).

Education and Religion, *Independent, 55:*3095–3098 (Dec. 31).

Address delivered at the Second Presbyterian Church of Philadelphia.
Reprinted in *Baccalaureate Addresses.*
Unauthorized reprint in *Business Administration,* Vol. X.

Foreword to *Collier's* edition of *Tom Brown at Rugby,* 1903.

1904

Biographical Memoir of James Hadley, 1821–1872. Read before the National Academy of Sciences, Apr. 21, 1904, *National Academy of Sciences, Biographical Memoirs*, 5:247–254 (1905).

Also issued as a separate reprint, Washington, Judd & Detweiler, printers.

Opportunities for Political Influence, *Yale Alumni Weekly*, 13:351 (Jan. 20).

Address at the Harvard Union, Jan. 13, 1904.

The Conflicting Claims of General Education and Professional Education, *Yale Alumni Weekly*, 13:399–400 (Feb. 3).

Address before the Medical Society of the State of New York at Albany, Jan. 26, 1904.
Also published in *Journal of the American Medical Association*, 42:373–375 (Feb. 6), and in *The Post Graduate*, Mar., 1904.

The Changed Yale Course, *Yale Alumni Weekly*, 13:508 (Mar. 9).
Speech at the Harrisburg Yale Dinner, *Yale Alumni Weekly*, 13:593–594 (Apr. 6).
The University and Free Speech, *Collier's* 33:10:14 (June 18).
The Public Purpose in College Education, *Independent*, 57:254–259 (Aug. 4), under the title "Public Purpose in Education."

Address before the Phi Beta Kappa Society of Amherst College, May 26, 1904.

Educational Methods and Principles of the Nineteenth Century, *Educational Review*, 28:325–334 (Nov.).

Address before the Education Section of the Congress of Arts and Sciences, St. Louis, Sept. 26, 1904.

1905

President Hadley on College Athletics: a Personal Letter to the Editor, *Illustrated Sporting News*, 4:2 (Jan. 7).
The Public Conscience, *Independent*, 58:641–644 (Mar. 23).
The Public against the Railways, *Boston Evening Transcript*, Apr. 1, 1905, p. 30.
The Immediate Future of the American College, *Century*, 47:864–867 (Apr.).
Mental Types and Their Recognition in Our Schools, *Harper's Monthly*, 111:123–129 (June).

The Study of Greek in American Colleges, *Independent*, *59*:244–246
   (Aug. 3).
A New Departure in Education, *Standard* (Nov. 9).

1906

Speech before the Denver Chamber of Commerce, Jan. 4, 1906, *Yale
   Alumni Weekly*, *15*:299–300 (Jan. 17).
Efficiency in Education. Address at Youngstown, Ohio, Jan. 30, 1906.
On the Hepburn Bill, *Boston Evening Transcript*, Pt. 3, p. 2, Feb. 24,
   1906.

   Reprinted in *Railroad Gazette*, *40*:198–200 (Mar. 2).

Address at St. Louis on the Establishment of the Yale Alumni Advisory
   Board, Feb. 24, 1906, *Yale Alumni Weekly*, *15*:463–465 (Mar. 7).
Old and New Education, *Yale Alumni Weekly*, *15*:502–503 (Mar. 14).
To What Extent Should Professors Engaged in Research Be Relieved
   from the Work of Instruction? *Educational Review*, *31*:325–332
   (Apr.).
The Purpose of College Study. Address at Vassar, Apr., 1906.
Wealth and Democracy in American Colleges, *Harper's Monthly*,
   113:450–453 (Aug.).
Administration Problems, *Yale Alumni Weekly*, *16*:212–213 (Nov.
   28).
Moral Duties of a Free Citizen, in Vol. V. of *Self Culture for Young
   People*, 1906, 2 pp.

1907

Intelligent Preparation for Public Service, *Independent*, *62*:17–19
   (Jan. 3).
Ethics of Corporate Management, *North American Review*, *184*:120–
   124 (Jan. 18).

   Reprinted in *Representative Essays in Modern Thought*, ed. by H. R. Steeves and
   F. H. Ristine, New York, American Book Company [c.1913], pp. 412–429.

The Purpose of Yale, *Yale Alumni Weekly*, *16*:546 (Mar. 6).

   Address delivered at Philadelphia, Mar. 1, 1907.

The Best College Life, *Yale Alumni Weekly*, *16*:590 (Mar. 20).

   Address delivered at Plainfield, N.J., Mar. 15, 1907.

James Dwight Dana, *Popular Science*, *70*:306–308 (Apr.).

Professional Ideals, *Yale Alumni Weekly*, *16*:710 (Apr. 24).

Address delivered at the dedication of the Engineering Society Building, New York City, Apr. 16, 1907.

The National Yale, *Yale Alumni Weekly*, *16*:734 (May 1).

Address delivered at Cincinnati, Apr. 27, 1907.

Address at Stratford Parish, Apr. 25, printed in *The Connecticut Churchman*, June 21, 1907, p. 47.

Baccalaureate Address, *Yale Alumni Weekly*, *16*:985–987 (July 10), under the title "Cleanliness in Life,"

Not reprinted in collected baccalaureate addresses.

Matriculation Address, *Yale Alumni Weekly*, *17*:40–41 (Oct. 2), under the title "The Right Perspective."

Not reprinted in collected baccalaureate addresses.

1908

Constitutional Position of Property in America, *Independent*, *64*:834–838 (Apr. 16).

Reprinted in W. H. Hamilton, *Current Economic Problems*, 3d ed., Chicago, University of Chicago Press [c.1925], pp. 764–770.
This article embodies one of the lectures given by Hadley as Roosevelt Exchange Professor at the University of Berlin in the winter of 1907–08 on "Industrial History and Industrial Legislation in the United States." Another lecture was published in the *Internationale Wochenschrift für Wissenschaft, Kunst und Technik* in Oct., 1907, under the title "Die Eigenart des Amerikanischen Wirtschaftslebens."

Facilities for Study and Research in the Offices of the United States Government at Washington, *U.S. Department of the Interior, Bulletin, 1909*, No. 1. Whole Number 398, Washington, Government Printing Office, pp. 1–73.

The Public Duty of Newspaper Readers, *Youth's Companion, 82*:555 (Nov. 5).

The Obligations of the Prize Winner. Address at Harvard, Dec. 11, *Harvard Bulletin*, *11*:11:1–3 (Dec. 16).

1909

The Library in the University, *Yale Alumni Weekly*, *18*:490–491 (Feb. 3).

Address delivered in New Haven before the Connecticut Library Association, Feb. 3, 1909.
Also printed in *Public Libraries*, *14*:115–117 (Apr.).

Two Sides of University Life, *Johns Hopkins University Circular*, New Series, *3*:4–14 (Mar.).

Commemoration address at Johns Hopkins, Feb. 22, 1909.

President Taft and the Yale of His Day, *Yale Alumni Weekly*, *18*:662–663 (Mar. 26).

The Influence of Charles Darwin upon Historical and Political Thought, *Psychological Review*, *16*:143–151 (May).

Reprinted in *Some Influences in Modern Philosophic Thought*, 1913.
Also reprinted as a separate pamphlet, Lancaster, Pa.

College Education and General Culture, *New York Times*, Aug. 28, 1909, p. 9.

Reprinted in *Yale Alumni Weekly*, *19*:31–33 (Oct. 1).

Matriculation Address, *Yale Alumni Weekly*, *19*:58–59 (Oct. 8).

Not reprinted in collected baccalaureate addresses.

A Liberal Education: What It Is and What It Is For. [n.p., n.d.]

Address delivered at the Hotchkiss School, Oct. 19, 1909.

Address delivered before the American Economic Association, Dec. 28, 1909, *American Economic Association Quarterly*, Third Series, *11*:94–98 (Apr., 1910).

In *Webster's New International Dictionary*, Springfield, Mass., Merriam. Revision of definitions relating to economics.

1910

Education in Germany, *Youth's Companion*, *84*:3–4 (Jan. 6).
An Educated Democracy, *University of California Chronicle*, *12*:207–222 (July).

Address at the University of California, May 17, 1910.
Reprinted as a separate pamphlet, Berkeley.

The Alumni and the University, *Yale Alumni Weekly*, *19*:947–948 (June 10).
College Democracy, *Century*, *58*:254–255 (June).

1911

Report of the Railroad Securities Commission to the President. *U.S. Sixty-Second Congress, Second Session, Document No. 256,* Washington [Government Printing Office].

Reprinted as a separate pamphlet, Washington.
Dutch translation published in Amsterdam, 1912.

The Yale Ideal, *Yale Alumni Weekly, 20:*899–900 (June 2).

Address at Chicago, May 20, 1911.

The College in the Service of the Nation, *Youth's Companion, 85:*591–592 (Nov. 2).

1912

The Government and the Railroads, *Youth's Companion, 86:*205–206 (Apr. 18).
Speech at the Inauguration of President Hibben of Princeton, May 10. *Princeton Alumni Weekly, 12:32:*529 (May 15).
James Dwight Dana, *Bull. Geol. Soc. Am., 24:*55–56 (Dec., 1912).

1913

Methods of Ascertaining and Apportioning Cost of Instruction in Universities, *Educational Review, 45:*58–69 (Jan.).

Reprinted in *Columbia University Quarterly, 15:*241–248 (June).

Some Current Educational Fallacies, *Yale Alumni Weekly, 22:*600–601 (Feb. 28).
The Relation of Science to Higher Education in America, *Science,* New Series, *37:*775–779 (May 23).
Matriculation Address, *Yale Alumni Weekly, 23:*57–58 (Oct. 3).

Not reprinted in collected baccalaureate addresses.

Learning to Read and Write, *Youth's Companion, 87:*523 (Oct. 9).

1914

The Object of Education, *Youth's Companion, 88:*31 (Jan. 15).
Yale's Professional Schools, *Yale Alumni Weekly, 23:*618–619 (Feb. 27).

The Undergraduate of Today, *Yale Alumni Weekly*, 23:640–642 (Mar. 6).

What Do the Social Changes in American Life Demand of the Higher Education? *Yale Alumni Weekly*, 23:677–678 (Mar. 13).

Address before the convention of the Religious Education Association, Mar. 5, 1914.
Also printed in *Religious Education*, 9:103–107 (Apr.), under the title "Education and the New Morality."

The University and Its Students, *Yale Alumni Weekly*, 23:678–679 (Mar. 13).

Dynamiting the Peace Palace, *Independent*, 80:126 (Oct. 26).

Research and Teaching, *Science*, New Series, 40:853–855 (Dec.).

1915

The Political Teachings of Treitschke, *Yale Review*, New Series, 4:235–246 (Jan.).

The Organization of Public Opinion, *North American Review*, 201:191–196 (Feb.).

Education and Public Service. Address at Fiftieth Anniversary of St. Mark's School, *Vindex*, June, 1915.

Matriculation Address, "The Duty of Straightforwardness," in *The Moral Basis of Democracy*, 1919.

Also printed as a separate pamphlet, Indianapolis, Bobbs-Merrill, 1915, under the title *Truth, a Civic Virtue*.

What Our Colleges Are For, *Hotchkiss Literary Monthly*, Oct., 1915.

Salaries at Yale University, *School and Society*, 2:751–752 (Nov. 20).

Based on a portion of the *Report of the President of Yale University* for 1914–15.

1916

Twentieth-Century Yale, *Book of the Yale Pageant*, ed. G. H. Nettleton, New Haven, Yale University Press, pp. 119–121.

Changes in University Life, *Youth's Companion*, 90:3–4 (Jan. 6).

The University and the Nation, *Yale Alumni Weekly*, 25:585–586 (Feb. 4).

Yale's Educational Problems, *Yale Alumni Weekly*, 25:640–641 (Feb. 18).

Address delivered before the Hartford Alumni Association, Feb. 11, 1916.

Choosing a Career, *Yale Alumni Weekly*, 25:698–699 (Mar. 3).

The University's Ideals, *Yale Alumni Weekly*, 25:962–963 (May 12).

Address at the Funeral of Timothy Dwight, May 29, 1916, *Timothy Dwight, President of Yale University, 1886–99. Memorial Addresses.* [New Haven, 1916.]

Preparedness for Peace and War, *Youth's Companion*, 90:411–412 (July 27).

Matriculation Address, *Yale Alumni Weekly*, 26:62–63 (Oct. 6).

Not reprinted in collected baccalaureate addresses.

Anniversary Sermon, Oct. 23, 1916, on the Two Hundredth Anniversary of the Removal of Yale to New Haven, *Yale Alumni Weekly*, 26:148–150 (Oct. 27).

1917

The University and Its Graduates, *Yale Alumni Weekly*, 26:462–463 (Jan. 19).

Development of the Professional Schools, *Yale Alumni Weekly*, 26:628 (Mar. 2).

National Defense and Yale's Preparations, *Yale Alumni Weekly*, 26:683–684 (Mar. 16).

War-Time Yale, *Yale Alumni Weekly*, 26:941–942 (May 25).

Intelligent Service to Country, *Yale Alumni Weekly*, 26:999–1001 (June 8).

College Studies and College Tests, *Harper's Monthly*, 135:537–542 (Sept.).

Reprinted in *Education and Government*, 1934.

Matriculation Address, *Yale Alumni Weekly*, 27:60–61 (Oct. 5).

Not reprinted in collected baccalaureate addresses.

1918

A Statement to the Teachers in the Associated Colleges and Universities, *The Carnegie Foundation for the Advancement of Teaching. Thirteenth Annual Report of the President and of the Treasurer*, New York City, pp. 41–56.

Written in collaboration with the other members of the Executive Committee. Also printed as a separate pamphlet, New York, 1918.

Yale's War Services, *Review of Reviews*, 57:518–519 (May).

Matriculation Address, *Yale Alumni Weekly, 28:*62–63 (Oct. 4).

Not reprinted in collected baccalaureate addresses.

1919

Yale Reconstruction from the Standpoint of the University Administration, *Yale Alumni Weekly, 28:*593–594 (Feb. 28).
Reconstruction at Yale, *Yale Alumni Weekly, 28:*963–965 (May 30).
The Colleges and the Nation, *Harper's Monthly, 139:*106–112 (June).

Reprinted in *Education and Government.*

The Purpose of College Study, *Vassar Quarterly,* July, 1919.

Address before Phi Beta Kappa Convention, May 25, 1919.

1920

The Spirit of Our Education, *Yale Alumni Weekly, 29:*539–540 (Mar. 5).
Modern University Life and the Graduate, *Yale Alumni Weekly, 29:*803–805 (May 21).

1921

University Leadership, *School and Society, 13:*508–509 (Apr. 23).
Induction Address at the Inauguration of President Angell, *Yale Alumni Weekly, 30:*1084 (July 8).

1922

A Call to Internationalism, *Yale Alumni Weekly, 31:*1182–1183 (July 7).
What Is Education? *Harper's Monthly, 146:*13–22 (Dec.).

Reprinted in *Education and Government.*

1923

The True Purpose and Value of a College Education, *Yale Alumni Weekly, 32:*745–747 (Mar. 16).

Reprinted as a pamphlet, as supplement to *Yale University Bulletin.*
Also reprinted in *Education and Government.*

Factors in the Railroad Situation, *Yale Review,* New Series, *12:*449–468 (Apr.).

Reprinted in *Education and Government.*
Also reprinted as a separate pamphlet, New Haven, Yale Publishing Association.

Our National Character, Its Strength and Its Weakness, *Current History*, *19:*1–9 (Oct.).

1924

S. Wright Dunning, an Appreciation, *Railway Age*, *76:*1368–1369 (June 7).

State versus Private Management of Power Plants, *Transactions of the First World Power Conference* (London, 1924), New York, Van Nostrand, 1925, *4:*1568–1579.

> Reprinted in *Nation's Business*, *13*, No. 1, pp. 15–17 (Jan., 1925), under the title "Where Public Ownership Fails."
> Reprinted in *Education and Government*.

1925

American Nationalism, *Yale Review*, New Series, *14:*787–791 (July).

> Review of W. C. Abbott, *The New Barbarians*, and of William McDougall, *The Indestructible Union*.

Law Making and Law Enforcement, *Harper's Monthly*, *151:*641–648 (Nov.).

> Reprinted in *Education and Government*.

1927

Principles and Methods of Rate Regulation, *Yale Review*, New Series, *16:*417–432 (Apr.).

> Reprinted as a pamphlet [New Haven], Yale University Press [c.1927].
> Also reprinted in *Education and Government*.

1928

The Meaning of Valuation, *American Economic Review, Supplement*, *18:*173–180 (Mar.). Paper read Dec. 29, 1927, at the annual meeting of the American Economic Association.

> Reprinted as a separate pamphlet, New Haven.
> Also reprinted in *Education and Government*.

Training in Political Intelligence, *Yale Review*, New Series, *17:*625–637 (July).

INDEX

CK COLLECTIONS

THIS BOOK MAY NOT BE RENEWED

A fee of 2 cents will be charged for each day
this book is kept beyond the date due.

DATE DUE		
▮▮Fe '49▮		
FEB - 1 1950		

Form DS 300M 4-48 T